Marjorie
HER WAR YEARS

PATRICIA SKIDMORE

Marjorie
HER WAR YEARS

A British Home Child in Canada

FOREWORD BY GORDON BROWN

DUNDURN
TORONTO

Cover image: (top) Fairbridge girls with a cottage mother on the steps of Pennant Cottage. Right–left: Jessie Newbold, unknown, Audrey Richards, Lillian Kemp, Marjorie Arnison, Mrs. Williams, Joan Vallintin, Betty Lenton, Winnie Hardy, Lily Clabby, Catherine Stoker, Mary Kewan, unknown. (Courtesy of the Cowichan Valley Museum and Archives, 999.10.15.42) (bottom) Fairbridge children heading back to their cottages at the end of the day. (Fairbridge Farm School, *Annual Report*, 1940, 8)

Back cover image: (top) Kenny, Marjorie, and Audrey at the Prince of Wales Fairbridge Farm School, circa 1942. (Skidmore family collection) (bottom) Audrey, Kenny, and Marjorie, free from the Prince of Wales Fairbridge Farm School, circa 1947. (Skidmore family collection)
Printer: Webcom

Library and Archives Canada Cataloguing in Publication

Skidmore, Patricia, author
    Marjorie her war years : a British home child in Canada / Patricia Skidmore; foreword by Gordon Brown.

Includes bibliographical references and index.
Issued in print and electronic formats.
ISBN 978-1-4597-4166-9 (softcover).--ISBN 978-1-4597-4167-6 (PDF).--ISBN 978-1-4597-4168-3 (EPUB)

    1. Arnison, Marjorie. 2. Home children (Canadian immigrants)--British Columbia--Biography. 3. World War, 1939-1945--Children--British Columbia--Biography. 4. Biographies. I. Title.

HQ792.C3S53 2018   362.7'7912092   C2018-902016-4
                                            C2018-902017-2

1 2 3 4 5   22 21 20 19 18

We acknowledge the support of the **Canada Council for the Arts**, which last year invested $153 million to bring the arts to Canadians throughout the country, and the **Ontario Arts Council** for our publishing program. We also acknowledge the financial support of the **Government of Ontario**, through the **Ontario Book Publishing Tax Credit** and the **Ontario Media Development Corporation**, and the **Government of Canada**.

Nous remercions le **Conseil des arts du Canada** de son soutien. L'an dernier, le Conseil a investi 153 millions de dollars pour mettre de l'art dans la vie des Canadiennes et des Canadiens de tout le pays.

Care has been taken to trace the ownership of copyright material used in this book. The author and the publisher welcome any information enabling them to rectify any references or credits in subsequent editions.
— *J. Kirk Howard, President*

The publisher is not responsible for websites or their content unless they are owned by the publisher.

Printed and bound in Canada.

VISIT US AT

dundurn.com | @dundurnpress | dundurnpress | dundurnpress

Dundurn
3 Church Street, Suite 500
Toronto, Ontario, Canada
M5E 1M2

*This book is in memory of my mother, Marjorie, her siblings —
Frederick, Norman, Phyllis, Joyce, Kenneth, Audrey, Jean,
Lawrence, Richard, and David — and to my grandfather,
Thomas Frederick Arnison. However, this book is most especially
dedicated to my grandmother, Winifred Arnison.*

Contents

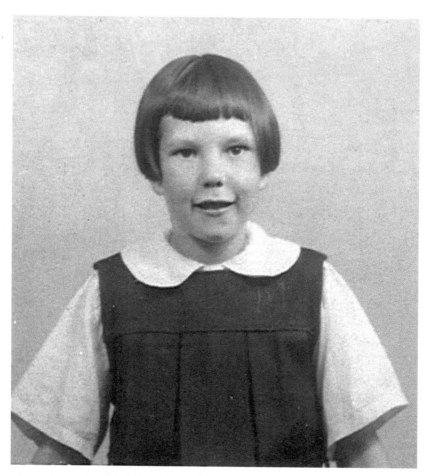

This is the earliest photo we have of Marjorie Arnison, taken at the Middlemore Emigration Home in Birmingham, 1937. The *M* on her tunic stands for "Middlemore."

Author's Note

While only a child, Marjorie was removed from her family in the Tyneside area of northeastern England and sent to Canada as part of the British child migration scheme. She was doing her duty to her king and country and, as Kingsley Fairbridge in 1909 and then the Prince of Wales in 1935 both emphasized, she was seen as an "imperial investment" in the British colonies.

Marjorie arrived at the Prince of Wales Fairbridge Farm School near Cowichan Station, Vancouver Island, British Columbia, Canada, on September 22, 1937, one day after her eleventh birthday.

Propaganda, in a variety of forms, such as brochures, newspaper ads, as well as newspaper and magazine articles from the philanthropic organizations seeking to be involved in the migration of children to the colonies, portrayed British child migration in the brightest of lights. Opposition was voiced but rarely heeded.

> This venture is backed by His Majesty's Government ... the consent of the Canadian Government and of the Provincial Government in British Columbia has already been secured for the starting of a school in that great province in the Great West.
>
> — "Fairbridge Farm School,"
> *The Times* (London), July 25, 1934

Marjorie's mother had little power to prevent three of her young children from being sent overseas to be trained as domestics and farm workers in the colonies, as this family was up against a system that was supported by the powerful in both Britain and Canada. Marjorie told me in an interview in January 2015 that she wasn't brought up, *she was dragged up* at this Canadian

This full-page article leaves no doubt that the Fairbridge Farm School scheme was fully endorsed by the Royal Family. Surrounding these three men are hundreds of donor names. The Fairbridge Society (a.k.a. The Child Emigration Society) had the backing of many influential people.[1]

farm school. She survived because that is what her instincts told her to do. She had her two siblings and a few close friends in her cottage, and she "got by because we had each other and because we had no choice."

Britain alone of the European Colonial powers seems to have made an industry of the export of its children.

— Geoff Blackburn, The Children's Friend Society, 1993

Strictly speaking, the Fairbridge Farm School is somewhat in the nature of a broker. They ask these public assistance authorities, who are like wholesalers, to supply the children to ourselves, who are the retailers.

— Letter to Frederick Charles Blair, Canadian Department of Immigration and Colonization, Ottawa, Ontario, regarding the material submitted for the Fairbridge Farm School, 1935

Farm School Plan is British-Backed. Number of English Children will be Trained on Vancouver Island to Become Canadians.... They will know Canadian farming thoroughly when they are through with us.

— *The Gazette* (Montreal), February 14, 1935

What better for the Empire than that in the newer lands it should be fed with trained material from the homeland, and its scattered elements united by the common culture and loyalty of those who from childhood had owed everything to St. George's England?

— "Youth and the Empire," *The Times* (London), April 25, 1935

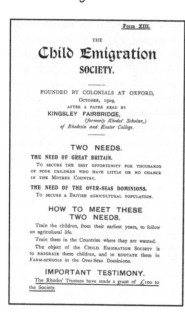

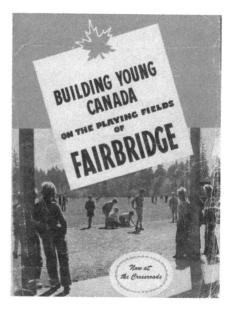

Child emigration pamphlet, circa 1910, and Building Young Canada on the Playing Fields of Fairbridge, circa 1949. Both images were from the Fairbridge Society's appeal for support, one at the beginning of Kingsley Fairbridge's campaign and the other when the Fairbridge Society found itself at a crossroads in Canada.

Foreword

This is a worthy sequel to *Marjorie Too Afraid to Cry*, which told a painful but critically important story of lives turned upside down by the then U.K. government's policy of sending children overseas and away from their families forever.

In February 2010, when I made a formal, full, and unconditional apology to the victims of the child migrant program on behalf of the British people, Marjorie's life was one of the stories at the forefront of my thoughts.

What happened at the Prince of Wales Fairbridge Farm School, where 95 percent of the 329 children sent there were not orphans but had families from whom they were cut off, continues to distress everyone who hears what went on there.

It was right that we said sorry to Marjorie and to all those who were truly let down.

Now we have another important chapter in her story. *Marjorie: Her War Years* recalls a childhood filled with loneliness, pain, and a sense of rejection. The children had no one to turn to and did not feel that anyone cared. Communication to the outside world was censored. Letters home had to give glowing reports — or the children were punished. Letters coming to Marjorie from her mother had sections blacked out or cut from the page.

This account shows how wrong it was that Marjorie and so many others like her were sent away at the time when they were at their most vulnerable. It was wrong that our country turned its back and did not see the tears or hear the cries for help. It was wrong that it took so long for an apology to be made and for Marjorie to be united with her brother.

The determination shown by Marjorie and all former child migrants to have the failures of the past acknowledged challenges us to do more. Like so many others, I am inspired by her spirit and resilience.

Marjorie Too Afraid to Cry shared a moving story of courage in the face of suffering, and this important sequel educates us about the callous and cruel mistakes that were made by decision makers — mistakes that should never happen again. While we cannot wipe out the pain, we can show that we understand it, that we are trying to make amends, and that we really do care.

— Gordon Brown, prime minister of the
United Kingdom, 2007–2010

Marjorie (Arnison) Skidmore receiving a personal apology from the former British prime minister, Gordon Brown, London, February 2010.

Winifred's Children

She wrapped her heart
Around their imaginary little bodies
If she held them too tight
Their essence would disappear
If she fought too hard
To hold them in her mind
She would squeeze the life out of them
And they would vanish like the mist
Her memories of them were illusive
Best seen out of the corner of her mind
Like a mirage
They could not be touched
Like the end of the rainbow
They could not be reached
She never stopped needing
To reach them again
To touch them again
To hold them again.

Introduction

THERE IS NO ONE MORE VULNERABLE THAN A CHILD

Unless the children are very carefully selected in England, some of them may have nervous breakdowns.

> — Harry Morris Cassidy, British Columbia's director of social welfare, was opposed to the opening of the Fairbridge institution. February 14, 1935[1]

All will not be rosy for these little girls and boys ... but they will be of an adaptable age.

> — *Daily Province* (Vancouver), September 21, 1935

Nowhere in the annals of British emigration history is there a more calloused expulsion of children, and nowhere in Canadian history is there a more shameful response to and treatment of the young and vulnerable.

> — Rooke and Schnell, *Discarding the Asylum*, 1983

The tale of my mother, Marjorie's, 6,600-mile journey as a ten-year-old girl in 1937, from Whitley Bay in northeastern England to the Prince of Wales Fairbridge Farm School near Cowichan Station on Vancouver Island, British Columbia, is told in my book *Marjorie Too Afraid to Cry: A Home Child Experience*.

Most of the children, once they arrived in their "new homeland," found themselves locked into a form of slavery until they reached adulthood. For so many, running from this past, burying the shame and the cruelty they had faced as defenceless children, was the only route to a sane future and a way to make a life for themselves. It was a childhood that far too few spoke of, and this worked to ensure this shameful episode of history was kept hidden from public view. The children who were sent away to help build Canada between the early 1830s and the late 1940s now need to find their proper and prominent places in the history lessons of the Canadian schools.

Even today I have people look me in the eye, their body language and tone of voice daring me to disagree, and claim: *It was the very best thing for each and every one of them. Those children were all better off.*

Others have challenged me: *Those children had nothing, they came from nothing, and whatever they found here had to be better than what they were removed from. Do you have any idea of the conditions in Britain at that time?*

What time? When? In 1618–1619, when King James I set in motion a policy of shipping children to the colonies? This policy was embraced, and as a result, child migration continued right into the 1970s.

This 1618 letter written by King James I authorizing sending British children to Virginia appears to be the starting point of British child migration to the colonies.

Trustie and well beloved we greet you well, whereas our Court hath of late been troubled by divers idle young people, who although they have been twise punished still continue to followe the same having noe employment.

We having noe other course to cleer our Court from them have thought fitt to send them unto you desiring you att the next opportunitie to send them away to Virginia, and to take sure order that they may sett to worke there, wherein you shall not only do so good service, but also do a deed of charity by employing them who otherwise will never be reclaimed from the idle life of vagabonds.

Given att our Court att Newmarket the thirteenth day of January 1618.

There were some difficult economic times over that 350-year period, I am sure. The poor were underpaid, and families could work together for twelve to sixteen hours a day and still not make enough to get by — and not getting by was seen as their fault.

However, the conditions that the children faced without their families, all alone, thousands of miles from anything that was familiar, were often terrifying, and the loneliness was soul destroying.

They had nothing!

Not true. They had families, they had identity, they had a community, they had their culture, and they had a country. They had roots.

It was the very best thing for each and every one of them!

Again, not true. My mother had the love of her mother. It was never replaced. My mother had the love of her siblings. They were torn apart. My mother was cast adrift at a very early age to find her own way. Once exiled to this strange country, she really did have nothing.

Marjorie's bearings were gone. She struggled with who she was without her family and the protection they offered. Her identity was lost as a new one was being crammed down her throat. She might have wondered, *If I try to be who you want me to be, then who will be me?* And like the children in the bottom photo on the front cover, she was forced to become a mere shadow of her former self. She was given the tools for her new life — mops and brooms, shovels, rakes, and hoes — while the tools they used to control her were threats, fear and isolation.

As Marjorie left Liverpool, her ten-year-old heart heavy with grief, her tears flowing into the River Mersey, she knew she had to forget her family, her country, and her roots in order to move forward and face her frightening and uncertain future, or all would be lost. She struggled to make sense of what she had done to deserve this fate. She worried about how to avoid repeating her unknown mistake, as from the start her captors made sure she knew that it could get worse, far, far worse, if she disobeyed them.

My mother was sent thousands of miles away from all that was familiar and brought up in an institution where most of her new "mothers" reminded her each and every day that she was a wretched British orphan. Marjorie screamed to herself, *But I am not an orphan,* her voice echoing with nowhere to go but inward. She was told regularly that she was a no-good guttersnipe, barely worth the effort it took to care for her.

The very best thing? For *all* those children over that *entire* 350-year period?

No one seemed to care how the children fared. The loneliness mixed with fear and confusion. The loss. The shame. The powerlessness. Missing identities. Homesickness. The abuse. The adult workload that so many were forced to do. No voice. Silenced. The lack of love and care.

Yes, it is true that some of the 120,000 children sent to Canada between 1833 and 1948 made good homes, and it's also true that regardless of their situation, many had a good life. But what choice did they have? The human will to survive can be strong. However, many did not or could not talk about their past, and they kept their "child migrant" history hidden from their new Canadian families. They tried to hide their British accent that would not go away, bury the pain caused by deportation, and conceal who they used to be because they could not make peace with their lost past and forced future.

It took me the first fifty years of my life before I was finally able to gain enough insight into my mother's hidden past to find out who she really was. My mother, Marjorie, was well into her seventies before I had a breakthrough. For years I faced the wall of silence. Nevertheless, I persisted, looking for a crack in the wall, as my need to have answers didn't diminish over the years, but grew. When my mother finally told me that she would get into trouble for speaking about her Fairbridge years, I realized the complexity and depth of her fear. I expected the silence to continue, but naming her fear helped to dissipate it. Thus, finally my mother was able to go back to that time, and slowly her memories emerged. Then, with research of my own, I was able to discover the many pieces of her lost childhood, and, at last, I was able to fully accept that former stranger who was my mother. Finding her past ultimately opened an avenue into who I am: now a person with roots, albeit severed, a person with a family — grandparents, aunts, uncles, and cousins — even if they are mostly unknown to me. But they are mine, and I now know who they are.

How could I know *me* fully without knowing the circumstances of my mother's life? They not only took the child migrants' roots away; they also denied these roots, the sense of family and identity, to the next generation.

Although the practice of child migration was strongly opposed throughout its history, its critics' opinions never seemed to carry as much weight as those of its supporters. Throughout the 1600s the practice of deporting Britain's unwanted children to the colonies expanded and it appeared that there was little control over the process, and the kidnapping of children became commonplace. The earliest newspaper record that I have located regarding the kidnapping of children was printed in London's *The Flying Post* on August 30, 1698. A vessel near the Thames was found to have two hundred kidnapped boys on board. The defence given to the judge by a crew member was that "he and three others, have for some time made it their practice to Kidnap boys, in order to sell them to the West-Indies." The article did not mention whether the crew were held accountable or whether the children were released.

Today we are aware that for eons Britain successfully hid some of the more sordid pieces of its past, and child slavery was just part of this hidden history. Historically, the negativity surrounding slave ownership has been placed, for the most part, on the United States, while the history of Britain's slave ownership during the seventeenth and eighteenth centuries has largely gone unknown, just like its child migration schemes, which began around the same time.

David Olusoga, in an article titled, "The History of British Slave Ownership Has Been Buried: Now Its Scale Can Be Revealed," stated that "geographic distance made it possible for slavery to be largely air-brushed out of British history, following the Slavery Abolition Act in 1833." Olusoga went on to say that for the forty-six thousand British slave owners,

> The Slavery Abolition Act of 1833 formally freed eight hundred thousand Africans who were then the legal property of Britain's slave owners. What is less well known is that the same act contained a provision for the financial compensation of the owners of those slaves, by the British taxpayer, for the loss of their "property." The compensation commission was the government body established to evaluate the claims of the slave owners and administer the distribution of the £20 million the government had set aside to pay them off. That sum represented 40 percent of the total government expenditure for 1834. It is the modern equivalent of between £16 billion and £17 billion.[2]

The well-established child migration scheme took a different turn when the abolishment of slavery left a labour shortage. The Children's Friend Society was one agency that began to ship children to South Africa in the 1830s to fill this need. This agency was also one of the first to send child migrants to Canada in 1833. They sent approximately 230 British children, mostly to Upper Canada (present-day southern Ontario), between 1833 and 1836. This sending agency was assailed with criticism from the start. The accusations included the kidnapping and selling of children. However, they had the support of many important patrons, including Queen Victoria,[3] and we must keep in mind that they were following an established tradition that had been in place since 1619. Kidnapping was an accepted part of the process. The authorities either sanctioned it or turned a blind eye. In May 1839, an article in a London newspaper, *The Operative*, titled "Transportation and Sale of the Children of the Poor," showed that not everyone supported the removal of Britain's children: "These traffickers in juvenile human flesh, who now stand convicted before the country, not only of transporting the poor children, but of selling them to the Dutch boors at the Cape, at prices varying from 8/ to 10/ (shillings) per head." The anti-slavery movement of the day might have influenced the British public, as the opposition to The Children's Friend Society was strong, and in 1842 it was dissolved.

The loss of one society may have stalled the deportation of children to the colonies, but it did not stop it. It had not only become commonplace, it was also a lucrative practice and many agencies sprung up to carry on this work. By 1869, a number of philanthropists in Britain began to round up children to send to Canada. The children were powerless, and their voices were not heard. And as former British prime minister Gordon Brown stated in the foreword to this book, "It was wrong that our country turned its back and did not see the tears or hear the cries for help."

In 1875, at the height of child migration to Canada, a man named Andrew Doyle was sent from Britain to report on how the child migrants were faring in their job of helping to settle the Canadian frontier. The resulting Doyle Report addressed the question of how to improve the process of child migration and included a number of observations that no one seems to have paid much heed to: "There appears to be nothing in the laws either of England or of Canada to prevent any person of a philanthropic or speculative turn, who can collect money for the purpose, from gathering any number of 'waifs and strays and street arabs,' and with their easily obtained consent shipping them to Canada."

As Doyle visited the children in their Canadian work placements, he observed: "Some of the places indeed, are worse than a Board of Guardians would consent to place a child in England." He criticized the fact that the children were presented in Canada as objects of pity: "It would surely be better to keep them at home, letting them take their chance of what Guardians can do for them amongst their own people." He felt that the children, taken from the British streets and placed on Canadian farms without any training, "will be less fit for service in Canada than they would be in England, and to send them as emigrants can be regarded not as a way of improving their position, but simply of getting rid of them at a cheap rate." Doyle felt that the placements the children were put in were "quite hard as, and in some respects more uninviting to the children, than the service in which at the same age they might be placed out in England." He reported that he "was often painfully struck in speaking to children … with the sense of loneliness manifested by them."

Doyle concluded that the employer often "gets the child's service merely for its maintenance. Employers may naturally feel that none but children the most destitute would in such a country as Canada be bound to serve upon such terms. No class of Canadians would consent to accept such terms of service for their own children."[4] Doyle openly criticized two philanthropists, Maria Rye and Annie Macpherson, for sending children to homes that were not vetted properly and for not being diligent in following up on how the children were managing in their work placements.

Maria Rye was responsible for shipping 4,200 to 5,000 children to Canada between 1868 and 1896. In a letter to *The Times* in London on March 29, 1869, entitled, "Our Gutter Children," Rye argued, "Can anything I introduce them to in Canada or America be worse than that to which they are doomed if we leave them where they are now?" Interesting that this attitude has carried through in some circles, to this day. Through her use of the possessive *our* in describing the children, Rye let the world know that she felt entitled to claim ownership of the children's future. Rye's work, like Macpherson's, had the support of the wealthy, and both continued shipping children to Canada in spite of the criticism. Rye sent children to Canada until 1896 and after 1896 the Church of England Waifs and Strays Society (The Children's Society) took over. Rye died in 1903, but the Children's Society continued to export children until the late 1930s. Even though Macpherson died in 1904, the Macpherson Homes carried on, and between 1870 and the 1920s close to ten thousand children were sent to Canada under this scheme.[5]

The children of the poor were treated as if they were expendable. They were unwanted material whose presence needed to be removed from the streets of England and carted away, as in Cruikshank's depiction of "Our Gutter Children."[6]

Rebecca Ward, in *An Alternative Approach to Child Rescue*, argued that "by vilifying the children they worked with and alleging that they were the paupers and criminals of the future, emigrationists in Birmingham and Manchester promoted themselves as offering a cost-effective alternative

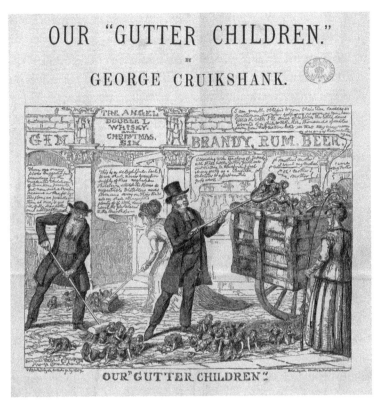

OUR "GUTTER CHILDREN."

Cruikshank was against the transport of England's innocent children to the colonies to be *white* slaves: "The proposition appears to me, like sweeping up the little girls, as so much mud out of our gutters, and pitching them into a mud cart, to be 'shipped aboard of a ship,' like so much guano, or like so many cattle, for a foreign market."

approach to child rescue that contributed to the gradual purification of society." The ongoing cost of caring for children in Britain versus the one-time cost of shipping them to the colonies was often put forth as an argument for the continuation of child emigration.

Authors Bean and Melville, in *Lost Children of the Empire*, argued that "all the organizations concerned with child migration differed in quality, methods, and philosophy, though for the children the end result was still exploitation and cheap labour.... Those who praise the philanthropists ignore one brutal fact: the children invariably didn't want to go."

Helen Boucher, in *Empire's Children*, tells us that in Britain, "between 1885 and 1913, Parliament passed more than fifty pieces of legislation pertaining to child welfare, including the landmark 1889 Prevention of Cruelty to Children Act, which empowered local authorities to remove boys and girls from parents convicted of neglect as well as the 1908 Children and Young Persons Act which obligated official intervention in such cases. This flurry of lawmaking emboldened many child savers." British law-makers appeared to ensure that the sending agencies were protected but not the children, nor their parents.

Children of the poor were sent to reform schools for slight infractions, and many reform schools had the authority to transport the children in their care to the colonies. Parents were judged against a system that gave them little power or control over their children. The list of those sending children to Canada had grown to over 110 agencies by the time the Fairbridge Society started their farm school in British Columbia. Some agencies only dabbled at migrating children, while others shipped out thousands. The British government's support of child migration was consistent throughout its 350-year history.

Almost fifty years after the Doyle Report, another study was requested in the face of continuing opposition to child migration to Canada. In 1924 the Canadian government invited the British Overseas Settlement Department to head a study to look at how child migration into Canada was being handled. A delegation led by Labour MP and trade unionist Margaret Bondfield was sent to Canada in November 1924. After a six-week tour of the children's work placements, she presented her report. The Bondfield Report concluded that the existing system was "liable to abuse." It recommended that no more children should be transported until they had reached the age of fourteen, the school-leaving age in Britain. The British government withdrew its financial support, and in April 1925, a Canadian Order in Council placed a three-year ban on unaccompanied children under the school-leaving age coming into Canada. In 1928 the ban was made permanent.

However, this did not stop the migration of British children to Canada. Barnardo Homes continued to send children, as did the Children's Society. When the Fairbridge Society approached Thomas Dufferin Pattullo, premier of British Columbia in 1934, about opening a farm school for child migrants in that province, Pattullo had "no objection to children of the required age being brought from Great Britain to be cared for" by this society.[7] And so the Fairbridge Farm School was established near Cowichan Station on Vancouver Island in 1935, a full ten years after the initial Canadian government ban. (This was the second such school; the first Fairbridge Farm School opened in Pinjarra, Western Australia, in 1912.) Premier Pattullo allowed the age restriction to be bypassed because the Fairbridge Society claimed they would be responsible for the children in their care until they reached age twenty-one.

The Prince of Wales Fairbridge Farm School barely got off the ground before it started to crumble, and many of the safety nets promised to its inmates were not there when they were needed. The Second World War and changing ideas about child rearing were major factors in its collapse. Sherington and Jeffery, in *Fairbridge: Empire and Child Migration*, argue that the 1933 Children and Young Person's Act "raised the question of the role of parents and the family ... in the general welfare of children. Whereas much of the older policy of child welfare had depended upon the removal of children from their families, the modern conception now emerging suggested that the family and family relationships were crucial in the development of a child welfare system." If anyone had taken the time to ask the children, most would have responded that their family was very important to them. Regardless of the shifting attitude against the removal of children from their families, the first party of forty-one child migrants arrived at the Fairbridge Farm School on September 25, 1935. All the children were under the age restriction suggested by Bondfield, and nineteen were between the ages of four and nine, with the eldest being thirteen. The Fairbridge Society sent Marjorie and her brother Kenny to this farm school in September 1937.

In 1944, twenty years after the Bondfield Report and almost seventy years after the Doyle Report, a B.C. superintendent of child welfare, Isobel Harvey, visited the Fairbridge Farm School. Harvey was asked to inspect the school after a member of the staff contacted the B.C. provincial child authorities to report ongoing instances of sexual perversion among the children under her care. There was also a sexual misconduct charge against one of the staff members at this time. This was the "in" that the province needed to make it past the wall of seclusion that the Fairbridge Farm School had maintained since its 1935 opening.

Harvey spent several days observing the day-to-day running of the farm school. The children were housed in cottages on the farm, with twelve to fourteen children per cottage. At the head of each cottage was a cottage mother. Harvey paid close attention to the dynamics in each cottage. The report of sexual perversion had to be investigated, but she found the reaction of the principal baffling. In her *Report on a study made of Fairbridge Farm School during the month of August, 1944*, she states, "When ... homosexual activities which have so alarmed others were discussed with him [the principal], he stated that the British people are over-sexed." The principal was the immediate head of the farm school, and his attitude toward the children would influence his staff. It was not just the hired hands and the older bullies that had their way with the children; I have been told by a number of former Fairbridgian males that they had their first sexual encounter with their cottage mothers. I don't know if the boys saw it as abuse, but today we certainly recognize the dangers and the imbalance of power.

Harvey's report criticized many aspects of the farm school life. Most importantly to me, her report confirmed the stories that my mother told me about much of her own life while in the hands of her wretched cottage mothers. Harvey stated that the "cottage mothers have too much power with the younger children, whom they discipline as they please. They lack sensitivity to the emotional needs of children, scream and shout at the children constantly, and are imbued with the Fairbridge doctrine that these children are different from Canadian children and must be shouted at and disciplined firmly, and that you must not be too kind to them."

It is not difficult to imagine what the cottage mothers were like when they were not being scrutinized. The farm school was isolated, and there was little interaction with the outside community. Old Fairbridgians (children who had been placed out to work away from the farm school) told Harvey that "they were handicapped by their lack of knowledge of Canadians, their accents, their clothes and their inability to make friends."

The children were sent away to be little Canadians, Britain's empire builders, yet they were kept isolated at the farm school for several years, treated like worthless trash, given little knowledge of what they might find when they were placed out to work in the larger community once they turned sixteen, and expected to be model citizens for Fairbridge. There are a number of cases where children, two of whom had arrived at the Fairbridge Farm School at the age of four, knew nothing of the world beyond the gates. The principal, Harry Logan, had to admit, "It was found that several of the older boys had never left the Farm School during the whole of their stay at Fairbridge and were quite ignorant of such elementary things as using the telephone or buying their own street car or bus tickets."[8] This isolation was a huge drawback for the children and added to their fear and loneliness once they were sent out to their work placements.

Harvey concluded:

> A Child Welfare worker viewing Fairbridge is left with a feeling of helplessness. The basic idea, antagonistic to every concept of Canadian Child Welfare, that these children are poor English children and, therefore, different from the ordinary child, is rooted so firmly in practically every staff member's mind that there is no use arguing against it. I was told over and over again by the Principal that I was incapable of understanding these children because they were English children. Anything they do, any trait they develop, is laid to the class from which they come.

The children were constantly reminded that they were second-class citizens in a country that did not want them in the first place. They were unworthy of kindness and love. Not all staff members in charge of the children took advantage of this attitude, but those who did were given a free rein, and the children were left to their own devices as to how to cope with the cruelty.

* * *

There are moments in history when past wrongs surface and refuse to remain concealed. British child migration to the colonies has been brought out into the light, and former child migrants and their families are gaining ground in their quest for answers and for this history to no longer be kept hidden. We will not be silenced any longer. The shame, so deeply rooted in many child migrant's hearts, was for many passed down to their offspring, but today we know this is not our shame and we will not rest until it has been placed squarely on the backs of the governments involved, where it belongs. There has been some progress, but as yet, it is not enough.

In 2001, as a result of the parliament of Australia's report on child migration, "Lost Innocence: Righting the Record," two major sending agencies went on record stating that it was wrong to send children overseas. In 2001, Barnardos Australia stated: "We have no hesitation in saying that it was a shameful practice, that it was barbaric, and that it was completely against any practices that we would currently uphold." Barnardos sent some of the last child migrants to Australia in the late 1960s and early 1970s. The National Children's Home also went on record, stating that it "is firmly of the view that child migration was a major mistake and we now deeply regret having taken part in it."

Public apologies to Britain's child migrants were given in November 2009 by the Australian government and then in February 2010 by the British government. This enabled many former child migrants and their families to begin to speak out about the betrayal and injustices brought about by this scheme. Instead of quietly fizzling out, the stories grew. Pandora's Box had been opened and it was not possible to shut it again. On February 27, 2017, the Independent Inquiry into Child Sexual Abuse, based in England, began its public hearings into the abuses so many children endured after being deported to the colonies. Such high-profile public apologies and inquiries have brought to light the darker side of British child migration, enabling a platform for the voices and stories of the former outcasts, which show clearly that deportation was certainly not the very best thing for each and every child.

It is time for the Canadian government to admit to its unwavering role in the migration of British children to this country for the purpose of their labour. In truth, some efforts have been made. On February 16, 2017, there was a motion in the House of Commons for such an apology. Luc Thériault (Montcalm, BQ) stated:

> Mr. Speaker, I ask for the consent of the House to adopt the following motion, with the support of the MP from Humber River–Black Creek [Judy Sgro], the MP from Chilliwack–Hope [Mark Strahl], the MP for Vancouver East [Jenny Kwan] and the MP from Saanich–Gulf Islands [Elizabeth May]:
>
> That the House recognize the injustice, abuse and suffering endured by the British Home Children as well as the efforts, participation and contribution of these children and their descendants within our communities; and offer its sincere apology to the former British Home Children who are still living and to the descendants of these 100,000 individuals who were shipped from Great Britain to Canada between 1869 and 1948, and torn from their families to serve mainly as cheap labour once they arrived in Canada.[9]

The following February, a private members' business motion, M-133, was sponsored by MP Guy Lauzon to recognize the British home children's contributions to Canadian society. Having this in place would enable a platform for educating the Canadian public about the British child migration program to Canada. I contacted my local MP, Elizabeth May, to ask her to support Lauzon's M-133. May responded, "Too few Canadians are aware of the BHC program's existence, let alone the horrific treatment so many of them endured. I will proudly vote in favour of M-133 in the House of Commons."

Lauzon encouraged all members to vote in favour, stating:

> Until recent years, very few Canadians knew about the British home children. Their stories of hardship, courage, determination, and perseverance are not part of Canadian history books. This needs to change. We owe a

great deal to these children for their contributions to our country. So far, we have been failing them. I encourage all members to make an effort to learn more about the story of the British home children, to share that knowledge with their constituents, and to do all they can to ensure that this chapter of their collective story is never forgotten.

On February 7, 2018, an important milestone in the fight for recognition of the contributions made by the British home children in Canada was realized:

> Pursuant to Standing Order 93(1), the House proceeded to the taking of the deferred recorded division on the motion of Mr. Lauzon (Stormont–Dundas–South Glengarry), seconded by Mr. Strahl (Chilliwack–Hope), — That, in the opinion of the House, the government should recognize the contributions made by the over 100,000 British Home Children to Canadian society, their service to our armed forces throughout the twentieth century, the hardships and stigmas that many of them endured, and the importance of educating and reflecting upon the story of the British Home Children for future generations by declaring September 28 of every year, British Home Child Day in Canada. (Private Members' Business M-133)

The motion was unanimously passed. September 28 of each year will be known as British Home Child Day across Canada.

On March 1, 2018, the Independent Inquiry into Child Sexual Abuse: Child Migration Programmes published its report. The inquiry heard evidence that the Fairbridge Society in England knew of the alleged sexual abuse of child migrants in both Canada and Australia from as early as the 1930s. With regard to the Prince of Wales Fairbridge Farm School on Vancouver Island, B.C., the report states:

In March 1938, Duties Master CM-F219 left the school after he had admitted, *"serious and gross misconduct with ... boys"* there. After the incident, Harry Logan (Fairbridge B.C. Principal) was clearly concerned to *"avoid talk of scandal as much as possible"* and to protect the *"good name of Fairbridge from being besmirched by the failure of one of her servants."* The Bishop of Victoria wrote to Gordon Green (Fairbridge U.K.'s Secretary) suggesting that CM-F219 should have been sent to prison, and that Mr. Logan should be replaced, but neither of these events occurred.

In July 1943, Duties Master Rogers was convicted of *"immoral relations"* with Fairbridge boys and imprisoned. He was also suspected of *"alarming behaviour towards older girls."* During a previous period of employment, he had been dismissed because of concerns of other staff members about sexual misconduct, and Mr. Logan's decision to re-appoint him had been controversial among the staff and the Canadian Welfare Council. Mr. Logan again hoped to avoid a scandal and that the affair would *"be viewed in its true light as something which may occur in work of the kind which we are doing at Fairbridge."* The evidence shows that: Mr. Logan later explained his decision to re-appoint Mr. Rogers by referring to the difficulties in obtaining trained staff (which we see to be a recurring theme in the child migration programmes); and he had obtained several references for Mr. Rogers on his re-appointment.[10]

The Canadian government needs to acknowledge that the voices of the British child migrants sent to Canada for the purpose of their labour are, for the most part, missing. Today most of these fractured stories need to be told through the descendants of the British home children. The history of British child migration and the part these children played in building this country needs to be taught in our schools. I want to hear the Canadian government say that it was wrong to receive young children in this manner and to acknowledge that more could have been done to ensure the safety of the children once they landed in Canada.

Life in the colonies was not rosy for all the children. Those who were more adaptable to their new environment fared better. The older children had a better understanding of what was happening and why, and those with siblings of the same gender had each other, giving a little comfort, but the younger the child, the more battles he or she faced. There was no one to turn to as they navigated through this new, sometimes terrifying and unfriendly environment that they found themselves placed in. The overworked and often untrained and unsuitable cottage mothers and duty masters rarely discouraged the bully system, and in fact they often encouraged it. The children were on their own and needed to quickly learn how to take care of themselves.

It is impossible to know the full extent of the abuse faced by the inmates of the Prince of Wales Fairbridge Farm School. Some former Fairbridgians remain vehement that no abuse ever happened anywhere on the farm school at any time and do not want to hear the stories of abuse and cruelty. This silencing from their peers has worked to stop some former Fairbridgians from speaking out about the abuses they faced during their Fairbridge days. The refusal by some to acknowledge that others experienced abuse at this farm school might be the outcome of years of control and brainwashing inflicted on them while they were inmates at the farm school. The children were told what to think, what to say, and how to feel … all handed out with a healthy dose of verbal abuse. Only glowing reports of happy, healthy, stable children were allowed to reach the public. It is little wonder, then, that the truth remained hidden all these years. In June 1934, Prince Edward, the Prince of Wales and future king, stated that "it is no exaggeration to say that the Fairbridge Farm School scheme is the only completely successful form of migration at the present time."[11] Public statements such as this would allow the belief to spread that British child migration to the colonies was a success. Likely, few bothered to look into it further; thus, perhaps the idea of it being the best thing for each and every child migrant was allowed to permeate society's consciousness.

The 329 children who went through the Fairbridge Farm School system near Cowichan Station have 329 different stories to tell. This book is based on what for me was the most important story to come out of that institution — my mother, Marjorie's. She raised me, and I knew her for sixty-six and one half years. I know first-hand the damage that was done by her deportation to Canada as a ten-year-old child. I lived with her fears, her anxiety, and her cringing in the face of authority. I still recall her nightmares as she ran through the house, tears streaming, screaming at an invisible assailant and begging for them not to take her children as she was taken all those years ago. And I, too, lived without my family, my English grandparents, my aunts, uncles, and cousins. We knew so little about each other because none of us fully understood the long-standing program of British child migration. My family did not know what to say, so they said nothing.

Home is where your stories begin. Without this base, your stories are severed, your identity shattered, your roots broken. We all need to hear the beat of our own drum, but when my mother lost her family, she lost everything, including the ability to make strong new sounds that she could relate to. Her voice and most forms of communication were silenced at the farm school. My mother was forced to reinvent herself in a critical and unsympathetic environment. She felt unsafe. She was placed in an institution where the only familial bonds she had left — to her younger brother and sister — were severed as much as possible. She had to look for a new identity, but unfortunately the parameters given to her at the farm school were a bad fit. She was reminded on a daily basis that she was of little importance. For many, a determination to survive grew within, and they fiercely fought for a life that they could relate to, not because of the Fairbridge Farm School but *in spite of it*.

Marjorie was at war with her "new life" throughout her five years at the farm school. Settling in and accepting this life meant giving up her dream of finding her family again. That dream faded over the years, and it became buried among her childhood memories and eventually lost to her as she looked toward her future and the day that she would finally be rid of the shackles of the farm school. She had no idea what she might find beyond its "walls," but anything would be better, and she was anxious to experience her freedom.

How can anyone believe that child migration was the best thing that ever happened to these young children?

It was certainly not the best thing for my mother, Marjorie, or for our family.

Who is more vulnerable than a child?

Chapter 1

WINIFRED'S CHILDREN

We insist that parish officers have no right to send children of the poor abroad; we protest in the name of the working classes against this scandalous abuse of their authority … indict the officers for child-stealing; this would probably bring the affair to an issue, disclose the names of some parties who are yet behind the curtain, and prevent this kidnapping of her majesty's subjects, which we believe is carried to a greater extent than the public are at present aware of.

— "Transportation of Children by Parish Officers,"
The Operative (London), February 3, 1839

The children on the Tyneside must be shewn the way to Fairbridge.

— Fairbridge Farm School, *Annual Report*, 1935

It was January 1937 when the lives of the eleven members of the Arnison family of Whitley Bay in the Tyneside area of northeastern England changed forever. It all began when the father, Thomas Arnison, received a letter asking him to give up four of his children. His wife, Winifred, and their children were living in Whitley Bay while he was in the London area working, saving for the day when he could bring his family down to be with him. Thomas replied to the letter, saying, "Providing my wife and the children are willing, I am quite agreeable to what you propose if my wife thinks that they will be better off away any how you have my full permission."[1] The emigration official that received the letter, unconcerned about the willingness or approval of his wife and children, scrawled across the top "This is a consent." The father's permission was all that was required.

Marjorie was in her eighties before she read a letter from her niece stating that it was to her mother, Winifred's, "eternal distress" that she had lost her children to Canada. Until that moment, she had not known that her mother's distress matched her own. It took my family many years to understand all the reasons and circumstances that underlay the deportation of Winifred's children to Canada. Winifred went to her grave with the loss permanently etched on her heart. It has been impossible to heal all the scars, although today we have come to a form of acceptance, easier now with the passing years and a greater understanding of the circumstances. Fortunately, the family no longer blame themselves for failing the children, as they now see, as Prime Minister Gordon Brown publicly admitted on February 24, 2010, that it was "the British government's fault for failing in the first duty of a nation, which is to protect its children."[2]

In February 1937, four of the Arnison children — Joyce, Marjorie, Kenny, and Audrey — were removed from their mother's care and sent to the Middlemore Emigration Home in Birmingham, where they were prepared for emigration to the colonies.

Canadian officials based in London, who had the final say on those who would be admitted into Canada, examined all the children that the Fairbridge Society selected for the Prince of Wales Fairbridge Farm School. Only children who passed the thorough investigation into their background and the testing of their mental and physical abilities were accepted. The children were vaccinated just prior to leaving England.

The use of immigration screening to enact a form of eugenics was not stated, per se, but the belief in it was alive and well in the offices of the Canadian government. Frederick Charles Blair, assistant deputy minister, Department of Immigration and Colonization, Ottawa, Ontario, worked to tighten Canada's immigration doors throughout his time in office. He not only made it his business to reject "substandard" British children, but he also attempted to keep out all who did not fit his image of the ideal Canadian citizen. Blair's policies had the support of the Canadian prime minister, Mackenzie King, who, while at the Évian Conference in 1938,[3] instructed his representatives not to support measures to assist refugees. The anti-refugee sentiment was strong in the Canadian government, and in 1938 Blair said, "Ever since the war, efforts have been made by groups and individuals to get refugees into Canada, but we have fought all along to protect ourselves against the admission of such stateless persons without passports for the reasons that coming out of the maelstrom of war, some of them are liable to go on the rocks and when they become public charges, we have to keep them for the balance of their lives." Allowing only the right stock into Canada was a priority for this government.

Given that, it is interesting to note that most, if not all, of the Fairbridge Farm School children were sent to Canada without birth certificates or passports.

Of the first 176 children presented by the Fairbridge Society for consideration for their Canadian farm school in 1935, the Canadian immigration officials rejected close to 75 percent. Reasons for rejection were varied; following are some examples:

> Younger brother mentally defective: rejected. Dislocation of hip — disability will tend to get worse: rejected. Father a soldier, but mother a neurotic hysterical woman: rejected. Underdeveloped: rejected. Nearly dumb, doubtful mentally: rejected. Tuberculosis in family: rejected. Bright but delicate: rejected. Good sharp boy but small. Wears glasses: rejected. Incontinence: rejected. Not good type, parents in trouble with the law: rejected. Child has half-caste appearance. Underdeveloped: rejected. Parents bad type: rejected. A backward child: rejected. Only a fair type of boy and does not impress as being at all bright: rejected. Poor physique: rejected. Physically defective: rejected. Poor musculature: rejected for the time being. Well-built, wears glasses, boy pilfers: rejected. Appears rather a stupid lad: rejected. Fish skin (ichthyosis

vulgaris), did not appear very bright: rejected. Mother has epilepsy: rejected. Boy backward and lacking in intelligence: rejected. A dull boy, underdeveloped: rejected. The boy is not up to standard: rejected. Deafness: rejected. Varicocele, flat feet: rejected. Defective heart: rejected. Only fair intelligence: rejected. Poor vision: rejected. Unsatisfactory condition of nose. Not impressed with this boy: rejected. Otitis media: rejected. Backward for age: rejected. Lordosis: rejected. Tic on right side of face: rejected. Below standard: rejected. Too small: rejected. Sulky and a fighter: rejected. Weak type: rejected.[4]

The Canadian government was after the brightest and the strongest of the poorer classes to do Canada's farm labour and domestic work. Siblings were separated, as the Canadian officials accepted one from a family but not the other. Some younger siblings were left behind at the Middlemore Emigration Home for years while their older siblings were sent to the colonies. Some were sent to Canada while their siblings were sent to Australia. The society claimed they made an attempt to send siblings to the same farm school in the same country, but in many cases this did not happen. Likely it simply came down to when a child was passed for emigration and where the next boat was headed. There are also a number of accounts where siblings were separated and put in different cottages once they arrived at the farm schools in Australia, effectively breaking their family bond.[5]

I have not heard of this happening at the Prince of Wales Fairbridge Farm School, but in Marjorie's case, she was separated from her brother, and her cottage mother made negative comments about her sister, Audrey, being too reliant on her. This was noted in Audrey's Fairbridge Farm School progress report dated March 31, 1939. One would think that siblings looking out for each other and relying on one another would ease the work of the adults in charge; however, from the start, this was not allowed.

When the three Arnison sisters were put in the Middlemore Emigration Home in February 1937, they were given cots in the girls' dormitory that were placed as far away from each other as possible.

Siblings were forbidden to comfort one another. Marjorie's older sister Joyce was punished a number of times when she was caught comforting her young sister, seven-year-old Audrey, once the dorm lights were out. They further punished Joyce when her three siblings were sent to Canada, leaving her behind because they thought she was thirteen and thus too old for the program.

Well into her senior years, Joyce never forgot the depth of distress that overcame her when she realized, after watching her sister Marjorie and brother Kenny walk away from the Middlemore Emigration Home in September 1937, that they were not coming back. In 1994 she wrote a letter to me: "It was the worst day of my life. I was ill in sick bay a long time, they said I was ill with a broken heart because they had taken them away and left me." Then, in August 1938, they sent her younger sister Audrey to Canada, leaving Joyce all alone this time. The children were herded and prodded and moved about with little concern for their needs.

Ten-year-old Marjorie and her eight-year-old brother, Kenny, left Birmingham for Canada in September 1937. It was traumatic for Marjorie and her brother to leave their sisters, Joyce and Audrey, behind at the emigration home. They had no say in their lives; they were not given the chance to say goodbye or to take any little treasures that they may have accumulated during their six-month stay. They were not told where they were going or why. The only avenue open to them was to do as they were told. By the time Marjorie boarded the ship in Liverpool, on September 10, 1937, at 6:00 p.m., she had shut down her emotions and pulled a cloak of protection around herself as the shores of her country disappeared. Trying to forget her past was the only way she knew how to face her uncertain future.

Crossing the Atlantic Ocean on the shallow-bottomed Canadian Pacific Railway (CPR) vessel the *Duchess of Atholl* left Marjorie in a haze of seasickness, as the vessel pitched and swayed its way through the September storms. Marjorie's seasickness was mixed with acute homesickness and a longing for her family, most especially her two sisters left behind in Birmingham. On the evening of September 18, after disembarking in Montreal, the group boarded a CPR car reserved for them and headed west. Once in Vancouver, British Columbia, they boarded the CPR ferry the *Princess Elaine* to Nanaimo, and then the Vancouver Island Coach Lines Limited bussed them on the last leg of their journey.

Marjorie and Kenny arrived at the Fairbridge Farm School near Cowichan Station on Vancouver Island on the afternoon of September 22, 1937. Marjorie had turned eleven on the train the day before. The twenty-eight British child migrants had travelled over six thousand miles from England. They were little empire builders with the purpose of maintaining "white stock" in the colonies.

Marjorie's first year at the farm school was fraught with fear, frustration, loneliness, anger, homesickness, and a growing resentment toward all the adults in her new life. Nightmares plagued her sleep, and a struggle to accept her new life plagued her days. Her younger brother Kenny was placed in a boys' cottage, and she had very little daily interaction with him. In a January 2014 conversation, Marjorie recalled that time:

> I couldn't do anything for Kenny at the farm school. He was on his own. I think that is what ruined him. No one understood him when he grew up. No one knew what we had all been through. He tried to tell me about the bad stuff on the boys' side, but he always held back, and we were always interrupted. I could never help him. It kills me to this day to have to admit that. You didn't dare walk over to the boys' section, so I couldn't help him. The boys and the girls at the farm school had separate pathways, and we were punished if we were found on the wrong path.

It was a bittersweet day when Marjorie's younger sister Audrey (now known as Bunny, a nickname she received during the voyage over to Canada that has stayed with her) arrived in August 1938. My mother recalled that day in an interview with me:

When she got off the bus, Kenny and I were there to meet her. She was so scared she peed her pants as she grabbed my hand and hung on desperately. She was so little. She was only eight years old. Once she got off the bus, she was told to go and stand in a certain spot, and I went with her. She wouldn't let go of my hand. She was glad to see me. She recognized me right away. Bunny was too afraid to cry; she just hung on to me.

She was so afraid that she used to sneak into my bed at night. My first cottage mother, Mrs. Read,[6] wouldn't allow this, and we were both punished when she found Bunny snuggled in with me. Then my next cottage mother, Miss Bishop, who we called D. Bitch, behind her back, of course, was even worse. She was a horrid, crazy, cruel little bitch of a cottage mother. She was just plain mean. She would sneak into our dorm room and check, and if she found Bunny snuggled with me she would make her get out. Then I had to listen to Bunny sobbing. But she had to cry quietly because if D. Bitch heard her, she would be strapped for crying. It was hard. I promised Mum I would look after her, so that is what I kept trying to do. Some of them were real bitches. Some of them? No, most of them. They were bitches from hell.

Having her little sister with her gave Marjorie someone to love, someone to care for, and a little sense of family. It was also someone to build memories with. However, it did not take away the pain of the loss of her family nor the frustration of being sent so very far away.

Marjorie tried to keep her memories of her family alive, but the pain and passing of time were more than she could control. It was a double-edged sword: keeping her memories of her family helped her feel less abandoned in her new world, but the memories were too painful to hold on to, and terror filled her as the loneliness stole in and engulfed her. She couldn't win. The details of Marjorie's childhood in Whitley Bay and her months at the Middlemore Home became deeply buried, but she clung

FAIRBRIDGE FARM SCHOOLS INC.
SAVOY HOUSE, STRAND, LONDON, W.C.2

The following ___HALF YEARLY PROGRESS___ Report, dated 31st March, 1939, has been received from the Prince of Wales Fairbridge Farm School, Vancouver Island, British Columbia.

Name ARNISON, Audrey.   Date of Birth 8.1.30.   Party 23.8.38.

COTTAGE Attwood.   SCHOOL STANDARD 3

COTTAGE MOTHER'S REPORT:
    A bright little girl, willing and obedient, is inclined to depend too much on her sister.
        R.E.RANDLESOME (Cottage Mother)

Fairbridge Farm School half-yearly report for Audrey, March 1939.

FAIRBRIDGE FARM SCHOOLS INC.
SAVOY HOUSE, STRAND, LONDON, W.C.2

The following HALF YEARLY PROGRESS Report, dated MARCH 1940, has been received from the Prince of Wales Fairbridge Farm School, Vancouver Island, British Columbia.

Name ARNISON, Marjorie   Date of Birth 21.9.1928 Party   Sept. 1937.

COTTAGE: Pennant.

Marjorie has not fitted into the cottage life as well as the other girls. She gets herself into so many arguments and quarrels with the other girls by being too officious and inquisitive. These two traits make them very rebellious towards her. She is very quick and willing in her work but generally it lacks thoroughness and she resents being told about it. Marjorie is very clean in all her habits. It is very difficult to keep her occupied as she does not seem to be able to concentrate on reading, games or sewing.

    (SD) D.BIRCH. Cottage Mother.

Fairbridge Farm School half-yearly report for Marjorie, March 1940.

to an emotional attachment to her family even when she could no longer conjure up a clear image of them.

In the spring of 1940, her progress report from her cottage mother told of her ongoing inability to settle in and accept her new life: "Marjorie has not fitted into the cottage life as well as the other girls."[7]

Marjorie's formal education ended with the June 1941 school term. It was farm school policy that when children turned fifteen years old they were called trainees and spent the next year working on the farm in preparation for their placement in the community the following year. Jock Bennett, a former Fairbridgian, said of his final year at the farm school that they worked hard for twenty-five cents a week; he called it slave labour. It may be that the farm school relied on the free labour of the trainees in their yearly budget and as a way to keep costs down.

At sixteen, the girls were put in private homes as domestic servants and the boys as farm hands on various farms and ranches on Vancouver Island, the lower mainland outside of Vancouver, and in the interior of British Columbia. The Fairbridge Society took half of their low wages with the promise that it would be returned to them when they turned twenty-one, but few ever saw this money again.

The story told in this book opens with Marjorie's arrival at the farm school and documents her day-to-day life and the struggles she faced during her incarceration there. It ends in the winter of 1942, when she was placed out to work as a domestic servant in Victoria, on southern Vancouver Island, British Columbia.

Chapter 2

A DIFFICULT YEAR: FORCED ADAPTATION TO A NEW DAILY ROUTINE

The difficulty of providing employment at home, under existing circumstances, we admit, but that difficulty is an argument, not for emigration, but for a change in our social system. We deny that there is a surplus population in England.... There is a part of the population ill-fed, but not because there is not enough food, but because the wealth of the country is locked up in a few hands.

— Quoted in Blackburn, *The Children's Friend Society*

Children, who are still growing in body and mind, take to their new lives ... as easily as putting on a new coat.

— Fairbridge Farm School, *Annual Report*, 1936

Marjorie lifted her head to look out the bus window. Mistrust of the world permeated every fibre of her being. She could no longer rely on her own senses. Unfamiliar feelings caused chaos within. She felt mixed up. Exhaustion filled her. She squeezed her eyes shut. She felt like crying, but even her tears were confused and dried up. Homesickness was so thick it filled her belly, threatening to come up all over the front of her travelling coat. Where had they sent her? She was so far from Whitley Bay, and the land was very strange. The view out the window grew bleaker and bleaker the farther they travelled. Where were the houses? Where were the towns? Where was she? Could she trust these people not to harm her? Hansel and Gretel came to mind, and she tried to push away the gnawing fear. The forests were unlike anything she had ever seen before.

The bus stopped at a rugged, wild, and unfamiliar place, and the chaperone told the children, "Here is your new home."

Marjorie clung to a little white box as she stepped from the bus. In it was a piece of birthday cake that the chef had handed her as she got off the train in Vancouver that morning. It was in celebration of her eleventh birthday. Her birthday had been the day before, but she hadn't said anything to anyone until breakfast that morning, and she'd just blurted it out because the chef was nice to her. He also gave her a Canadian penny as a souvenir. It had leaves on it and was inscribed with the word "Canada." Marjorie was surprised at how small it was. The chef said that it had her king on it, King George VI. She wanted to say that he wasn't her king — she didn't have a king anymore — but she quietly slipped the penny into her coat pocket. She carried her cake on the bus tour around Stanley Park during their morning's drive. She carried it onto the eleven o'clock sailing of the *Princess Elaine* ferry between Vancouver and Nanaimo. She almost dropped it on the ferry, when, for a brief moment, she dared to hope. As the ferry passed some land just before docking in Nanaimo, she heard someone call it Newcastle. Maybe, just maybe, it was her Newcastle, and this nightmare was about to end. But it was Newcastle Island and not Newcastle, England, and having this bit of familiarity ripped away left an empty feeling. She carried her cake off the ferry and onto the waiting bus. She looked at her cake on the bus and could see that it was getting battered, and the icing was sticking to the lid. She tasted the creamy icing, but it stuck to her throat and she couldn't swallow. She dropped the box when it was jerked out of her hand as the bus careened around a bumpy, winding section of the dusty dirt road. She would have lost it for good if Kenny hadn't caught it as it skidded down the aisle. She held her cake tight, crumpling the box a little, as she stood panic-stricken on the bus, terrified to walk down the steps. Holding this box was like holding on to hope. Would eating her cake mean that she accepted her new life?[1]

As she stood, she said over and over to herself: *I don't want a new home. I want my home. I don't want a new life. I want my mother. I want my family. I don't want a new family.* She watched her little brother Kenny. He looked as worn out as she felt. They had been travelling for ages now; she had lost count of the days. Where were her sisters? Did they miss her as much as she missed them? She tried to remember what her mother looked like, but the image was already becoming faded.

"Okay, children. Quiet now. When I call your name, step forward and I will tell you which cottage you will be in and who will show you to your new home. You will find your suitcases with your house leaders. Quiet, please! Just listen for your names. Kenny Arnison, Strathcona Cottage; Marjorie Arnison, Attwood Cottage; Frederick ..."

In her heart, Marjorie knew her nightmare was just beginning, and it was one that she could not wake herself from. She stood where she was told to stand. Obedience was akin to survival. She felt light-headed, alien, alone, and uncertain. Cautious. She watched her younger brother move over to his group. They gave each other a slight wave. They were discrete, as they had learned early on not to draw unwanted attention to themselves, but the little wave was an acknowledgement that they both still had each other, giving them one known person here in this strange land and a connection to their past, to *their* family.

When all twenty-eight newcomers were assigned to cottages, two girls already at the farm school led Marjorie and the new girls down the path. Kenny and the group of new boys followed the two older boys they were assigned to in the opposite direction from his sister. He was used to being separated now; it was just part of the drill. The lead girls whispered to one another as they neared one of the buildings. Marjorie stopped dragging her suitcase and tried to hear what they were saying. It sounded like "Should we warn them?" *Warn us about what?* Marjorie's tired heart sank. There seemed to be so much to be afraid of now.

Marjorie looked up, saw a large woman standing in the doorway, and automatically scanned her face, trying to get a sense of what to expect and to see if she looked friendly. On this journey she had come into contact with some who put her at ease, while others put her in immediate survival mode as she kept out of striking distance. The woman before her waddled like a duck when she walked. Marjorie gasped as she attempted to stifle a panicky giggle. Her nerves had become unreliable and she couldn't foresee whether laughter or tears would pour out when faced with alarming situations. Mostly she just tried to remain silent, but that wasn't always possible. This woman did not look welcoming. There was only sternness in her face with no trace of a smile. Marjorie's instinct was to run; yet she knew she had nowhere to run to.

"Hello, girls. I am your cottage mother, my name is Mrs. Read. Come in and I will explain the rules. I expect obedience and absolutely no nonsense. Do I make myself clear?"

"Yes, ma'am."

The girls were shown where to hang their coats. It was a warm September day, so they were happy to be free of the heaviness. Next they were shown where they could unpack their suitcases. The tour continued up the stairs. As Marjorie climbed, she counted eighteen stairs. Next the girls were shown into a dorm crowded with cots. The cottage mother assigned a cot to each new girl. Above each cot was a small shelf for a few personal items. All the while she rattled on about the rules: Make your bed, and make it properly the first time or there will be penalties. Keep your area tidy. No talking after lights out. Dinner is in one place and breakfast and lunch in another, and the schedule changes for the weekend. The bell by the dining hall[2] must be obeyed. Do not be late for meals, for school, for chores, for church. Do not walk on the boys' path. Do not fraternize with the boys. There will be no hanky-panky allowed. The cottage mother pressed again that obedience would be the key to their happiness.

"Do I make myself clear?"

"Yes, ma'am," a chorus of tired voices responded.

"Okay. I will show you the kitchen. Follow me." Mrs. Read stepped quickly from the room, and the new girls instantly followed. They passed a closed door.

"This door leads into my rooms, and you must never enter unless you are invited. Do I make myself clear?"

"Yes, ma'am."

As the girls approached the kitchen, they were told, "You will learn how it works and what you each need to do every day starting tomorrow.

But now it's time to go to the dining hall where there are some refreshments waiting. Okay, girls, line up and let me look at you."

The tired newcomers were used to being lined up; they automatically formed a row.

"You. What is in that dirty, crumpled box you're carrying? Are you bringing filth and germs into my cottage?"

"No, ma'am." Marjorie looked at her precious box with horror. "The chef gave it to me because it was my birthday yesterday." Her voice trailed off.

"Your what? Speak up. How do you expect me to understand the lot of you if you don't speak clearly? Give that to me you little street urchin." Mrs. Read wrestled the box out of Marjorie's hand and crammed it into the wood stove before Marjorie could utter a word of protest. One lone tear slid down her cheek. What did it matter? Everything else was gone.

As Kenny reached his cottage, he looked up and saw a thin woman standing in the doorway. She looked like a mad little bird. Her sharp features were anything but inviting. Kenny had no idea how astute his initial observation was, as this cottage mother turned out to be wickedly mean and had a foul temper. Miss Bishop acted like a vulture and would swoop down and strike when the children least expected it. Before Marjorie left the farm school, she, too, would endure years of abuse from this woman.

And so began Marjorie and Kenny's first day at the farm school.

The next morning was Thursday, a school day. There was no time for the new children to get used to the farm life; it carried on, and they had to catch up to it and fall in line as quickly as possible. The fall school term had already begun, and morning classes started right after breakfast. The clanging of a metal spoon on the frame of one of the iron cots jarred Marjorie from her fretful sleep. The cottage mother ordered everyone up. The girls scrambled to get dressed, get washed, and make their beds, and then they lined up by the door, ready to go to the dining hall for breakfast.

Marjorie shivered in the cool morning air. She looked for the coat she had been wearing yesterday, but it was no longer there. In its place was a row of different coats, not the nice ones that they wore to travel in. The ones hanging now were ragged and worn. She wanted to take one, but she didn't know whether she was allowed. Then she remembered her penny. She had forgotten to take it out of her pocket. Nothing mattered. It was just a silly penny. And besides, she could not see any shops where she could spend it.

Marjorie walked out with the girls and joined the other groups making their way to the dining hall. She automatically looked for Kenny, but he was nowhere to be seen. When she entered the dining hall, she saw him already sitting with his cottage mates. Marjorie found out later that his cottage, Strathcona, was at the opposite end of the village from hers.

Marjorie quickly fell into the routine at the farm school; the children were kept so busy that they had little time for reflection. Her day was regulated from the moment the cottage mother woke them up in the morning to the moment Marjorie lay her head down at night. The dining hall bell, the day school bell, and her cottage mother's yell further regulated the day.

All freedoms, especially the freedom to be herself, had been taken away. Her opinions, her needs, her wants and desires were not important to the plans that her new wardens at the farm school had in store for her. She was a number, a cog in the child migration wheel, and the system only worked if she obeyed.

She had no choice but to go along with their demands; there was nowhere to go and no one who cared to hear what she wanted. Fighting the system took away the few moments of play that she was lucky enough to get. Punishment for fighting the system came with the knowledge that it would only get worse for those who did not comply. Each day that Marjorie awoke at the farm school, she fought it less and less. It was pointless. She would bide her time, bury what she couldn't cope with, and keep hope alive for a time when she could get away.

The fall went by, and soon it was early December and talk of Christmas had begun. It would be her first Christmas away from her family. As the snow fell silently outside, Marjorie decided to write a letter to her mother. Her chores were done for the day, giving her a bit of time before bed. She needed to try to keep some memories, because without them, her family in Whitley Bay was fast becoming a dark hole. Nothing. A type of amnesia.

Dear Mum,

I miss you. Why did you send us to this horrible place?
Don't you love me anymore? I love you and miss you so
much. I hate our cottage mother. She is mean and ugly,
and I want to come home. Kenny's cottage mother is an
old witch, too, and he hates it here and wants to come
home, too. I miss Joyce and Audrey, and I can't look after
Kenny because they keep him separated from me. Please
can you come and get us? There are some bad people
here. We need you. I don't want to be here for Christmas.
I want to be home with my family.

Love from your daughter, Marjorie

She sealed her letter and put it in the cottage mail basket, feeling happy
for the first time in ages.

The next morning Mrs. Read pulled Marjorie out of her bed. She could
see in her cottage mum's eyes that she was in trouble. She quickly searched
her mind, trying to remember what she might have done.

"You horrid little liar! How dare you write such rubbish?" Marjorie
could see her opened letter in Mrs. Read's hand!

"Why did you read my letter?" Marjorie was angry, but her voice
cracked, showing she was more frightened than furious.

Mrs. Read didn't reply. She tore Marjorie's letter up and threw it at
her. "Pick that up and put it in the fire. You can miss breakfast, and while
we are gone I want you to mop the kitchen floor and fill the woodbins as
punishment. If you dare to write such rubbish again, you will be sorry.
You are an ungrateful little wretch after all that we have done for you. No
more lies! Have I made myself clear?"

"Yes, ma'am." Marjorie wanted to wipe off some of the cottage mum's
spittle that had landed on her face, but she was too afraid to move. Mrs.
Read turned and stomped back to her sitting room. Marjorie wiped her
face and bent down to pick up the pieces of her letter. Her hopes of rescue
were gone. How could her mum rescue her if she didn't know that she

needed to be rescued? Tears welled up and couldn't be stopped no matter how hard she tried.

"Stop that snivelling, you little guttersnipe." The witch had suddenly appeared behind her. "You were brought here to learn to work, and by my word I am going to see that you do it properly. Pick up that mop and get started. If I see any streaks, you will mop the floor again. Do I make myself clear?"

"Yes, ma'am."

Marjorie watched the girls from another cottage with envy. It was a lovely spring day, the air was warm, and the leaves were starting to bud out. It was the kind of day that made you forget all about the long, cold winter. The girls' laughter reached across to Marjorie. She watched as they surrounded their cottage mother. One girl had linked arms with her cottage mum, and another held her hand; their arms swung gaily as they walked along. At lunchtime, on the way to the dining hall, Marjorie grabbed her cottage mother's hand but was quickly slapped away.[3]

"Don't you touch me!" Mrs. Read hissed.

Marjorie jumped back, hurt and confused. She needed someone to care. Why wasn't she in the other cottage with a nice cottage mother? At that moment she missed her sisters more than anyone. *Where are they? What did they do with them?* she wondered.

Later in the day, two cottage mothers were chatting over coffee: "Can you believe one of my girls tried to hold on to me today! I can't allow myself to get close to any of these girls. How on earth could I keep control over them?" Mrs. Read's eyes rolled skyward.

"Yes, you have to keep your distance. The next thing you know they'll want to climb up on your lap." Miss Austin laughed.

"Oh my goodness, what a thought! Nestling with a guttersnipe! What is this world coming to? The problem with being trapped way out here, miles from even the small town of Duncan, is that we can't look for a better job. We're stuck here with these wretched British brats."

"Well, we'll just have to stay on our guards while we're here. I don't trust my girls. Some mornings I think they would just as soon knock me down the stairs as say hello."

"I know what you mean. One of my girls tossed a piece of firewood at me, and it nearly hit me. They're little animals! Anyway, I taught her a lesson; she'll think twice next time. I swear that these children are the spawn of the Devil.[4] And getting them to do their chores on time and properly! Well, I could pull my hair out at times, I get so mad. Useless British trash, really. They should have stayed in the old country; then they wouldn't be our problem. Why they were brought here, I really cannot understand. I bet England is getting the better deal — cleaning up their stock and keeping this country British at the same time. Mark my word, it will be Britain that comes out on top, not us."

"I thought Canada needed these workers to take the jobs that our children refuse to do?"

"Yes, I guess we need workers, but what kind of workers will these children become? Well, just let me say it won't be my fault because they are almost impossible to teach."

The two cottage mothers chatted on, sharing the bits of news that circulated around the farm. One had heard of parents trying to have their child returned to them in England. It was funny, as they knew that the farm school was not about to give up any of its wards. This made Marjorie's cottage mum recall a letter she saw by mistake in the principal's office. The mother of one of her girls was using a friend to try to get her daughter.

"Imagine." Mrs. Read smirked. "The mother wanted her back, and this girl was born out of wedlock. I saw the mother's letter, too," she continued. "Here, I'm quoting, 'I will be glad if you are able to get my daughter.' What on earth was she thinking? The girl was hardly worth the effort it took to look after her, and the mother was in no position to take care of her daughter let alone come up with her fare back to England."

"Really? Which girl was it?" News like this interested Miss Austin.

"I better not say. I think the administrators told the parents that it would be most disturbing for a child to make a readjustment, and they assured the mother and her friend that children, without exception, prefer to stay in Canada. They told the mother that the girl must remain in Canada and learn at the farm school to make her way as a Canadian."[5]

"Canadians, my foot. It will take more time than we have to turn these brats into something useful to Canada."

The cottage mothers may have been able to chat to each other, but Marjorie had no one. Still, she had to unburden herself. Cottage life unsettled her. She couldn't write to her mother — not the truth, at any rate — and she was afraid to confide in the other girls. Shortly after she arrived, a girl in her group spoke openly when asked how she liked her cottage mother. Without hesitation, she said that she thought she was a mean old witch. She was punished for it, as the conversation was reported back to her cottage mother, and the retaliation was harsh and quick. The news spread in the cottage, letting all the children know that it was best to bury feelings and be very careful about whom you trusted. It was the same for the boys. On one of the rare occasions that they were able to sneak in a quick visit, Kenny told Marjorie that he'd tried to talk to his teacher about the unfair treatment he was given when he was strapped for something a big kid had done, but instead of any understanding he was punished again and told he wouldn't have been punished in the first place if he didn't deserve it. The rules were unfair. At times Marjorie felt completely bottled up and ready to explode. Then, an idea came to her. She couldn't send a real letter to her mum, but she could write a pretend letter to her. No one could stop her. No one could read her thoughts. She could pour her heart out without fear of being punished. Marjorie lay back in her cot and began:

Dear Mum,

Why did you send us away? I want to come home. I hate it here. I miss Joyce and Audrey every day. I miss you, and it has been over one year now since I last saw you. I feel so alone. I hardly ever see Kenny, and he seems so sad. There are so many bullies here, and they go after the little ones like Kenny.

The girls in my cottage are mostly okay. Some are bossy, and I don't know who I can really trust, but the mean thing in my cottage is the cottage mother. And she is not a mother. She is a nasty old thing, and I hate her. And I am not the only one. The other day she was fighting with one of the big girls and the girl tossed a large piece of firewood at her, almost hitting the cottage mother on the head. The old witch deserved it, but, of course, the girl was really punished and we all had to watch. There is no fairness here.

I will tell you about a normal day at this awful place — well, there is nothing normal about anything, really. We are forced from one thing to another. Go here, go there, do this, don't do that. Our cottage mother yells at us all the time, even when we try our best to do our jobs properly. For a normal school day, we get up and make our beds. Then we get dressed and washed. We have twelve cots jammed into our dorm, so we have to be careful when we make our bed. We have no privacy to get dressed. We go to the dining hall for breakfast, and we take our dishes and cutlery from the cottage, and then we come back to our cottage to return the dishes and cutlery to get them washed. While the dishes are being done, the ones not on dish duty bring in firewood, sweep the floors, and clean the bathrooms and the cottage mother's room. I hate going into her room. It is smelly just like she is. Then we go to school for the morning, and for lunch we go back to the dining hall. My cottage mother put me at the end of our table, and when the food is served I usually get mine last, and the oatmeal never has any sugar left, and the best things are already taken. I don't care. I get so mad it feels like an explosion, and so I try very hard not to care.

Remember how we would always share everything and make sure we all got some? We don't do that here. We have to fight for everything, but you get punished for fighting, so you have to make sure no one sees you fighting. And the cottage mother has her favourites, and I am not one of them, so it doesn't matter if she doesn't see me 'cause I get blamed anyway.

After lunch we go back to school, and after school there are chores. If we are on punishment duty, we stack firewood or chop kindling and fill the furnace room and bring in wood for the cottage mother's fireplace. I carry a lot of firewood. The chores change all the time. If you're on supper duty in your cottage, you help get supper ready. We call it tea, but they call it supper. Everyone has supper in the cottage during the week.

The kitchen stove in our cottage is heated with wood and not coal. I had to chop and carry all the wood last Saturday. I did chores all day, and I didn't have much free time. Sometimes we get to play in the playing fields. The boys and girls are allowed to play together on the playing fields, and I sometimes get to talk to Kenny when he is there. Not much, though. Big kids call him a baby if he wants to talk to me. On Sunday we go to church. Some kids go into Duncan for church. And, Mum, there is one duty master who the big girls call a sex maniac and say that he tries to get his jollies with the girls. The big girls told us to avoid him. This is not a good place. Please come and get me.

Love,
Your daughter, Marjorie
P.S. I hope you remember me.
P.P.S. I dreamed about you the other night. You were singing. I was in a different room, but I could hear you clearly as if I was right beside you.

Marjorie would have given anything to be able to see her mother, to talk to her, to hug her and let her know that her new life was horrible. She would have held her and not let her go. She fell asleep that night with a lighter heart. It felt good to tell someone her troubles, even if it was just herself.

Spring turned to summer. The day school's second wing was being built. Other cottages were being built, too. The farm was in full swing with the days devoted to garden chores and preserving the food they were growing. The farm school had lots of visitors and everyone had to be on their best behaviour. Several photos were taken where the children were told to smile their biggest smiles. Marjorie and Kenny had to be in two group photos. One was of all the children who had come from the Tyneside area of England where she and Kenny had come from, and one was of all the children who had come from the Middlemore Emigration Home. Marjorie didn't want to be reminded of Middlemore, and seeing all the Tyneside kids together just made her sad. Marjorie was also introduced to the swimming hole on the Koksilah River. She had learned to swim in the pools at Whitley Bay and was already a strong swimmer, so she was allowed to swim out to the raft. Swimming was the best part of summer.

One afternoon in mid-August, Marjorie came in from the fields, hot and dusty and in no mood for anything other than a cooling swim in the Koksilah River. As she neared the cottage, she could see her cottage mother in the doorway. She eased away, thinking she might avoid her, but no luck. Mrs. Read had to repeat herself before Marjorie fully understood what she was saying. She stood stunned. Her cottage mother told her to close her mouth or she'd be catching flies.

Her sister Audrey was coming. They had left Liverpool the day before and would arrive at the farm school in a couple of weeks. Marjorie didn't know whether to laugh or cry. She was excited that she would get to see her sister but felt bad that Audrey had to come to this place. She asked about Joyce, but Mrs. Read said that she had heard nothing about a sister named Joyce. Marjorie turned and ran, wanting to tell Kenny the news. She didn't even care if she had to break the rules by going on the boys' path to find him.

Every day Marjorie asked the same thing: "Is Audrey coming today?" "No, not today," was always the answer. Then one morning Mrs. Read said, "Not today, but today we are going to walk to Cowichan Bay to pick blackberries." Marjorie protested, crying that she didn't want to go in case Audrey showed up, but the cottage mother told her to stop being so silly.

The girls stopped by the old Stone Butter Church[6] in Cowichan Bay to have their lunch. The church was just an empty shell of a building, but there was something fascinating about it. The large openings for the windows had no windowpanes. Marjorie and some other girls climbed up on the windowsill to eat lunch. Their feet hung into the church, and the warm afternoon sunshine fell on their backs. Why someone would build the walls and ceiling of a church and then go away and not finish it simply did not make any sense to her.

After lunch Marjorie was thrilled to walk down the road to the beach at Cowichan Bay. It was a long walk, but it was worth it. For a moment the beach smells and the sounds of the seagulls brought her right back to her home at Whitley Bay, and she was playing on the sands again. She closed her eyes and breathed in the salty ocean air. She wanted the moment to last and last. She stood and savoured this treat. It was powerful and familiar and so unexpected. She stood quietly with her eyes closed tightly. Her

Sisters Audrey (Bunny) and Marjorie at the Old Stone Church, 2014. The waters of Cowichan Bay can be seen on the far right of the photo.

The Vancouver Island Coach Lines arriving at the remote Prince of Wales Fairbridge Farm School with another party of children.

Audrey

Audrey (Bunny) and her party of twenty-eight children on the *Duchess of York* (left). The girls are reunited. Audrey (Bunny) and Marjorie at the farm school (above).

senses tingled with happiness as she felt the ocean breeze on her face. She kept her eyes closed and smiled to herself. The magic was broken when Mrs. Read shouted at her, asking her if she was daft, standing there with her eyes closed. She felt her balance slipping; she opened her eyes and looked around. Marjorie tucked this special moment away to savour later. She was finding that there were some things that no one could take from her. She picked up a few seashells and put them in her pocket. Her Whitley Bay beach had the best sand in the world. Cowichan Bay was muddy, but the salty ocean smell touched her like a present. The seagulls swooped and dove in the sky just like her Whitley Bay gulls. They made her homesick, but this new homesickness, when mixed with the ocean smells, had a strange comfort to it. She was on the beach and away from the farm, and that was all that mattered for the moment. She hadn't known the beach was so close to the farm school and close enough to walk to. The girls headed the five miles back to the farm, carrying their buckets of blackberries, but Marjorie carried a lot more than blackberries back with her. She was happy for the outing and a break from the garden chores.

Marjorie heard the bus coming before she could see it. Her sister Audrey was almost here. She had helped to get her cot arranged. She wanted it to be placed next to hers, but that was not allowed. She asked her cottage mother over and over again about whether Joyce would be coming with Audrey, too, but was told that Joyce was not assigned to the cottage and if she kept asking she would have to do extra chores. Mrs. Read hoped that Marjorie might settle in better once her sister arrived. It had been almost a year now, yet she still acted homesick and was difficult and argumentative.

DOCTOR BARNARDO'S "AFTER SAILING" NOTIFICATION

18 to 26 Stepney Causeway,
London, E.
1888

To _____(Parent or Guardian)_____

I am desired to inform you that in accordance with the terms of the agreement entered into when

_____(Name of Child)_____

was received into this Institution, the Managers included her in the party of girls who left these Homes for Canada.

Should you desire to write to her, the address is the

The Secretary, "Dr. Barnardo's Homes, "Hazel-brae, Peterborough, Ontario, Canada. Your letter will need a penny stamp.

DRH

Malcolm Jackson, Esq.,   29th
35 Dean Street,   July,
Newcastle on Tyne.   1938.

Dear Mr. Jackson,

I have to confirm that arrangements have been made for Audrey Arnison to be included in the party of children due to sail for the Prince of Wales Fairbridge Farm School, British Columbia, on the 11th August.

Audrey will not be coming to London to stay with Dr. Jeffs as previously arranged, as he wants Bobby Cockburn instead. She will therefore come to London with the other Middlemore children on the 10th August.

Yours sincerely,

SECRETARY.

P.S. Do you think we should notify the mother?

Dr. Barnardo's Homes sent "After Sailing" notifications to parents. It appears that the Fairbridge Society followed their lead, as is evident in this letter from the Society's office at 35 Dean Street, Newcastle-on-Tyne, regarding Audrey Arnison's imminent departure for the colonies, which questions whether to inform her mother before or after sailing.

Chapter 3

BUNNY'S BIRTHDAY

We are merely transferring them from part of the Empire
to another — from our own England where they have
no prospects, to our own Canada, where their prospects
are as bright as the flame that glows on the maple leaf
in the fall.

> — Arthur Chilton Thomas, manager of Father Berry's
> Homes of Liverpool, cited in Rooke and Schnell,
> *Discarding the Asylum*, 1902

Nature abhors a vacuum; sooner or later Destiny presents
its account to those countries which neglect to populate
themselves.

> — "Those Empty Spaces,"
> *Morning Post* (London), May 10, 1935

With the arrival of her little sister at the farm school, Marjorie
finally had new memories, recent memories, that gave her joy
without the pain. Today was Sunday and a beautiful day for a birthday.
The valley was having its first winter storm of the new year. Yesterday,
the girls had run to their cottage after school as the wind howled, but
by bedtime there was a strange calm. Marjorie slept fitfully when the
wind blew fiercely through the trees around the farm school cottages.

She would lie awake some nights just worrying about things. She was thankful for the calm, yet last night she was restless and her sleep was full of dreams. She was excited about Bunny's birthday, but with it memories of other birthdays with her family crept in, threatening to spoil everything. The worry was pushed away when she looked out the window. What a bonus for Bunny's birthday that snow had crept in while they were sleeping. The sun's rays jetted through the clouds and lit up the snow that lay over the land like a brilliant, shimmering white blanket. Little footprints in the snow dotted the area around their cottage. *Are they from the deer that live in the nearby woods?* Marjorie wondered.

Her thoughts were interrupted when Bunny came up to her. "Marjorie, I made up a poem and some came true. Do you want to hear it? It's called 'Dreams for My Birthday.' *There are only two things that I want for my birthday; I want snow, and I want my family.* Do you like it?"

They had snow, but getting their family back was as remote as ever.

Marjorie and Bunny stamped the snow off their boots before they went into the dining hall for the Sunday morning church service. The girls pulled off their mittens and stuffed them into their coat pockets. The morning prayer service was about to begin. They scurried to their seats.

"Marjorie, let's make a snowman if the snow doesn't melt," Bunny whispered.

"Okay, Aud, I mean Bunny." Marjorie worked at using her sister's nickname, but it was hard. "Let's put two black rocks for his eyes."

"And maybe we could find an old hat and scarf and a carrot for a nose." Bunny wiggled in excitement. Snow on her birthday was a special thing.

Marjorie let her mind wonder. Having her sister here with her made a world of difference. She had been alone at the farm school for a long time before Bunny arrived. She felt it was selfish of her to be happy about Bunny's arrival — because who would wish this place on anyone? — but the day the bus pulled in with the new group of kids was the best day ever. She and Kenny waited for ages down by the school gates. Finally, a rumble in the distance let them know that the bus was coming. They could hear it before they saw it because of the bend in the road.

Kenny yelped with excitement, "Marjorie, I can hear the bus! Audrey is almost here. Do you think Joyce will be on the bus, too?"

"I don't think so, Kenny. The cottage mum told me that she's not on the list. But maybe they made a mistake. Do you think she'll recognize us?" Marjorie was almost as worried as she was excited. She really wanted Joyce to be coming, too, but deep down she knew better. She would not give up all hope until the bus came, though.

The two children watched for their sister as the new group climbed off the bus. There was Audrey! "Audrey. Audrey! Over here!" Both Kenny and Marjorie yelled at the same time. They pushed past the other kids and ran up to her.

"Marjorie! Kenny! Is it really you?" Audrey looked at them, terrified, too afraid to even cry. She peed her pants as she grabbed Marjorie's hand and held on tightly, her eyes showing the depth of her fear, a fear that kept her rooted to the spot. Other children pushed past her, trying to get off the bus.

"Yes, it is. Quickly, come over here. Oh, Audrey, we missed you."

"My very own sister and brother. I missed you too!" They laughed through their tears and hugged and then hugged again. "It was such a long trip, the train and the ferry, and, oh, the huge ocean liner. I didn't know where they were taking me. I was so scared." Audrey stopped to catch her breath.

Marjorie was listening, but she kept looking back at the bus.

"What are you looking for?" Audrey asked her.

"Oh, nothing. I was just wondering if Joyce came, too." Marjorie's voice trailed off. She had hoped that her cottage mother was wrong, and maybe Joyce was coming and she was going to stay in a different cottage, and that was the reason she wasn't on her cottage list. Marjorie thought that would be okay. The important thing was to see her again. She watched as the bus driver got off the bus and shut the door.

"No Joyce," Marjorie said aloud.

"No, they wouldn't let her come. They said she was too old. I put up a big stink because I didn't want to leave her, but they wouldn't listen to me. I told them I didn't want to come all by myself. I tried to get away and run back to get Joyce, but they held my arm. Why didn't you wait for me? I didn't even know you were gone, and when I got out of sick bay, I looked for you and looked for you, then they told me you were gone and Kenny, too. Oh, Marjorie, it was so awful coming all by myself, and they wouldn't let me say goodbye to Joyce. The nurse said it would be best, as it would just upset Joyce, but I don't think that was fair, do you?" Audrey sobbed and looked up at her sister. Disbelief covered her young face. She looked around as if trying to understand where she was.

"No, it's not fair at all. They didn't let me say goodbye to Joyce or you, either. I just thought we were going for a picnic or something, but we never came back. How do you know you have to say goodbye when you don't know you're going? When we first got here, they told us you would be coming when you got better, but it has been months and months, and Kenny and I decided that it was a lie to keep us from having a fit, and you were not really coming at all. I can't believe you're here!" Marjorie hugged her little sister again.

Marjorie, Kenny, and Audrey were not the only family members reunited that day. Billy, a boy who came out with them on the boat last year, called out, "Bobby! Eunice! I can't believe you're here!" Then Jimmy and another boy named Kenny yelled out, "Amy! It's good to see you." And Olive and Tom grabbed their younger brother George. Tom said, "George, we thought you'd never get here! I'm so glad to see you. How long has it been?"

His sister replied, "Well, we've been here almost two years! It has been a long time. Did Kenny come with you, too? Where is he? Why isn't he here?"

"Nah, he couldn't come yet. They told me he was too young. They said he'd get to come out when he's older. I didn't want to leave him, but I had no choice, did I?" George looked at his older brother and sister and hoped they agreed with him. He'd tried his best to look out for his brother after his other siblings had left, but what could he do now? "He's still just a little guy; he's only five years old, I told them. I said he should have come with me, but they never listen to kids. I hope he's okay. I wasn't allowed to say goodbye."

"Listen, children. Line up and I'll tell you which group you will be in. Audrey Arnison, Attwood; Lionel ..."

"Audrey, let's get you to our cottage quickly and get you changed." As Marjorie pulled her sister away from the group, she glanced over at the bus. There were a few children standing around, looking very uneasy in their new surroundings. Marjorie's chore for the afternoon was to take care of Audrey and show her around. She looked for Kenny, but he had already run off with a couple of his pals. "C'mon. Give me your suitcase and I'll show you our cottage. I've got your cot all ready for you."

As Audrey walked through the new group of kids, one of the girls turned and said, "Bunny, is that your sister?" Marjorie was surprised when Audrey answered.

Bunny smiled. "Yes, that's my big sister Marjorie." Bunny grabbed Marjorie's hand, and they headed off toward their cottage.

"See you later, Bunny," the girl yelled after her.

As Bunny skipped alongside Marjorie, she yelled back, "See you later. I'm going to my cottage now."

Marjorie looked puzzled. "Why did she call you that?"

"What? Bunny?" Audrey asked. Marjorie nodded. "Well, that's my name now. A sailor started calling me Bunny on the boat, and now everyone calls me that. I don't mind.

"What boat were you on? Was it really huge? My boat was called the *Duchess of York*, and it was really, really huge. I was seasick a lot. I blubbed all over the place." Bunny made a face as she remembered how she'd felt.

"Yuck, Audrey. I don't want to hear about you barfing! Kenny and I came over on the *Duchess of Atholl*. It was huge, and I was seasick a lot, too. I don't think Kenny got sick, though. The sailors said he got his sea legs right away. They said he would make a good sailor, and they offered him a job on the boat, but they were just teasing him. I think Kenny would have stayed, though; he liked it that much. They let him go down and see the engine room and everything.

"Well, here we are. This is our cottage. Attwood Cottage.[1] Mrs. Read, the cottage mum, can be an old witch at times, but you get used to her after a while. You just have to learn to keep out of her way. She's not like a real mum, you know. We just have to call her that." Marjorie was unsure how to explain their cottage mum to her sister.

"Did you see our mum at all?" Marjorie turned away, trying to hide her tears, her fears. She had to be strong for her little sister.

"No. Not even once." Bunny brushed her hand across her eyes. "Is Mrs. Read anything like our mum? Does she give you hugs? What happens if we're sick or something? I hated being sick at Middlemore. They shaved my head and put blue stuff all over it. It was awful in the sick room. I couldn't play with anyone. I hated it. They left me all alone. Do you miss our mum, Marjorie? I still do." Bunny looked up at her sister.

"I miss her all the time. I will never forget her. Never! She is still my mum, even though she sent us away. Sometimes I think I hate her, and at the same time I love her, and I miss her so much it hurts and I have to stop thinking about it." Marjorie wiped her eyes. "Well, our cottage mum is not like our mum at all. Sometimes I think she hates us. She never hugs us, and if we get sick, we go to see the nurse. Nurse is pretty nice."

"Where is the nurse? Is she like the Middlemore nurses?" A shudder ran through Bunny.

"She's close by. The hospital is in Douglas Cottage, on the other side of that cottage, right over there. That side is called Pennant. It's really two houses stuck together at the middle, but you have to go outside and up those stairs to get to the other side. There's no doorway to each cottage from the inside." Marjorie pointed to the building next to theirs. "They're going to build a proper hospital, and then that side can be for another girls' cottage. Our nurse is different from the Middlemore nurses. It's like she's a real nurse — one that belongs in a hospital, not a home."

Marjorie put her arm around her little sister's shoulders and gave a squeeze.

"Ow!" Bunny jumped away. "My arm hurts where they jabbed me. I screamed when they did that. Did they do that to you, too?" Marjorie hadn't thought about her vaccinations for months. The four huge scabs had been sore for ages. Hearing her sister shriek brought back the painful memory. She grabbed her sister's hand.

"Yes, and it hurt. Here we are. If you ever get lost, you can ask for the way to Attwood Cottage."

"This is a pretty nice house." Bunny held tighter. The sisters stepped over the sill.

Marjorie and Audrey in front of the second cottage they were placed in: Pennant Cottage, 2014.

* * *

Bunny tugged at Marjorie's sleeve. Marjorie had forgotten where she was. Everyone was standing up to sing the next verse. She quickly followed and got ready to sing with the rest of them. Really, she just mouthed the words because her teacher had told her that would be best. The day was etched in her mind when, during choir practice, her teacher had said, "You don't have a very good singing voice, Marjorie. Why don't you just mouth the words?" Her teacher patted her on the shoulder and walked away. She did not see Marjorie's face turn red or the tears forming in her eyes. Was her singing that bad? She had enjoyed singing up to that point. Ever since then, her voice was stuck and she could not sing at all, not even "Happy Birthday" to her cottage mates.

After the service, the children quickly changed out of their church clothes so they could play in the snow until lunch. There was a competition between the cottages to see who could build the biggest snowman. Marjorie hoped that maybe later they could take the sleighs up to the hill behind the cow barn. This was one of the areas where the boys and girls could play together. They were watched, but maybe she could get in a quick visit with Kenny if she was careful. Sledding was the best fun, and Bunny would love it, too.

As Marjorie piled up the snow, she thought about the surprise for Bunny's birthday. She and the older girls were going to bake a chocolate cake — with the help of the cottage mum, of course. She had gone to the supply building to get some cocoa yesterday. A duty master was standing in the doorway blocking her way. Fear of what he might do to her ran up her spine.

She tried not to be around any of them when she was alone. The girls had rules to avoid several of the men at this farm school: "Always travel in pairs," an older girl in her cottage had whispered to her, "and never go into any man's rooms by yourself or else." Marjorie had passed this on to Bunny right away.

And now here she was, stuck. She grabbed the tin of cocoa, knocking supplies off the shelf, but instead of picking them up when he yelled for her to do so she squeezed past him. He reached out for her, but she wiggled out of his reach and ran. She was safe this time.

Now they had all the ingredients they needed in their cottage kitchen. They were going to start the cake right after the afternoon Sunday-school class. She had a little gift for Audrey, and so did their cottage mum.

Her present was a special seashell from the beach at Cowichan Bay. The girls had walked for ages to get there last summer, but it was worth it. They were away from the farm for the entire day. They stopped at the river along the way for a cooling swim. Marjorie hoped that they might go again. She wanted to show Bunny the old Stone Butter Church near Cowichan Bay where they had stopped to eat their lunch. But mostly she wanted to show her sister the beach. Marjorie vividly recalled the smell of the ocean as it slapped her in the face and stopped her in her tracks, and once again she allowed memories of her Whitley Bay sands to flood every corner of her mind.

As she had prepared for bed that night last August, Marjorie felt something in her pocket. "My shells!" she whispered to herself. She had forgotten that she had slipped a few seashells into her pocket. She quickly dusted off the bits of mud and seaweed and placed them on the shelf above

Girls shovelling a path at Fairbridge Farm School.

her bed, and there they had remained for months, hidden in the back. She had not shown them to Audrey, so giving her a seashell for a birthday present would be a perfect surprise. They were just like the shells at Whitley Bay. Imagine these two beaches so far apart having the same kind of shells. Oh, then she could tell her all about their beach adventure. How strange to be rolling snowballs now and remembering how hot it was then.

"C'mon, Marjorie, help me with this. I can't lift it up by myself."

"Oh, this is heavy." The two girls held the snowman's head steady while the others packed snow to hold it in place. Bunny stuck a stick in for his nose.

"Good work, Bunny. That's better than an old carrot. Here are some rocks for his eyes. Can you reach?"

The girls stood back and looked at their creation. It was a good snowman, even if they did say so themselves. They walked over to the nearby cottages to see how the other snowmen were coming along. "Ours is much better!" yelled Bunny when she saw the first one. Then, suddenly, a group of girls ran out from behind the building and began pelting snowballs at them. It was an ambush. They had been stockpiling snowballs and waiting for the other cottage girls to show up. The girls ducked the flying snow and scooped up handfuls for themselves, quickly forming them into little balls and letting them fly.

All too soon, playtime was over. The cottage mums were calling for the girls on lunch duty. This signalled the time for all the girls to start their chores.

"What are your chores this week, Marjorie?" Fanny Apple asked as she sucked on a piece of snow.

Marjorie asked, "Did you check to see that it wasn't yellow?"

Marjorie laughed as Fanny Apple threw her snow to the ground. "Yuck! Gross! I was enjoying it until you said that."

Marjorie was still chuckling when she said, "My chores this week are kindling and firewood."

Girls on firewood duty had to get up at a quarter to six to get the fire going so the cottage would be warm when it was time for everyone to get up. They also had to ensure that the cottage's woodbins were filled for the furnace and the cookstove and the cottage mother's sitting-room fireplace.

"C'mon, Bunny. You gotta help me, too. I'll split kindling if you stack it. Let's hurry so we can be done before lunch."

As the three girls started walking back to their cottage, Marjorie asked Fanny Apple, "What are your chores?"

"This week I'm on cottage cleanup. I like that better than laundry duty. How about you? I hate laundry duty. Except I hate cleaning up the cottage mum's rooms more. It's not fair! She should clean up her own mess, especially her bathroom. It's not fair that she has a bathroom all her own while the rest of us have to share ours. You know why I hate laundry duty?" Fanny Apple looked to see if Marjorie was paying attention.

"Why?" Marjorie was listening.

"Because I hate all the ironing and the mountains and mountains of stinky boys' laundry." Fanny Apple laughed.

"Do you remember last winter when we hung some clothes outside to dry and they froze solid? We stood them up in the laundry room, and they stayed standing until they warmed up and fell over."

Marjorie scooped up a handful of snow and sucked on it.

"I don't believe you." Bunny looked at the two of them.

"Yeah, it's true. I remember that. Frozen solid, and they stood up all by themselves. When the heat got to them, they fell over."

Bunny still looked unconvinced.

"It's true, Bunny. Really. Marjorie, were you on laundry duty when we had a bunch of blouses hanging on the line and some of the boys started throwing rocks at them, and because they were frozen the rocks went right through them?"

Fanny Apple grabbed another handful of snow.

"Yes! Those creeps. We had to mend the holes!"

Marjorie laughed, remembering the laundry matron trying to catch the culprits.

"Yeah, they are creeps. They never have to work in the laundry. Still, I'm glad they never got caught."

Fanny Apple tagged Marjorie and said, "I bet I can beat you back to the cottage."

The two girls ran off. Audrey yelled for them to wait up for her, but they pretended not to hear.

That evening Marjorie snuggled into her cot and thought that it had been a good day. The cake had a big dip in the centre, but it still tasted great. Audrey opened her present, turned the shell around, and put it against her cheek. At first it seemed like she didn't like it, but then she whispered, "Whitley Bay. It's like I have a piece of Whitley Bay." A thank you was not necessary. She didn't need to say anything else; the tear that escaped down her cheek told Marjorie all she needed to know.

Marjorie took Joyce's picture down from her shelf. One of the girls in the picture had arrived at the farm school just after Bunny. So had one of the boys. Why not Joyce? The paper was starting to curl at one corner. Her mum had sent the picture of Joyce shortly after Audrey arrived at Fairbridge. It was the first letter that Marjorie had received from her mum since she left Whitley Bay. She was so excited that she was shaking when she pulled the letter out of the envelope. She was surprised that it wasn't sealed, but she was in a hurry to see what her mum had to say. It was impossible to read, though, as there were several big black lines crossed through her letter. She asked her cottage mum who had opened her letter and put the black lines all over it.[2]

"It's hard to read with the black lines on it."

Marjorie passed the letter to her cottage mum, who helped her to read it: "The end part goes like this: 'I hope you are well and that you look out for your little brother Kenny and little sister Audrey. I visited Joyce at Middlemore after Audrey left for Canada, and she gave me this photograph for you. She doesn't want you to forget her.' Then she says, 'Love, Mum.'"

Mrs. Read handed Marjorie back her letter.

Marjorie looked at it again. She could read those parts; she had hoped the mum could tell her about the blacked-out parts. She looked at the envelope. The place where her mum had written her address had solid black lines through it as well. The cottage mum didn't answer her about the black lines, and Marjorie knew that if she had to ask twice she wasn't going to get an answer.

Marjorie's sister Joyce, third girl from the right, at the Middlemore Emigration Home. Photo sent to Marjorie while at the Fairbridge Farm School, circa 1938, from her sister Joyce. She never let go of it.

She held Joyce's picture up to the light. It was a little out of focus, but her sister looked just the same as she remembered her. She would have to keep the picture safe because she was forgetting Joyce bit by bit, just like the rest of her family. She tried hard to remember all their faces, and it was scary because their features had faded and were becoming more and more unrecognizable. Sometimes she felt that her memories were all she had to cling to, and they kept her from feeling so alone … but there were times when the memories were too painful to hold on to and the loneliness took her breath away.

She talked to Joyce — in her mind, of course, not aloud — and she wrote imaginary letters to her. They were her private letters that the cottage mum could never see or read, so she couldn't tear them up or put black marks all over the paper. She told Joyce that they had a good day for Bunny's ninth birthday. *I mean Audrey.* Joyce probably didn't know that they called Audrey Bunny now. As she wrote her letter, she imagined Joyce reading it, and it took some of the loneliness away.

She tried to be happy for Joyce because they had let her stay in England, but it was hard. Had Joyce gone back home, or was she still at Middlemore? It would be nice to have a picture of her mum and the rest of her family. Kids should know about their families. Maybe she should write a real letter back so that she could ask her mum to send her some more pictures.

Chapter 4

EXILED: A ONE-WAY TICKET TO NOWHERE

Prince of Wales: "It is this great migratory stream which forms a personal flesh and blood link that will stand, I think, any strain put upon it."

Leopold Amery, secretary of state for dominion affairs: "We had boundless material resources and we had human resources, but they could only be wedded effectively if they were properly distributed."

— *The Times* (London), January 27, 1926

"Marjorie, wake up." The low voice echoed loudly in the midnight dorm room. "Marjorie! You're sleepwalking again. Get out of my bed." The little girl yawned as she pushed Marjorie away.

"Whisht! Will you be quiet? You'll wake up the cottage mum, and then we'll all be in trouble. Just help her back to her bed. She probably won't even wake up," an older girl whispered through the darkness.

"I can't do it."

"Little kids!" The girl groaned as she pulled back her covers and got out of bed. "Yikes! This floor is cold. How can it not wake up Marjorie?" She took Marjorie by the shoulders and gently but firmly led her back to her cot and tucked her in. "Now stay there!" she warned, but Marjorie just snuggled further under her covers without waking up.

The 6:45 a.m. wake-up call from their cottage mother was right on time. The girls began to stir in their sleep. Marjorie grimaced. "It can't be time to get up already," she mumbled to no one in particular, her face firmly planted under her cover.

"Well, if you would stay in your bed and not walk around all night, you would probably have a better sleep." The head cottage girl was the one to break the news to Marjorie that she had been walking in her sleep again last night.

"Oh, no! Not again. Really?" Marjorie hated it when the girls told her that. "Did I wake the mum up?"

"No, and you're lucky because you woke all of us up," Bunny told her sister. "I watched you walk around, and you couldn't find your own bed, so you just started to climb into her bed." Bunny laughed and pointed to a bed on her side of the room.

"It's not funny! I got that far without waking up?"

Marjorie had not walked in her sleep for ages. She'd thought for sure that she was over it. She hated that it had happened again last night. It annoyed everyone. The cottage mum had a fit the first time she caught her, and they all got into trouble. Ever since that first time, she knew the girls tried to get her back to bed as quietly as possible, before she woke the mum up.

"I'm sorry," she told them. "I don't do it on purpose."

Marjorie used to lie awake for hours, telling herself not to sleepwalk. She would have to start doing that again.

She sat up and stretched. There was that odour again. It had taken her a long while to realize what it was. It was like a baby's wet nappy. Yuck! Middlemore had some bedwetters, too, but that dorm was larger and the smell didn't get as strong as it did in this room. Marjorie was thankful that she didn't have that problem. All she had was sleepwalking and night-mares, and that was bad enough. Having the mum catch you with a wet bed was the worst. She watched as the girl hurried to hide the evidence. Most days she was successful because all the girls helped her.

That morning it was Marjorie's turn to get the tin dishes and cutlery ready to take to the dining hall for breakfast. She recruited Bunny to help her.

"Bunny, do you still miss our family?" Marjorie looked at her sister to see what she would say.

"Sometimes I do, but I hardly 'member them anymore. You and Kenny are my only family now. Do you miss them? I miss Joyce the most, because she was really nice to me when we were at Middlemore, just the two of us. I don't think Joyce can be happy that we're here and she isn't." Bunny looked back at her sister. "I'm glad you're with me. I hated it when I was coming over here and I didn't have anyone with me."

"I still miss them. The first year that I was here, before you got here, it used to make me feel really sad. Now I sometimes just feel mad. I feel mad at Joyce because she stayed at Middlemore. But I miss her so much. I feel mad at our mum because she sent us away. I feel mad when the cottage mum is mean. But mostly I just feel afraid because I don't know what to expect. Did you know that it was Lawrence's birthday last week?"

"Our Lawrence?"

"Yes, our Lawrence. I feel mad when I remember things like that. I didn't think about them for a long time, then, when it was Valentine's Day, I remembered about Lawrence's birthday. I don't remember what he looks like, and I don't remember how old he is now. He could be four or five. And I think about Jean and Phyllis and Fred and Norman. Do you think they remember us?" Marjorie felt the old prickle of tears coming for her. She stared up at the corner of the ceiling for a bit. That seemed to help to stop them.

"I don't know. I wonder if they're still living in the flat on Whitley Road." Bunny was beginning to feel sad. Marjorie could hear it in her voice.

"Probably not, but I don't know. When Mum sent me the letter with Joyce's picture, the place where the address should be was blacked out, so I couldn't tell what it was. I bet they moved again."

"Are you hungry?" Bunny patted her tummy. "I'm empty."

"Let's hurry. I'm starving, too. I'll race you to the dining hall."

The rest of the Attwood girls were right behind Marjorie and Bunny. The girls in charge of getting the food from the kitchen were heading to the table as Marjorie and Bunny set the cutlery and dishes in their proper places. Mrs. Read sat at the head of the table, sipping her tea. The girls served her first. She had a lovely china plate filled with bacon and eggs and toast. Marjorie looked at her tin plate and at her toast. No eggs or bacon. She took her spoon and started eating her porridge. Yuck! She hated porridge, but she was hungry.

Marjorie picked up her glass of milk. Mrs. Read was looking away. This was her chance. She took a mouthful and squirted a long stream of the milk through the gap between her two front teeth. It went clear across to the next table. The girls at her table choked back giggles.

"Marjorie!" The mum scowled at her. "Bring your things here and come sit beside me. You," she said, pointing at the little girl next to her, "move down the bench and make room for her."

"But, ma'am, what did I do?" Marjorie tried the innocent look; it was always worth a shot. Without replying, the mum pointed to the seat beside her. Marjorie stood up and gathered her things. She wondered how the mum knew who it was. She had been so careful not to be seen.

As Marjorie ate her porridge in silence, she contemplated being a cottage mum when she grew up. It would be better than being a farmer's wife. Cottage mums got their own rooms, a sitting room, a bedroom, and their own bathroom. The mum was the boss of the cottage. You got the best food and good dishes. You never had to tidy up your own rooms. You got your breakfast served to you in bed on Sunday mornings!

Oh! Marjorie choked as she tried to suppress a giggle and bits of her porridge sprayed across the table. The image of her cottage mother licking her lips with delight last Sunday morning as she took a spoonful of her soft boiled egg was still fresh in her mind. Marjorie had mixed a booger into the top and she stood transfixed, wanting to see if she could tell and hoping that she could not. She reprimanded Marjorie for breaking the yolk when she cut open the top, but that was all.

"Marjorie! For goodness sakes! Do you want to go eat in the piggery? One more outburst and that is where you will find yourself!"

"Yes, mum. I'll be good, mum." Marjorie looked away. Maybe she didn't want to be a cottage mum when she grew up. Sometimes the children spit on her food too — just little spits so that she couldn't tell. Yuck. No, not a cottage mum. What if everyone hated her and messed with her food?

Morning classes started at 9:00 a.m. The dishes were returned to the cottages, washed, and put away, ready for lunch in the dining hall. Morning chores were finished by 8:45, and the dining-hall bell signalled time for school. The girls went to their lockers for their notebooks and sewing

Promotional photo of a cottage mother and her girls learning to sew. Note how young the cottage mother looks (top).
Fairbridge Farm Day School (bottom).

supplies before sitting down. Their sewing class would be first, then their cooking class. The girls were making their own aprons and service uniforms. Marjorie pulled out her apron. It was almost finished. She would be able to start her uniform soon.

* * *

At 3:30 p.m. sharp the bell rang. Books were closed and children headed back to their various cottages to work on their afternoon chores.

Marjorie was on cottage dinner duty. Bunny stuck close and helped the best she could. Marjorie hated making meals in the cottage. They always had to get the key from the cottage mum for the supply cupboard. It just seemed wrong to keep everything locked up if this was supposed to be their home. Sometimes it seemed that no one trusted them.

The girls looked forward to having some free time after their dinner. Maybe a group of them would go to the gymnasium and play there. No! She recalled that tonight was movie night! Movie nights were the best nights. They had movie nights once a month in the wintertime. One of the day school teachers ordered in movies from the National Film Board.

The Attwood girls sat around their large cottage table. They had to be extra polite because the mum's sister was visiting for the night. Mrs. Read was telling her sister that her girls were placing high for the competition between the cottages this month and if they would only try a little harder they might come in first for a change.

The girl sitting beside Marjorie let out a loud burp. A little twitter went down the line of girls.

"Marjorie, not at the table!"

"But, mum, it wasn't me! I'm always blamed. It's not fair." Marjorie was indignant. She didn't do it this time, but she usually got the blame, and she hated that.

"Enough! You mannerless little guttersnipes! Don't you know how to behave?" Mrs. Read turned to her sister. "I have tried my best with them. They have no idea what good manners are. I think it's a lost cause. You can take them out of the gutter …"

"But you can't take the gutter out of them." The sister finished the sentence and they gave each other a knowing nod.

The girls were still giggling. "Quiet, the lot of you, or you won't be going to see the movie." Mrs. Read's tone left them with little doubt that she would have them in bed at six o'clock if they continued to misbehave.

* * *

It was a good evening. Marjorie was able to talk to Kenny while they put on the second reel. He seemed to be doing okay; at least that's what he told her. She asked him what chores he had for this week, and he told her he was on barn chores. He told her that the sheep in the bottom field were having the last of their lambs. It was cold going out at night to check on them. One of the babies died, and they found it with all this slimy stuff on it. He said cleaning up the barn was okay in the winter, but last summer it was hard to be inside when it was so hot. He just could not stand it.

"Marjorie," he whispered, "I don't want to be a farmer. I hate seeing dead baby animals, and I hate the smell. I will never like farming. I'm just not a farmer." Marjorie told him that she understood how he felt and they would have a hard time trying to make them into farmers. "As soon as I'm old enough, I'm getting out of here."

"If you get outta here, will you take me with you?"

"Of course I will, and Bunny, too."

Then he told her that one of the boys tried to run away last night. "The boy is in big trouble," Kenny whispered, "Marjorie, I think he ran away because someone did something bad to him."[1]

"What did you say? You're talking too low." Marjorie got closer so she could hear him.

"Never mind. I better get back to my seat." Kenny scooted quickly to his seat just as the second movie reel started.

The Attwood girls were walking back to their cottage after the film.

"Geez, it's cold out here! That was a good flick, wasn't it?"

"Yeah, I liked it. Hey, did you hear that one of the boys ran away?" Marjorie was anxious to tell her news.

"I heard that. He didn't get far, did he?"

"No. Where could he go anyway? I heard the dirty duty master tried to touch him, you know, *there*."

"Oh, gross. Why can't these jerks leave us alone?"

"It was freezing cold last night. He was lucky they noticed and went out looking for him. He might have frozen to death."

Marjorie and a couple of the girls had talked about running away before, but once they got to the bottom field they had no idea which way to go, so they stopped talking about it.

"I heard that one of the little kids ratted on him."

"Do you know which one?"

"No."

"I'd hate to be him. He'll get it good now."

"Where was he going?"

"I heard he was going to try to get back to England."

"What a dolt. There is no way out of here. It's like when we left England we got a one-way ticket to nowhere and we're stuck here forever."[2]

"It won't be forever and ever. When we get older they can't tell us what to do, right?"

"They can until we're twenty-one, and that's a long time for me, and I'm older than you are."

"Oh. I thought we got to leave when we're sixteen."

"Well, we leave the farm school, all right, but we don't get to go on our own. We have to go to work in people's houses in Victoria."

"I think Victoria might be nicer than here. If it's a city, there has to be shops and things and more people. I think I'll like being in Victoria."

"You probably won't get much time off to go to the shops, and you won't have any money left over to spend. We don't get paid much."

"I thought we had to be a farmer's wife." The youngest in the group spoke for the first time.

"That's what they keep telling us, but I'm not going to be a farmer's wife. I want to be a nurse or a waitress or work in a shop maybe. They can't make us be farmers' wives, can they?"

"I don't think so. I hope not! Can you imagine never getting away from the smell of poo?"

"Oh, gross!" The girls were having a fit of laughter when the cottage door opened.

"Hurry up, girls. It's getting late. Time for bed." Their mum had heard them laughing outside, and it was simply too much noise.

Snuggled back in her sitting room, Mrs. Read felt happy for the first time in ages. Her sister's visit was exactly what she needed. The cottage mothers had very few visitors and needed to rely on each other for company, which was sporadic as they had so little time off. Outside visitors were discouraged, but she really appreciated some adult company every once in a while, especially during the long winter evenings after the girls were in bed.

Mrs. Read was looking through a stack of old newspapers and magazines. She pulled out Vancouver's *Daily Province*. "Listen to this: 'Church Plan for Fairbridge School.' I guess they should start the building soon."

"They're building a chapel?"

She turned to her sister. "Yes. Maybe then the fear of God can be instilled in these little heathens. It's like turning stone into gold to turn these children into anything useful, especially Canadian farmers."

"What do you mean?"

"I mean that they never should have been sent out here in the first place. Canada does not need them. We have enough unemployment here as it is. I wish I could get a better job. I hate being stuck up here in the wilderness with this riff-raff. I would love to work in Victoria. I miss the city. I never get any breaks with this job. They expect me to be on call twenty-four hours a day."

"C'mon, it's a decent job. What other kind of job could you do, anyway?"

"Look at this." Mrs. Read passed over the *London Illustrated News*. "It says, 'The Sun Never Sets on the British Empire.' I guess not if they keep sending their wretched unwanted children to all corners of the world." Her nose wrinkled in distaste.

"Oh, it's all about the 1936 coronation of King George VI. This school is named after his brother, the Prince of Wales, Edward VIII, who gave up the throne for a woman."

"The British are a strange lot. Do you think there'll be another war?"

"Another war? I doubt it. I don't know. I hope not. I guess I should be thankful that I've got a job, but it gets lonely up here and there's not much to do, even if I have little spare time to do it in. It's so isolated. It takes hours to walk the five miles into Duncan. Who wants to walk there in the winter? Being here makes me feel like I'm stuck at the end of the road. It's like I've bought myself a one-way ticket to nowhere."

Chapter 5

I Ain't Gonna Be a Farmer's Wife

Everyone knows that eventually these children will please themselves as to whether they will stay on farms or as house help after they are discharged.... Is British Columbia to become a dumping ground and be dictated to by Imperial dictators? ... Are there not thousands of our own idle and are there not thousands of children being born here every year to idleness?
> — *Daily Colonist* (Victoria), March 9, 1935

"New Fairbridge Girls Declare They Won't Be Farmer's Wives."
> — *Daily Province* (Vancouver), September 21, 1938

The children grow enamoured of the open life at once and learn to be farmers by preference.
> — "Little Empire Migrants," *London Spectator* (U.K.), reprinted in the *Evening Journal* (Ottawa), February 23, 1939

"Okay, girls, up you get. The bell rang a while ago." Mrs. Read walked down the row of cots, smacking a spoon on the metal bed frames. The girls began to stir. "C'mon, up and at 'em." She stopped by a young girl's cot. "Get up."

"I will in a minute, ma'am." The girl pulled the covers tightly around herself.

The mum could see it in the child's eyes. She hated bedwetters with a passion. She was sure this girl wet her bed just to spite her, wretched child. Well, she'd give her a lesson she wouldn't soon forget. The mum grabbed her covers and pulled them back. "Whatever is wrong with you, Miss Pissy Pants? Get up and get those wet things off. Look at the puddle under your bed! You dirty girl."

The girl jumped up and began to pull off her wet nightclothes. She stood there shivering, trying to hide her nakedness. Terrified, she remained glued to the spot, not knowing what to do next.

"Put your pissy knickers on your head and march around this room to show the other girls what a horrible child you are, and then get downstairs for a shower."

"But, ma'am, please …" As tears flowed, she choked back a sob. "I didn't mean to. I didn't do it on purpose."

"Get your knickers on your head, you smelly thing. You are a disgusting girl. Do you not have any control? Do you think the other girls like to sleep in the same room after you have soiled it? Take your sheets and get them scrubbed in the downstairs basin. Then get the mop and pail and mop up the entire dorm. *Go!*"

The girl put her knickers on her head and marched around the room. The rest of the girls chanted as she ran by, "Piss pot, piss pot, pissy bed, pissy knickers on your head."[1]

Mrs. Read demanded the teasing. The little girl grabbed her bedding and her soggy pajamas and fled the room; her loud sobs grew fainter as she reached the basement.

When she got downstairs, she ripped the knickers off her head and started the shower. When she was dressed, she filled the basin and put in her pajamas and then her sheets. She would have to bring her mattress down to the furnace room or else it would still be wet at bedtime. She headed upstairs with the mop and bucket. It was quiet in the cottage; everyone had gone to the dining hall for breakfast. She felt so alone, but she was glad that no one was there to see the irrepressible tears that flowed freely down her cheeks.

* * *

Marjorie grabbed the plates and the cutlery. It was Bunny's turn to set their table for breakfast. The girls ran along the path to the dining hall, and while Bunny set things in place, Marjorie walked over to the kitchen to get their food. Marjorie had to squeeze past one of the big boys in the doorway. He was carrying his cottage mother's plate; she could tell because it was china. He bent down toward the plate and gave a quick spit. Marjorie stifled a gasp. He looked up and winked at her. He was brave to do that so openly.

After breakfast, the girls headed back to their cottage to wash up. One of the girls tapped a spoon on her tin plate while she sang a little tune:

> We are Fairbridge folk, all as good as e'er,
> English, Welsh, and Scottish, we have come from everywhere;
> Boys to be farmers and girls for farmers' wives,
> We follow Fairbridge, the founder.[2]

"Why do you sing that stupid song? I ain't gonna be a farmer's wife, are you?" Marjorie scowled at her.

"No! Of course not. I ain't gonna be anyone's wife." The girl made a face. "I'm never getting married."

"Well, why do you keep singing that song then?" Marjorie asked.

"I don't know. It just gets stuck in my head, and I don't even think about what I'm saying."

"Why don't you ever want to get married?"

The girl's face clouded over and she whispered, "Because I don't like being touched. Never mind." She ran ahead but not before the others saw her tears.

Marjorie ran down to the basement. The girl who wet her bed was still down there. "You missed your breakfast."

"I know. I don't care. I'm not hungry."

"I brought you a piece of toast. Here, do you want it?" The little girl grabbed the toast and ate it quickly.

"I could help you hang out the sheets. It's easier with two people." Marjorie was used to helping. It was a leftover habit from when she used to help her real mum. Here, the kids were not encouraged to help each other with things like this. Marjorie knew that it just made the loneliness worse, though.

"Okay, but now the whole entire school will know that I wet the bed again last night because the only time the sheets get hand-washed at our cottage is when someone pees the bed." She choked back a lonesome sob.

"Well, we could say that you spilled something on them. No, we have to think of something else. No one is allowed to have anything to drink in bed." Marjorie tried to think of something, but nothing came to mind, so she said, "We better hurry or we'll be late for school."

As they hung up the sheets, the little girl said, "I hate being teased by you girls, but when the kids in all the other cottages start on me, I could just scream. It's not like I do it on purpose or anything."

Marjorie could see her sister coming out of the cottage. "Hey, Bunny, come here and help us. We'll get them up faster, then we can all run to the school together." The day had turned dark and stormy. It would probably rain before long.

"You'll definitely have to bring these in and hang them in the furnace room so they'll dry before tonight. I'll help you at lunchtime. You know, I didn't mean it when I called you those names. The mum said we had to call you that. She told us we had to do it for your own good. She doesn't understand anything, does she?"

Just then, Mrs. Read poked her head out the back door of the cottage. "Good for you. Your laundry is done. Have you washed the dorm floor?"

"Yes, mum. I did it while everyone was at breakfast. Can I go to school?"

"Yes, off you go now." The cottage mum closed the door with a resounding bang.

Mrs. Read was having her morning coffee with Miss Scott, one of the new mums. They had managed to get one of last week's newspapers from the principal's office. "Hey, here's an article: '$20,000 for Fairbridge. Anonymous Friend Gives Fund to Provide Chapel at Duncan. Pupils Will

Have Tea with Viceregal Party and Go to Victoria to See King and Queen.' It says that the boys and girls are wild with excitement because they are getting a chapel.[3] They are just wild!"

"Oh, so Fairbridge is getting a chapel, and Sunday service won't have to be held in the dining hall anymore?" asked Miss Scott.

"That's right. It goes on to say that the children will get to meet the King and Queen. Listen: 'The King and Queen mean more to the boys and girls at Fairbridge Farm School than to most little citizens … because they are away from their homes in England, away from their families, and sometimes a little lonely for the friendliness and familiarity of their motherland. A sight of the King and Queen in Victoria will be a great event in their lives. In the minds of the children at Fairbridge School … the King and Queen are coming to the end of the Empire to see them.' What nonsense! Maybe they will take them back to their motherland so the little darlings won't be lonely."

She didn't get a response from Miss Scott, so she continued. "I doubt that the children will even get a glance at the King and Queen. They aren't that important." Mrs. Read smirked.

"Do you ever feel stuck here?" Miss Scott wondered if it was a good idea to share her feelings. She really needed this job, even if she hated the isolation, but she knew that she should be careful with what she said.

"Oh, Lord, do I! Especially during the winter months. Just wait until you have spent a whole winter here! Sometimes in the middle of winter, I feel like the rest of the world doesn't exist. On our wages, we'll never save up enough to leave,"[4] Mrs. Read groaned.

The lunch bell rang out, summoning the children. Marjorie could see a boy pulling on the bell rope outside the dining hall. She wondered why she never had a chance to ring it. She had only ever seen the boys ringing it. As she got closer, she realized it was Kenny. She ran over to him. "Hey, Kenny, how come you get to ring the bell?"

"I dunno. It's my turn, I guess." Kenny grimaced as he moved away from the bell rope.

"What's the matter? What happened to your legs?" As Kenny moved, she could see dark red welts across the backs of both his legs.

"Miss Broad-ass, my cottage mum, thrashed me."

"Who?"

"We have another new cottage mum, and she is horrid. Worse than Miss Bishop. Her name is Miss Brown, but we call her Broad-ass because she's so big. She is a wicked, horrible old bag. I hate everyone here. They're mean," Kenny complained.

"What did you do? Did you do something really bad?" Marjorie wanted to give him a hug, but there were too many other kids going into the dining hall. She knew Kenny would be embarrassed.

"No, I didn't do anything, but the older boys said I did, and she believed them and not me. It always happens to us. The younger kids are always getting it. If we tell on the jerks, then they get us, too, and the cottage mum turns around and smacks us again." His sister was one of the few people who he could tell how he felt. It was too bad that they had so little time to talk.[5]

"Why don't you tell someone?" Marjorie looked at Kenny. She wanted to help him so bad, but she knew there was nothing she could do.

"I did, and I was called a baby and whiny and told to grow up and not to bother people with such nonsense." Kenny sucked back his tears. "Then I had to cut a huge pile of kindling because I was a tattler. I missed my supper that night because I had to keep working, and I didn't even do anything in the first place. You know, when you do something and you deserve some punishment, then you don't mind so much because you kinda asked for it, but when it wasn't me that did anything in the first place, it just makes me hate it here more. They all bug me! I wish I had my mum. She never whacked us or ..." Kenny's voice trailed off. He looked around to make sure the coast was clear. In a low voice he continued, "It's one of the little boys. Marjorie, I think, well, someone is doing bad things to him, you know. He cries at night after they bring him back, and he has bad nightmares, and he screams, 'no, no, no' ..." Kenny looked past his sister. He saw his cottage mum. "We better get inside, or we'll get into more trouble." Kenny scooted through the door and headed over to his table.

Kids cried at night. Kids had nightmares. What could she do about it? Marjorie felt a growing frustration because she could never have a good talk with her brother. One of the adults always interrupted. She wondered why Kenny rarely spoke above a whisper. Was he afraid someone would hear him? She had to fill in the blanks of what he was saying, and she didn't like how it sounded. She certainly couldn't protect him, but at least she could look out for Bunny, even if she got into trouble for it.

Marjorie and the other girls reported to the cottage mum after school to find out what their chores would be for the rest of the day. Some weeks they knew what their chores would be for the entire week, like when they were on laundry duty or helping the nurse or cooking, but some weeks their chores changed every day depending on what needed to be done.

"Well, girls, we'll get the cottage laundry done first. Here's a pile of socks, Marjorie and Bunny; you two can start with those, and Mollie and Betty, you two can do the kitchen windows. They really need a good cleaning." Mrs. Read handed over a soapy bucket and some rags.

"What are you two waiting for?" The mum turned to Marjorie and Bunny, wondering why they were still standing there.

"Why do we have to wash the smelly socks all the time? We did laundry yesterday."

"Well, because I said so, that's why. And you'll do laundry tomorrow and the next day and maybe all week, if you complain any more. Now get off with you two or you won't have it finished before dinner." Mrs. Read looked over at the two girls washing the windows.

"Scrub harder Betty. And Mollie for goodness sake wipe that nose, young lady. *No!* Not on your sleeve, you little heathen. You are more than I can take at times. Go inside and get some paper and do it properly."

Marjorie and Bunny pushed past Betty and Mollie, and ran down the basement stairs, dropping socks along the way and chanting, "Snotty nose, snot face."

"Don't you think that's gross, Marjorie? Why does she always have snot running down her face?"

"I don't know, but it's awful. It's always right down to her mouth." Marjorie shuddered. Having a snot or bedwetting problem only added to the difficulties here. It was hard enough without extra things to worry about.

She picked up a handful of socks. "God, these are crusty, too. I wonder if they have snot on them!" Marjorie laughed as Bunny threw her handful on the floor. "I'm only teasing you."

After they cleared away the supper things, the children sat around the fireplace darning their socks. The radio was on. The fireplace was casting a pleasant light and warmth. The night was stormy. The rain knocked at the windows before running down in sheets.

Marjorie and another girl were looking through their copies of the March issue of the *Fairbridge Gazette*. The very first issue had come out in February, and it was creating a lot of interest.

"Hey, is this going to be the new Fairbridge logo?" Marjorie asked. "That looks good with the leaves and the beaver."

"I believe so," Mrs. Read replied. "Have you other girls seen the *Fairbridge Gazette*? It's quite fun, really. You should make sure you get a chance to read it. Jimmy Lally, one of our older boys, is the editor." The girls ran over to see what she meant.

Marjorie passed her gazette over to the mum, who said, "I heard that Mr. Lort, the man who designed several of the school buildings, had a

Prince of Wales Fairbridge Farm School annual cross-country race and new Fairbridge logo in top right corner.

hand in drawing the new logo. I like the oak leaves and the beaver. I think it's appropriate." The mum handed back the gazette.

Marjorie leafed through the paper, just reading the headlines. She found a note clipped to the third page. "Hey, it's not fair! It says here that because I'm twelve I have to pay two cents for a *Fairbridge Gazette*. Well, I will just read my little sister's 'cause she can get it for one cent. Wow, look, the adults have to pay a nickel. That's a lot of money."

Marjorie showed the price to the girl beside her and then flipped to the next page.

"Look, Marjorie, they talk about the boys' last cross-country race on page four. Your brother Kenny came in first for the twelve-and-under boys. Isn't that great? He made the news."

"Well, Kenny will be pleased to see that." Marjorie thought about the race. Even though Kenny was just a little guy, he'd learned to be fast. It was a survival skill. He needed to outrun the bullies. He loved to run, and he was good at it. She wondered why they didn't allow the girls to run in the races. They would probably beat some of the boys. That would be a hoot!

Finally, Marjorie was given the opportunity to be the nurse's helper. It was better than washing crusty old socks. When her shift was over, she imagined writing a letter to Joyce and telling her about what she was doing at Fairbridge. She would tell her that all the girls had to spend time working with the nurse in the hospital. Well, it wasn't really a hospital; it was in one of the cottages, and it was a temporary hospital because they were building a real one. Being a nurse's helper was better than laundry duty, but it was still a long day.

No, wait — she should start her letter properly:

Dear Joyce,

How are you? I am going to tell you about my day as the nurse's helper, then you will know some of what we do at the farm school. First, I have to get over to the hospital at a quarter past six to light the fires to get the hospital warm. Sometimes I find a good bed of coals in the bottom of the stove, and then it's easier to light and you have a good roaring fire in no time at all. Next we have to prepare breakfast for the patients, and we eat our breakfast there as well and not in the dining hall as we usually do. Before we give the patients their breakfast trays, we take everyone's temperature, and then we take the trays around. After breakfast we change the beds and get the patients all clean and cozy. Next we tidy up the ward. When we're finished tidying, we have to disinfect the laundry. Nurse explained to us that the germs stay on the bedding and pajamas, and it's important to kill all the germs.

Then, just before lunch, if we have time, we have to fill the cod liver oil bottles for all the cottages. We use a huge jug. I thought of dropping it, but they would just get another one, and I would get into trouble and have to do other chores that would be worse. It is horrible, gross stuff. Whoever invented it must be an awful person. Someone who hates kids maybe. They make us swallow a huge ladle full, and then we have to say thank you. Can you believe that? You can't say thank you with a mouthful of cod liver oil, and that is how they make sure you swallow it. Most of us run outside right away and puke our guts out. Anyway, I put a funnel on the bottle, then I carefully pour the goopy stuff. The nurse told me if I spilled any, I would have to lick it up. She's nice, so I think she was teasing me, I hope. I poured out several bottles, then I came to our cottage's bottle — each bottle has a cottage name on it — and I was trying to think of ways to put in something else, like syrup or something that would look like cod liver oil so no one would know that I changed it. But I couldn't think of anything else to use. That would be a hoot, though. Don't you think so?

At lunchtime, me and two other girls go over to the main dining hall to pick up the food for everyone in the hospital. They cook it there. We usually have our breakfast and lunch in the big dining hall and our dinners in our own cottage. We bring enough food back for us and for Nurse and the patients. After lunch it's rest time for the patients, but there is no rest for us. We usually tidy up the ward some more and do some dusting and things like that. Rest time is supposed to be a quiet time, but with a hospital, you never know what to expect. Everything was real quiet and we were just mopping up the floors when the door flew open and one of the boys came running in, yelling, "Help me! Ow, ow, ow!" He was shaking his hand, and the blood was flying everywhere, all over our nice clean hospital. The nurse grabbed a cloth and ran to him. She told him to keep still, that he was getting blood everywhere and he was making it worse by shaking his hand like that, but he couldn't listen because he was too busy jumping around and yelling. She held him tight, and then she wrapped his hand in the cloth. She finally got him to sit down. She tied the cloth around his hand, but the red came through the cloth, and he started to yell again. "Am I going to bleed to death?" he screamed. What a big baby. I wanted the nurse to give him a needle because he was one of the big boys who bullies Kenny. The nurse told him that he would be okay, but he needed to sit quietly and calm down. The nurse cleaned it up, and it was only a little scratch, really. It didn't need stitches or anything. Boys can be such sissies when they see blood. She called for me to bring some bandages and disinfectant over to her, and she had him as good as new in no time. The rest time was nearly over, and the patients didn't have a very restful time, but that is what happens in a hospital.

After that I read some stories to the two little patients. My reading is pretty good now. They both wanted more stories, but I had to go help make dinner. We make the dinner in the hospital kitchen just as we do at our own cottage. All the cottages have kitchens. After dinner, we help clean up, and then we get the patients cozy for the night. We go back to our own cottage around 6:30 p.m. It's a long day, but it goes by fast when we're busy. We usually do one kind of chore for one week. That way everyone gets a chance to do different things. Then we have an hour to play or do what we want until bedtime. It's a wicked night out tonight, so we have all stayed in our cottage and are busy darning our socks.

From your sister, Marjorie

No, she thought — *Love from your sister, Marjorie.*
And, oh, she needed to add something.

P.S. The part I hate the worst are the bedpans.
P.P.S. They are going to build a new hospital. There will be more wards, and each ward will have a buzzer to call the nurse. And it will be on one floor so we will not have to keep going up and down the stairs with trays of stuff. The hospital will have isolation rooms for the really sick patients, just like at Middlemore.
P.P.P.S. I still miss you, Joyce, and I am glad I have a picture of you. Can you send me another one? This one is getting worn out.
P.P.P.P.S. They keep telling us that we have to be farmers' wives when we grow up, but not me, no way. They can't make me. That's our secret, okay? I hope they can't make me. What are you going to be when you get out?

Marjorie thought that would make a grand letter. She was better at writing letters in her head than writing letters on paper. She just couldn't seem to get started, and she didn't like the idea of her cottage mum reading her letters. She imagined Joyce getting her letter, opening it, and reading it. It helped her to feel closer to her big sister.

Chapter 6

A PARTIAL ECLIPSE[1]

A double service is rendered to religion, humanity and civilisation, in carrying off the children of distress to the open lands beyond the sea, to live in the open, to work with nature, to wrestle with forest, field and stream, to forget the fetid city slums, to think and strive and pray in the open, to grow strong and self-reliant, to be the guardians of the outpost of civilisation, religion and new endeavour ... every child a pioneer of the Empire.

— Father N. Waugh, *These, My Little Ones*, 1911

The children are "brought out into the sunshine, away from the darkness of the slum."

— Sir Arthur Lawley, *The Times* (London), May 9, 1927

"Marjorie, you forgot the cups." Mrs. Read stood at the back door, her lips pinched in disapproval as she passed Marjorie the cups. "If you weren't in such a hurry, you wouldn't forget things."

"Sorry, ma'am." Marjorie grabbed the cups, dropping one in her rush. The tin cup bounced off the stair and landed in the dirt.

"Slow down."

"Yes, ma'am."

"Dust off that cup."

"Yes, ma'am."

Marjorie ran to the dining hall. She wanted to get her table set first. They were having a competition to see which cottage did the best with their chores. Each cottage was given points, and at the end of the week they added up all the points. Right now, their cottage was in third place, but Marjorie thought with a bit of effort they could catch up because they were really close.

The head girl carried the flat pan full of porridge to the table. Marjorie could see the steam rising from the glistening pile of brown sugar in the centre of the dish. She wished she could be one of her cottage mum's favourites because then she would get some of the sugar, too. She and Bunny watched as the mum scooped out the porridge. The mum's favourite girls always got all the sugar. She served them first, taking their portions from the sugary centre.

Marjorie was used to it. She didn't know what sugary porridge tasted like anyway. She had learned to accept these things, to bury her feelings; otherwise, she would always be in trouble. But it hurt. The unfairness would grab at her and shake her. She had to let it go. At the end of the table, the mum's favourite was having fun teasing the rest, savouring every bite of her sugary porridge. When the pet saw the girls at Marjorie's end of the table watching, she stuck out her tongue. Melted sugar dripped off her chin. Marjorie took a drink of her milk. The cottage mum wasn't looking, so she let a stream of milk fly through her front teeth. It got the spoiled pet right on the head. She stuck her tongue out at the girl and went back to eating her bland, lumpy porridge.

"Eat up, girls. Quickly now. We don't want to be late." Mrs. Read stood up, putting an end to the table fight. She knew having favourites caused problems, but she needed to ensure she had some allies in her cottage. A full-blown mutiny could be disastrous for her.

"Marjorie, bring the dishes with you. Who's on dishwashing duty today?" Two of the girls raised their hands. "Good. Help Marjorie carry the dishes back to the cottage. Let's go. Quick! Quick!"

"Be careful! Don't look up at it without the smoky glass in front of your eyes." Mrs. Read was doing her best to keep the children from looking directly at the eclipse, but as usual, they were not listening to her. The children had never seen anything like it before.

"What's it called again?"

"It's called a partial eclipse of the sun. We are very lucky that we have a cloudless sky this morning; otherwise we would not be able to see it so clearly. You watch. Now let's see, it's a quarter to eight, and in fifteen minutes it should be at its height. More than half of the sun should be obscured."

"What does *obscured* mean?"

"Covered over. The moon will be standing in front of the sun, blocking out its light."

"Oh, I see, I think."

"Eclipses don't happen very often where we can actually see them. Hey, I told you not to look at it without the smoky glass in front of your eyes. You'll hurt your eyes."

The principal thought that viewing the partial eclipse would be a good educational lesson for the children. They put their chores and morning classes on hold so they could all watch it. Their cottage mum wished they would listen to her, though, so she didn't have to keep such a watchful eye on them. She wanted to see the eclipse herself.

"Marjorie, you'll burn your eyeballs right out of your head. You'll have nothing but smoking holes left." Marjorie quickly picked up her piece of viewing glass.

"Wow, it's getting darker. Look! The moon is blotting out the sun. This is neat."

The children stood quietly for a few moments, mesmerized by the scene in the sky. As the moon moved away and it began to get lighter, the kids started to lose interest.

"All right, girls. Pass me back the pieces of glass and get ready for your morning classes. We can catch up with the chores later."

Marjorie scrambled into her desk. Sometimes she felt just like an eclipse. Hidden. Covered up. Not herself anymore. How could her mother recognize her if she couldn't recognize herself?

The teacher they all called Legs — behind his back, of course — sat at his desk reading the newspaper. He told them to pull out their books without even looking up from his paper.

Finally, he put his paper down. "Who watched the eclipse this morning?" They all held up their hands.

"Well, then, who can tell me what an eclipse is?" All the hands quickly went down.

"C'mon, class, someone must have an idea. What did you see?"

"The sun got blotted out, sir."

"It got darker, sir?"

"Yes, that's correct. Now ..."

The lesson plan had suddenly changed for the morning. Legs decided that he would spend a little more time on solar eclipses.

"Um, now, can anyone tell me why you can't look at it directly with your eyes? Marjorie, why do you suppose you can't?"

"Well, sir." Marjorie's voice was barely above a whisper. "Because, sir, if you do your eyes will burn out and you will have smoking holes in your head and you will be blind. Our cottage mum said so. Is that true?"

Marjorie had been sneaking a little peak when the cottage mum caught her. It had hurt her eyes, and she kept seeing spots in front of her face. She was waiting for the smoke to start.

"Well, Marjorie, you can do a lot of damage to your eyes, but I don't think they will start to smoke." Legs gave a little chuckle and went on with the lesson.

At lunchtime, the girls of Attwood Cottage were sitting at their table in the big dining hall. Their plates were full, but they had to wait until everyone was sitting down. When they were, the headmaster said grace.

"For what we are about to receive, may the Lord make us truly grateful. For Christ's sake. Amen."

For a moment, all you could hear was the sound of cutlery against the metal plates. Many slices of the one hundred pounds of bread that the baker produced daily were consumed.[2] As the stomachs filled up, the sounds changed to children whispering with their neighbours. They had finished

Marjorie, left, with two Fairbridge girls. Pennant Cottage is on their left, and Attwood Cottage is on their right.

The interior of the dining hall.

their main meal, and the girls waiting tables had gone to the kitchen to get their dessert.

Marjorie looked around. She and a group of girls had had the chore of cleaning the dining hall yesterday. They had polished the tables and waxed the floor. It was a huge floor, but polishing it went quickly when there were many girls to do it. The sunlight was streaming through the large windows, making the linoleum shine.

"Oh, yuck!" Marjorie said as a bowl of tapioca pudding topped with prunes was put in front of her. They had to eat whatever they were given regardless of whether they liked it or not or even whether they were hungry or not. "Look at the size of the tapioca. It looks like frog eggs!"

"Is that what frog eggs look like?"

"Exactly. Haven't you gone down to the scummy pond and seen the floating piles of frog eggs? That's probably where they get this stuff from; they just scoop it up from the pond and pull off the bits of leaves and twigs and serve it to us."

"Oh, they do not. Are we really eating frog eggs, Marjorie?"

Bunny looked ready to throw up. Marjorie had a sudden idea. Maybe if she could get her to throw up, it would distract the mum and she could get rid of her pudding in the confusion.

"Yes, silly, of course we are. People eat frog legs, too." Marjorie grinned at her sister.

Bunny was looking more and more green. "You're lying to me, Marjorie."

"No, I'm not lying. Eggs are good for us. People eat chicken eggs and chicken legs just like frog eggs and frog legs." Marjorie tried to keep a straight face.

"Well, that's different. I think you're teasing me." Bunny turned the other way and refused to listen to her sister anymore, and Marjorie's hopes of using her as a distraction were dashed.

Marjorie picked up a slimy prune on her spoon. The thought of it slipping down her throat was enough to make her gag. She played with it on her spoon, wondering how to get out of eating it. The spoons were made of thin metal, and that made them good for flinging things. She held it close to her and pulled the spoon back, aiming high. Bingo! She got it. The prune stuck up on the ceiling. The girls beside her giggled softly.

Mrs. Read knew something had happened, but she'd missed it. She looked up and down the table. She suspected Marjorie was the culprit, but it didn't really matter; she'd make an example of her anyway. Marjorie could get even later herself if she was accusing the wrong girl. "Marjorie! Get down here and sit beside me. Should I have you sitting beside me at every meal?"

"No, ma'am. I didn't do anything." Marjorie stood up and grabbed her bowl of pudding.

"Nonsense. You look guilty. Get down here. Okay, girls, get your dessert done without any further chatter."

As Marjorie placed her tin bowl beside the cottage mum, she heard something plop on the table next to theirs. She didn't look over; she knew what it was. Her prune had become unstuck from the ceiling. As the cottage mum glanced over at the other table, Marjorie saw her chance to say good riddance to the unwanted pudding. She slid her bowl to the edge of the table and let it fall.

"You clumsy, stupid girl! Look what you've done now. Get a rag and get it cleaned up. Now!" Mrs. Read continued, "It's a good thing you have a tin bowl. We'd have no china left with guttersnipes like you breaking it at every meal." She stood up and glared at Marjorie. Some of the frog eggs had landed on the bottom of the mum's skirt. The girls were trying their best to finish their pudding. They found it difficult to eat and suppress their giggles, but months of practice helped.

The children at the other tables cleared up their dishes. The girls and boys assigned from each cottage grabbed their cutlery and dishes to carry back to their own cottages. The dish duty children raced to wash up so they could get to their classes or afternoon chores. As Marjorie ran to the kitchen for a rag, she heard some of the big boys say that they would be working in the fields this afternoon. Then she heard them say that they liked it much better than sitting in a stuffy classroom. Marjorie was surprised, as she hated working in the dusty fields. She would much rather be in a classroom. Well, really, she would much rather be down at her Whitley Bay sands. Marjorie sighed; those were the best days.

* * *

After school the children lined up at their cottage door, waiting for their mum to assign them their afternoon chores. "It's a beautiful day, and it's been quite dry lately, so I think we can get started on our Victory Garden. I want you all to put in a special effort this year. We have a good chance of taking the first-place ribbon this time. We were close last year, coming in second, but nevertheless, that's the first loser. Right, girls?"

"Right, ma'am," they chorused back at her.

"Okay, then you will need to pull out all the weeds and pile them away from the garden. Then you need to take your spades and forks and turn over the soil. I'll come out and check on you shortly. Off you go now."

The girls ran to the basement to get their gardening tools. They only had an hour before dinnertime, so they would have to work quickly. They had started working in the big fields this past weekend. Last year the weeding in the big garden was back-breaking work. The celery was tough, too, because you had to put up boards to keep the sunlight off the stalks, and the boards didn't stay up easily. But picking up potatoes after the potato digger was the hardest work. You got dust in your mouth and in your nose and in your clothes. The girls didn't have to do as much fieldwork as the boys, but still they did enough, and it was not easy. There were fifty-three tons of potatoes dug up last year, and they were all stored away in the root cellar. That was quite a mountain of "taties." She shuddered to imagine having to peel them all.[3]

Kenny once told her that the boys stole potatoes and snuck away to cook them in their forts in the nearby woods. They made a small fire and made sure that it wasn't too smoky, just in case someone looked up there and saw them. They didn't want any unexpected visitors. He said that the potatoes tasted best when cooked outside. "And anyway, we're not really stealing, are we, Marjorie? We plant the taties and hoe them and weed them and pick them. It's kinda like they're ours, right?" Kenny looked at her with that worried look of his. She assured him that it wasn't really stealing, not the kind of stealing that sent you to hell. Kenny looked relieved. "Well, I gotta go now. Bye, Marjorie."

She had watched her brother run down the boys' path. *He might be small, but he's fast,* Marjorie thought as she stood on the girls' path, watching him disappear. The best chance she had of speaking to Kenny was by the communal area in front of the dining hall before the pathways went in separate directions. She would never understand why they weren't allowed to move freely about the farm. These Fairbridge people didn't seem to trust them at all. They watched the kids like hawks. Sometimes it seemed to Marjorie that she was yelled at before she even did anything wrong. It was like they expected her to make mistakes.

As Marjorie tried to dig her spade into the ground, she realized that it wasn't going to be that easy. Weeds had grown into a solid mass. "Oh, this is impossible," she complained.

"Use your fork; it'll be easier." One of the big girls showed her. Soon the group had a large section of the garden dug up.

"Look at the size of this worm." Marjorie held it up so they could all see it.

"Yuck! Get it away from me!" one of the girls screamed at Marjorie, giving her all the encouragement she needed. She flung it over, and the worm landed on the girl's head.

"Marjorie!" Mrs. Read yelled. "Why do you have to do things like that?"

The girl ran toward the mum. "She threw a worm at me on purpose," she wailed.

"I saw everything. You'll do extra chores, Marjorie!" The mum brushed the dirt off the girl's hair and led her inside.

Marjorie had not seen the mum come out. She would never have dared to throw anything, let alone a worm, at one of the mum's favourites if she knew the mum was watching. She hated that she wasn't one of her favourites. She missed her own mum — she could always run to her for comfort, and now she had no one. They had even taken away her big sister, who always looked out for her. She wondered what Joyce was doing right now. She would do anything to be with her.

That evening, after her extra chores were finished, Marjorie didn't join the rest; instead she stayed downstairs and curled up in a corner of the playroom. She wanted to think. The rest of the girls were listening to the radio with the cottage mum. They had all worked hard in the garden after dinner. Their garden was looking very smart. She hoped they would get first place this year; it would make their cottage mum happy, and when she was happy she was nicer to everyone.

Marjorie rarely had a chance to be alone, and she needed to be alone to think about her family. They were dim in her memory, more shadows than real people. It seemed like the more memories she had of Fairbridge, the fewer she could remember of Whitley Bay and her family. She missed Joyce the most and still thought of her almost every day. She looked at her picture every night before she went to bed, at least on the nights that she remembered. She wondered if Joyce was still at Middlemore or if they had sent her home or maybe to some other place. Did she still work in the kitchen? Did her mum ever go to see her?

As soon as she thought of her mum, she knew the sadness wouldn't be far behind. She blinked really quickly, trying to scare away the tears. She pretended to write a letter.

My dear Mum,

Oh, Mum, why did you send us away? Did you know Canada would be like this? It's so far away, and it's all trees, trees, and more trees. We're way out in the middle of a big forest. I've only seen the beach a couple of times when we walked for half a day. I miss Whitley Bay and the sands and the smell of the ocean. I'll never get used to the smell of a farm. I don't see Kenny very often, and when I do, he has horrible stories to tell me. If you could have seen the welts on his legs last month, you would not send us here. It was days before they got better. He ran a race last month. He came in first for his age group, the twelve-and-under boys. He's learning to run here because he has to be fast as he's too little to stand up and fight.

Mum, sometimes I think it's not so bad, really, but only because I've forgotten what you look like. I don't remember Lawrence and Jean, either, although I remembered that Lawrence's birthday is on Valentine's Day, but I don't know how old he is. I try to be brave about being here and say nice things about the school because I will get into trouble if I don't, but I hate it here and I will always hate it here. Nobody cares about us. I don't think anybody really likes us. Our cottage mum — I hate calling her our mum; she's not my mum! You are my mum! Our cottage mum doesn't like me very much. She treats the pretty girls better than the rest of us. They get the treats, and then they march around saying they are better than us, and we can't do anything about it because we will just get into trouble, and you don't want to get into trouble here as it simply makes your life horrid. And the mum gets the best plates and the best food. She treats us as if we are her slaves. We have to do everything she says, and when it's not fair she doesn't even care, and she even seems happier at those times. We have no one to talk to about our problems. No one listens to us. We just don't matter to anyone here.

I hate that you asked us to look after the little ones. Or at least you asked Joyce, and I guess I had to take over because Joyce isn't here. It's really, really hard. I'm doing pretty good with Audrey, but I can't look after Kenny. It's too hard. If the big boys find out, they just beat him up more. I try, but I mostly don't even get to see him. Sometimes we can talk, but just a little bit. Sometimes I think he is really sad. Oh, Mum, there is so much that is not good here. Some of the men try to get the girls into their rooms, and we try not to let that happen by never going anywhere alone, but sometimes the new girls don't understand that you cannot trust everyone. Afterward, I hear crying at night and we cannot do a thing. We have our suspicions, but no one will really talk about it. I wish you could come and get us. I don't feel safe here, and

I'm forgetting things about you because too much time is coming in between us, and I can't see you or Whitley Bay in my mind very good anymore. Goodbye. Do you still love me?

Love from your daughter, Marjorie

Marjorie sniffed back a tear and curled up tightly in the corner. She was convinced that if she were able to talk to her mum, and if she could tell her what this place was really like, she would rescue her and Bunny and Kenny. She remembered the first letter she wrote to her mum shortly after she arrived at Fairbridge. She tried to tell her mum how she was feeling and asked her to get her out of there. She felt so much better about writing down her feelings. Her mum would understand. She knew she would. She would help her. But the cottage mother tore up her letter. It was hopeless.

That was the last real letter Marjorie wrote. She wrote other letters, saying, "How are you? I am fine," but she never dared to put her feelings down on paper. Instead, she wrote her real letters in her head. That way she could say exactly what she wanted and not get punished.

The girls found Marjorie snuggled up in the corner when they came down to wash up and brush their teeth before bed.

"Marjorie." Bunny gently shook her sister. "Wake up. It's time to brush our teeth."

Marjorie woke with a start. She wasn't sure where she was at first. She stretched and stood up. She was feeling stiff. "Hi, Bunny. I guess I fell asleep down here."

Marjorie smiled at her sister. She had been having a nice dream about her family. Her mum, Phyllis, Joyce, Jean, and even little Lawrence had come to Fairbridge to take them home. Her mum told her that Fred and Norman were at home waiting for them. She was happy to see her family. The nice feeling stayed with her even after she woke up. As Marjorie brushed her teeth, she realized that it was getting harder to remember her family, especially the little ones, but she had to keep trying. She didn't know what she would do if they were totally gone from her memory. She needed to cling to the few memories she had left.

A Partial Eclipse
A partial eclipse of my mind.
I've hidden the hard thoughts.
A partial eclipse of my heart.
I've buried the hard feelings.
A partial eclipse of my soul.
A part of me is buried and gone.
I am no longer complete.
I am a shadow of my former self.

Chapter 7

LITTLE FARMERS

The Society must understand that we are not taking either defective or border line children. Much has been said about the large number of splendid children available in the Mother Country. The whole approach to the Department for the acceptance of the Fairbridge Farm School here was based on the claim that only first class children would be sent.

— Frederick Charles Blair, Canadian Department of Immigration, August 10, 1935

Marjorie did not understand why they had to move from their cottage. She had been in Attwood Cottage ever since she got to the farm school. She had not realized just how much she had come to think of that cottage as home. She did not like being in Pennant Cottage.

The cottage mum said that because of the war they had to economize. The farm school had to do their bit for the war effort, so they needed to shut down some of the cottages to save money. Because of the war, they were not sending over many children, but the children who had reached sixteen years of age were still leaving to go into service in homes and farms, and that was leaving empty beds with no one to fill them. But why couldn't they shut down someone else's cottage? Why did they have to shut down her cottage? It was not fair!

The very worst part of the move was their new cottage mother. Marjorie had heard all about her from Kenny. He hated her. And it didn't take Marjorie long to understand why. Their new mum seemed to hate everyone more than their old one did. The girls called her D. Bitch behind her back, and she was a bitch through and through. She was a hundred times worse than their other mum.

It took a lot of energy for the girls to keep out of her way. Marjorie's nightmares returned. Bunny cried at night again. And the cottage bedwetter, Miss Pissy Pants — that is what their new mum called her — started peeing her bed again. The little girl had not had any accidents for ages, but she started again almost as soon as they moved to Pennant Cottage.

Their mum was not going to put up with any of it. Marjorie was slapped for waking everyone up with her shrieks, and Bunny quickly learned to stuff her scratchy grey blanket in her mouth to hide her sobs to avoid punishment. But the bedwetter suffered the most. "Oh, no! I won't have a bedwetter in my cottage!" Miss Bishop shrieked. "No way, young lady. Get those knickers on your head and clean up this mess."

When it kept happening, the mum's fits grew wilder, and she yelled and screamed out her threats to the poor girl. One morning, after being dragged from her bed, the girl stood shaking in her wet pajamas and peed again, all over the floor. The mum's rage escalated. It was the worst fit yet! Her speckled red face looked ready to explode. Ever since that morning the mum would sneak into the dorm just before the bell to check if there was a puddle under the girl's bed. The girls tried to get up earlier to help her get rid of the evidence, but the mum just kept getting up earlier than they did.

One morning the mum snuck in while it was still dark. Her footsteps creaked on the floorboards and woke Marjorie. She watched Miss Bishop tiptoe into the room. She held a flashlight in her hand, but she held it low so it wouldn't wake the girls. She shone the light under the bed, and when she saw a puddle, Marjorie heard her suck in her breath. She pulled the girl right out of her cot. Marjorie bolted up. What was she going to do? The commotion woke everyone up. The little girl stood there as if she was in the middle of a nightmare. Her eyes looked wild, like she had seen the Devil. The mum tossed the wet bedding on the floor, and then she pulled up the soggy mattress and strapped it to the girl's back!

"There. Maybe that will teach you!" Miss Bishop shrieked.

The bedwetter didn't say anything. She just stood there. The mum made her put her pissy knickers on her head and carry her pissy mattress on her back all morning. Luckily, the mattress was thin, so it was not too heavy, but it was awful for the other girls to watch her. Finally, the mum said, "Take it off and put it outside where it can air all day."

Tears streamed down her face, but she made no sound as she walked to the back door. The girls had to watch so they could all learn a lesson. As she walked down the stairs, the mum started the chant and the girls knew to follow; they had no choice. "Pissy pants, piss pot, wet your bed, pissy knickers on your head."

After breakfast, the younger girls lined up outside their cottage for their daily chores. Today the older girls knew they were not going into their classrooms because it was the week for getting the big garden planted. Most of them would spend today and tomorrow gardening.

> **Down on Misery Farm (girls' version)**
> Down on Misery
> Down on Misery
> Down on Misery Farm School
> Where you work all day
> And get no pay
> We wax the floors
> And scrub the doors
> Down on Misery
> Down on Misery
> Down on Misery Farm School[1]

Marjorie really did not like working in the big garden, but at least she was away from her cottage mum all morning. She grabbed another handful of weeds. White fluffy bits covered everything. She looked up and thought it was snowing. The air was full of the tiny white bits of fluff. "Look," she yelled to the girls. "It looks like snow, doesn't it?"[2]

The girls stood up and tried to catch the fluffy stuff. "This is neat stuff. I wonder what it is." They laughed as they jumped up trying to catch the light fluffy bits.

"Hey, you girls, get back to work." The gardener did not put up with anyone playing around in his garden.

It was warm for the end of May, and the girls groaned as they went back to their work. *Well*, Marjorie thought, *they can't stop us from talking.*

"I hate our new cottage mum, don't you?" Marjorie asked the girl beside her.

"I'll say! She's a real old witch. I think she hates us, too. I hate that we have to bring her breakfast in bed on Sunday morning."

"I really hated it when we had to make her a special breakfast for Mother's Day. She's not our mum; she's an old hag."

The girls giggled. "Yeah, but we got her back, didn't we? I wonder if it is really true that if you use the water we boil her eggs in for her tea that it will poison her? It doesn't seem to be working. Maybe she's too strong, or maybe it's a slow poison and it doesn't work right away?"

Every Sunday morning, when the girls prepared the mum's breakfast, they made her tea with the same water that they boiled her eggs in. They heard that eggshells can carry a poison, and they wondered if using the egg water for her tea might poison her. Every week the girls watched as she sipped her tea, looking for signs that it was working. But she just smiled at them and took another sip. "You can go now, girls. I have everything I need."

"Yeah, maybe one day she will just drop dead! I hope I'm there to see it!" The girls laughed and all agreed that would be one thing they would not want to miss.

"Maybe they have to drink it every day for the poison to work. We only give it to her on Sunday. Maybe that's not enough. We gave our last cottage mother egg-water tea all the time and it didn't poison her either."

"Yeah, we did, too. I can't believe that she couldn't taste the spit in her food, though. We could barely stop laughing when we put her food on her bedside table. When we had to say 'happy Mother's Day' we were choking back our giggles." The group of girls fell in the dirt laughing. They had tears streaming down their faces. "Oh, my side hurts! Don't make me laugh anymore!"

"She's so dumb. I think she thought we were smiling so much because we were happy at being the chosen ones to serve her breakfast on Mother's Day. I'd like to serve her my fist. It's too bad that girls can't take up boxing. I'd practise every single day until I knew I could take her down with one blow." The girl stood up and punched the air.

"Well, what about the time Fanny Apple got really mad at the mum and threw the iron at her? Remember? The mum was going down the stairs. Fanny Apple was standing at the top of the stairs, and she just let it go. I think she meant to miss her, though. It would have cracked her head apart if she actually hit her. Can't you just see her with an iron sticking out of her head?"

"I thought it was a piece of firewood."

"That was a different time and different cottage mother. I'm surprised the old witch is still here. She has had some close calls."[3]

"Hey, you girls, stop fooling around. Get those carrots planted, and then you can start on the turnips. It looks like the weather might change, and we need to get this planting finished today." The gardener seemed anxious to get the work done. "C'mon. The boys planted the entire potato field quicker than you're doing this. They got the beets in, too. Let's go — no more fooling around."

"Well, what do you expect? There are a lot more boys than girls; so if you have twice as many people doing something, you'll get twice as much work done, dummy head!" one of the girls whispered, loud enough so the other girls could hear her but not the gardener.

The girls worked steadily while the gardener stood and watched them. As soon as his back was to them, they started to talk again. The senior girl in their group asked, "Wasn't it fun to go to the music festival? We came in second."[4]

"No, it wasn't fun for me. I hate the choir." Marjorie scowled. "During choir practice I was told to pretend to sing the words because the teacher said my voice was no good."

"Don't feel bad. She wouldn't let me be in the choir, either," the girl beside Marjorie responded. The two girls looked over with envy. Your life was a little easier if you were really good at something that the grown-ups wanted, and the senior girl in their cottage had a beautiful voice.

"Hey, did you like the sports day we had last weekend?"

Marjorie groaned. "No! I didn't get to go."

"Why not? Where were you? It was fun."

"Well, one of the trainee girls hit Bunny, so she came crying to me. I had to do something, so I beat the crap out of her. She told the matron, and I was the only one punished. The little pet didn't even get a talking-to about hitting Bunny in the first place." Marjorie flung a handful of weeds aside.

"Well, what do you expect? She's one of the matron's favourites. I'm not looking forward to staying at the matron's cottage when I'm a trainee."

"Me neither. But we don't have to be there all the time. Anyway, I missed the whole sports day, and I had to weed the matron's garden all day. I pulled out a bunch of her flowers and smashed them. I was so mad." Marjorie yanked out a few more weeds. She was still feeling mad about it.

"Well, it's too bad you didn't see your brother run. He sure can run fast. I think he came in first for his age."

"He always does." Marjorie felt proud of her brother. "But it's because he has to run fast to keep ahead of the bullies."

"Yeah, my little brother is always getting beat up by the bigger boys in his cottage. At least you can look out for Bunny."

"Yeah, but it isn't easy because I know I'll get all the blame. Have you noticed it's always the favourites who pick on Bunny? I think it's because they know they won't get into trouble. It's funny how they see every little mistake I make, especially Miss Bishop. God I hate her. I wish she'd just die." Marjorie looked around to make sure no one had overheard her. Sometimes, when you least expected it, the mum was standing right behind you. She would just appear out of nowhere. The coast was clear. "Maybe she's a witch — like, you know, a real live witch."

"She probably is. She's probably the Devil's wife."

"God, can you imagine her and the Devil kissing!"

"Oh, gross." The girls let out peals of laughter. "Stop it. I'm going to pee my pants!"

The gardener stood over them. "The lot of you are going to get into trouble if you don't get this finished!" He pushed his hoe at them in a threatening way.

The girls went back to their planting.

One of the girls began to sing their favourite song. The others joined in. It made them feel like rebels.

> Down on Misery Farm School
> Where you work all day
> And get no play
> We wax the doors
> And scrub the floors

"It's 'get no pay' and 'wax the floors' and 'scrub the doors,' silly."

"Well, we scrub the floors, too, don't we?"

"Yes, we scrub the floors and the stairs and the laundry and we weed and we plant and work all day on this miserable farm and get no pay. I hate it here. Hey, did you see the principal's office building when it was on fire? I was hoping the whole darn place would burn down. Maybe they would send us home then."

"Yes. I watched the boys form a line with their buckets. It's a good thing that they practise what to do in case of a fire."

"Who does?"

"The boys. It's part of their training. One of the boys told me that they used an old fire cart and hose. On Saturday morning their duty master tells them where the fire is supposed to be and how to get there and he makes them run as fast as they can as if there was a real fire. Sometimes the boys run away and the duty master gets real mad. The office isn't the only building that had a fire; the cow barn burned down and the sheep barn burned down, too. But they got all the animals out."

"I wonder if someone is lighting the fires on purpose?" She dug her fingers into the soil, deep in thought for a moment, before turning to Marjorie. "I like planting the seeds better than weeding. Don't you, Marjorie?"

"I guess so. I like eating the fresh carrots best, though, right from the ground. I had no idea that there was so much work in growing vegetables. I don't want to be a farmer, do you?"

Marjorie instinctively whispered. It was an unspoken rule among the girls that you kept it to yourself that you had no plans to be a farmer, and especially not a farmer's wife, when you got out of here. Most of the girls kept track of the years until they would be old enough to escape. Marjorie did not know what to expect once she was out. She had been to Duncan a few times, but really, she had little knowledge about life beyond the farm. She knew that they would probably send her to work in Victoria when she turned sixteen, and then she would find out. When she got out, would she know what to do? There was no one she could ask here because she was afraid that someone would guess that she was planning to escape.

Kenny told her that the boys tried to escape all the time. They never got very far because they had nowhere to go.[5] They could not carry very much food with them, either. They always came back, and they were tired, cold, hungry, and in big trouble. He told her that they really punished the runaway boys when they brought them back.[6] Kenny whispered to Marjorie that one day he would run away and they would not catch him — ever.[7] Marjorie watched his face. He was so serious and sure of himself that Marjorie hoped he was right. She saw that some of the boys just gave up after a while. They lost their spark. Their spirits seemed broken. She hoped that her brother would make it okay.

"Marjorie, why did you leave church last Sunday?" Her gardening partner tossed a clump of dirt at her.

"Yeah, how did you manage to get out of that, you lucky thing?"

Marjorie had been off in her own little world, thinking about things. She looked at the girls and tossed back some dirt. "What did you say?"

"How did you manage to get out of going to church the other day?"

"Oh, that. Well, I was standing there, and the room started to spin. It was like there wasn't enough air in there. It was hot and stuffy. But I was confirmed at the new font first. I don't know why. I don't believe in God anymore."

"Marjorie, he'll hear you. Maybe you're allergic to church? Don't you just love it? Everyone is so excited about having the new church, but to us it just means one more building to clean." She sang softly: "Where you work all day, and get no pay. We wax the floors, and scrub the doors."

"Yeah, it seems that the work is growing, but the number of girls to do the work isn't."

"Well, what about the new group of kids that arrived a couple of weeks ago?"

"There were not many kids, and only six were girls. We didn't get any new girls in our cottage."

"We didn't, either. I think they put them all together in one of the other cottages."

"Remember when there seemed to be new kids coming in every few months? I don't think we've had any new kids for a long time — maybe two years."

"Well, I think the last group that came out was when my brother came out, and that was before Christmas, not the last one but the one before that. It must have been 1938." She looked over at Marjorie. "Remember, I came out with your sister, and my brother came out a few months later."

"I think you're right. I don't remember anyone coming last year."

"Hey, look at the rainbow." It had started to sprinkle a bit, but the sun was trying its best to win. "Wow! I can see both ends. It's brilliant!"

"Do you believe in gnomes and the pot of gold at the end of the rainbow?"

"You're daft! It's not a gnome; it's a leprechaun. Have you ever tried to get to the end? It just keeps on moving. It's impossible to find the end. So if there's a pot of gold there, it's pretty safe."

"What would you do if you found a pot of gold, Marjorie?"

"I'd get out of here. I'd go back to England and find my family."

"Do you know where they are?"

"No, but if I had enough money, I could find them."

"Would you take me with you?"

"I'd take you all with me. We would show them all. We'd go home and help our mums, and then we could have our families back." She had often daydreamed about finding enough money to go back home.

Marjorie stood up and stretched her back. The horses pulling the ploughs in the lower field were sending up clouds of dust. It must have rained very little. She watched the horse-drawn hay cutter as it cut the hay in the other field and was fascinated by how smoothly they cut the hay and left it lying in a row. She watched the boys who were doing the stooking. It looked like it was back-breaking work. The trainee boys worked hard, all right, and she could see that they had better do it right because the head gardener always made them redo the stooks that failed to pass his inspection. When the hay was dry enough to bring into the barn, it was piled up into high hills and carted away by horse and wagon. The boys were also in charge of the chickens, cows, and pigs. The school was doing its best to turn everyone into farmers, but Marjorie didn't know of anyone who planned to be a farmer after they got out of here.

At the other end of the large garden field, a little band of boys was also nearing the end of their morning shift. The warm temperature made them mutinous at the thought of coming back out for the afternoon shift. The duty master had been pushing and prodding at them all morning, but they didn't feel like hoeing or picking peas, and the raking and weeding was back-breaking work. All they could think about was the cool Koksilah River on their backs, and they longed for its refreshing waters to surround their dusty, sweaty bodies.

Their duty master, Mr. Sampson, yelled out in frustration, got down on his knees, and began to furiously grab at the weeds. "You do it like this! It's not that hard."[8] Seeing him down in the dirt made some of the boys stifle their laughter, while others were alarmed into hoeing a little harder.

"Now get to work if you expect to get a swim in before your afternoon shift. Sing with me. Sing the Fairbridge March with me!"

> Cheerio!
> Here we are
> Working hard
> On our Fairbridge Farm …
> Our Empire home
> For we love our island home
> *Our Empire home in Canada*[9]

Marjorie turned away and ignored the commotion across the field. "Miss Bishop said she would walk into Duncan this Saturday with us so we can go to the movies."

"You guys are lucky. What do you think is showing?"

"I think the *Wizard of Oz* is on for the matinee."

"Oh, I want to see that movie."

Cottage mother and children. Perhaps they are getting ready to walk into Duncan. Marjorie is in the middle, fourth from the left.

"It's worth it to walk the five miles into Duncan for a movie like that. We walked all the way once and the movie was awful. I can't remember what it was called, though."

"Remember the time when we walked into Duncan for May Day? There was a maypole and everything." Marjorie thought of a group of the Duncan girls dancing around the maypole. They had on the prettiest dresses she had ever seen. She still remembered seeing a mother with her three daughters. It just made her miss her mum so much, especially when the lady sat on her blanket with the baby and watched her older daughters dance around the maypole. She wanted her mum to watch her. Maybe she would have avoided getting herself so tangled in the ribbons if her mum was watching. Maybe if she had on a pretty dress instead of her dingy old Fairbridge clothes she would have done better. Her cottage mum called her a clumsy oaf, grabbed her out of the circle, and made her sit and watch the others. The mother on the blanket smiled over at her. She wanted to run over and ask her … she wanted to ask her something, but what would she say? *Can you find my mum? Can you take me home? Can I be your daughter, too?* She looked at her cottage mum, who glared at her, and she knew that now was not the moment to try to escape.

"Oh, that was a great day, but do you remember when it started raining when we were walking back? We got soaked. Our cottage mum said she would never take us again."

"And I saved my allowance just so I could spend it at The Canoe."

"Don't be daft; that store is in Koksilah. We went there when we walked to the old Stone Butter Church in Cowichan, remember? We walked over that bridge and took shortcuts across fields."

"I dunno. Well, The Canoe is the best store."

"I never seem to be able to save my penny a week. I always get fined or spend it at the store by the dining hall on Saturday morning. Hey, don't we get more when we get older? I heard the older boys get five cents a week. That's not fair!"

"When you turn twelve, you'll get five cents a week. I already get a nickel. Boys and girls both do. When we're fifteen we get twenty-five cents a week."

"When we're fifteen we get to be a trainee, right?"

"Yes, and do you know what a trainee is?"

"What do you mean?"

"A trainee is someone who works all day every day and gets no pay!"

"We get a quarter, right?"

"Right, but it's not very much money for all the work we do. That's what's not fair!" Marjorie informed the younger girl. "You know, I heard one cottage mother telling a visitor that we might do more work than other kids but that work is like play to us! I wanted to wring her neck and yell that she is full of it. What a lot of rot."[10]

"It's all rot and rubbish. I'll tell you what's not fair. I had five pennies saved up, but my cottage mum fined me three of them for sassing her. What an old bitch."

"Yeah, they're all old bitches."

"Marjorie, hush! The gardener will hear you."

"I don't care; it's true. Aren't we supposed to speak the truth? I got fined twenty-five cents for not having my apron on when I was serving in the dining hall. I didn't get any allowance for weeks. It took me ages to pay it off." Marjorie looked at the girl beside her. "Didn't you get fined for not saying your prayers?"

"Yes, and I was gated[11] as well. What happened when you swore at the teacher?"

"I was gated for one week, and then when I broke my probation I got strapped. I guess I deserved it. I shouldn't have snuck out. I just can't seem to be good enough."

"Oh, the strap! That's the worst, especially when they get your legs. They're mean old bitches."

"What about the boys — they have to drop their trousers, and they don't wear any knickers!"

"Oh, how gross! Let's talk about something else!"

Marjorie looked at her and laughed. "I remember the first time we went to Duncan and stopped at the store. I had a penny, and I wanted to buy some lucky tatties, my favourite candy back home, but the woman behind the counter looked at me as if I was crazy. She pretended that she didn't understand me. Then she said, 'You're from that farm school, aren't you?' She had a snotty voice, as if she just wanted us out of there. I miss the candy that we used to have in England." It had been a long while since Marjorie had thought about it, but she suddenly remembered swinging on her gate in Whitley Bay and calling for some money so she could buy some lucky tatties with the fizz pops and a surprise toy.[12]

After their lunch break the girls headed back to the garden. Marjorie stretched her back and looked around the group. One girl had been very quiet and hadn't joined in with any of the chatter. She watched as the girl took handfuls of dirt and let it slip between her fingers. Silent tears ran down her face, leaving trails on her dusty cheeks. It was faint, but Marjorie was certain she was singing the new song they had learned in choir: "There'll Always Be an England."[13] A cloud of sadness surrounded her.

The afternoon wore on. The gardener walked over to inspect their work. He said they were nearly finished, then gave them another patch to plant. Now she wished she was working on the cottage Victory Garden.

At least you could see the edges of the plot. The huge fields had rows and rows that went on forever. She would be happy to go back to her day school routine on Monday. It seemed to take ages before the gardener walked over again. The girls knew they couldn't get away until they had his permission.

"Well, the rows could be straighter, girls, but I guess it will have to do. Off you go now. That's enough for today."

The girls didn't need telling twice. They jumped up and dusted themselves off. They grabbed their gardening tools, feeling full of energy again, and chatted happily as they headed back to their cottage. They were ready for the showers.

"Look at your knees, Marjorie. They're all brown."

Marjorie pointed to the other girl's knees. "So are yours." The sides of their baggy brown shorts, covered in dust and dirt, wore the evidence of where the girls had wiped their hands. The seats bore the evidence of where they'd sat as they worked. Their blouses had splotches of dirt as well. "We all look a fright. We're filthy. I'm going to enjoy a shower. Last one there is a rotten egg." The group of girls giggled as they tried to run with their shovels and hoes toward their cottages.

There were several children in front of Pennant Cottage. One was struggling with the old hand mower. A couple of girls were stacking kindling. The days were warm, but some of the evenings were still cool enough, so they welcomed a fire. The girls who had finished their chores were playing jump rope.

Bunny came running up to Marjorie. She was wearing her new Brownie uniform. Kenny was in the Boy Scouts. Her cottage mum told her that she should join something, but she didn't want to. It made her miss being in Whitley Bay and going to her Sunbeam meetings. They called them Brownies here, not Sunbeams.

"Hi, Marjorie. Do you like my new uniform?"

"You look smashing, Bunny!" Marjorie grinned at her sister. "How was your meeting?"

"Good. It was fun." Bunny skipped up to her.

"You better get your uniform off before the old battleaxe sees you. If you get it mucky you'll be in big trouble."

"In a minute. The duty master said to come by and show him my new uniform. He said he had a sweet for me." Bunny started to skip away, but Marjorie grabbed her roughly by the arm. She was shaking she was so mad.

"How many times do I have to warn you? Don't trust him. Never ever go there by yourself. Promise me." Marjorie wanted to say more, but the cottage mother stood in the doorway calling for the girls to get on with their chores. "Promise me," she whispered urgently.

"Okay! You don't have to pull my arm off. Your hands have muck on them. Let me go. He said he had some chocolate." Bunny frowned.

"Bunny, you must never go alone. It's not safe." Marjorie pulled her sister close and whispered, "He tries to grab your private parts." Treats were so scarce that sometimes the younger ones could forget the dangers.

"What? Really! I won't ever. I promise, Marjorie. I promise." Bunny's face showed disgust and fear. Marjorie hoped her sister understood now.

The girls on dinner duty had already started preparing the evening meal. They could smell the boiled cabbage as they raced by the basement stairs to the shower room. During the heat of the day they longed to jump in the river, but it had cooled off and now a hot shower was more inviting.

"When I grow up, I'm going to have a job where I stay clean." One of the girls groaned as she took off her dirty work clothes. "I hate having to scrub off this dirt all the time."

"Well, it's not just dirt, you know," Marjorie said.

"What do you mean?" the other girl asked as she tossed her clothes into the laundry basket.

"It's full of poop, too!" Marjorie made a face.

"It is not! Don't tell me that!"

"What do you think they do with all the poop from the cows and the chickens and the pigs? They spread it over the fields, and we were digging in that stuff all day. We were playing in poop!" Marjorie was enjoying the girls' reactions. One looked positively green.

"Yeah, and we eat food grown in poo!" said one of the other girls as she eyed Marjorie and grinned.

"Yuck! Stop it! I don't want to hear any more! No wonder they're trying to make us be farmers. Who else would choose to work with poop?" She

Working in the garden at the Prince of Wales Fairbridge Farm School.

Haying at the Prince of Wales Fairbridge Farm School.

jumped into the shower. The other girls followed. They quietly scrubbed and scrubbed, trying very hard to get the day's dirt off them.

Farming

Farming makes the world go 'round,
Feeds the city, feeds the town.
And you can worry, work and strive,
Yet farming keeps the folks alive.
Raising corn and raising wheat,
So the folks have 'nough to eat.
'Cause farming isn't any fun,
Keeps a fellow on the run.
Ploughing and sowing to be done,
And faith in the weather to be won.
Tending calves and milking cows,
Putting up and filling mows.
There's more work than you'll allow —
Doggone farming anyhow.[14]

Chapter 8

OFF TO FINTRY: NOW WHAT DID I DO WRONG?

> If they pass into the care of Fairbridge whilst they are
> still malleable, then their lives can be preserved for
> them.... Instead of being children of the dead-end in
> this country, they will become self-supporting settlers
> in the Dominions.
>
> — Fairbridge Farm School, *Annual Report*, 1936

It was the first Friday in June and Marjorie's last day on laundry duty. "We better get dressed quickly, Bunny. I'm on laundry today, and it's my turn to get the fires started to heat the water. Do you want to come with me?"

Marjorie peeled off her pajamas and quickly got dressed. She hoped Bunny wanted to come with her because she hated travelling across to the laundry building on her own. It was worse in the winter when it was dark in the mornings. The shadows held unknown dangers that could be better kept at bay when there were two of them.

Bunny jumped out of bed. She enjoyed going with Marjorie to the laundry building. She felt safest when she was with her big sister. The two sisters quickly folded their pajamas and tucked them under their covers. They pulled up their grey blankets, smoothed the tops, and then neatly tucked them in. "There. All done. Let's go."

The sisters ran to the laundry building. Bunny scrunched up some paper, and Marjorie grabbed a handful of kindling. The flames were soon

Fairbridge Farm School girls working in the laundry building.

licking at the dry cedar, and it began to crackle and pop. They worked quickly so they wouldn't be late for breakfast. The girls ran for the door. It opened just as they got to it, and in walked the laundry matron, Mrs. Baker.

"Good morning, girls."

"Good morning, ma'am. The fire's going really good; we'll have plenty of hot water soon," Marjorie told her as the two girls bolted out of the door. Mrs. Baker yelled after them to slow down, but they were gone. They made a beeline for the dining hall.

Marjorie headed back to the laundry building after breakfast. Bunny carried on to the day school. "See you at lunchtime, Bunny." Bunny turned and waved and then ran off. Marjorie was the first one to arrive back at the laundry. She put another log on the fire. As she shut the stove door, the matron walked in with five other girls.

"Well, girls, we had better get to work. We've got a lot to do today."

Marjorie and her co-workers started with sorting the laundry from the different cottages. They looked for the cottage initials on each item and put them all in separate piles. Marjorie knew not to look for anything under "I" because when the cottages were given letters, they left that letter out. Soon they had twenty-one huge piles of laundry, one for each cottage: 1935 cottages: A-Edith Attwood, B-Silver Jubilee, C-Queen Mary, D-Lady Houston; 1936 cottages: E-Liverpool, F-Saint George's, G-Richards, H-Lord Riddell; 1937 cottages: J-Strathcona, K-Lumley, L-Douglas, M-Pennant; 1938 cottages: N-Hill, O-Molyneux, P-Dulverton, Q-MacMillan; 1939 cottages: R-Laybourne and S-Davidson; plus one more for the principal's house and one for the bunkhouse workers.

As soon as the girls washed one load, they put it in the huge extractor to get out as much water as they could. When the weather was okay, they hung everything out the back of the laundry building until things were dry enough to iron. Some days the wet clothing hung all over the laundry room, with the wood stove cranked up until the top glowed red, ensuring everything would dry. The room became hot and steamy, the windows clouded over, and little puddles of water formed on the windowsills.

"Ma'am," one of the girls said, "someone told us that we wash about two hundred and eighty bits of laundry here every week. Is that true?"

"Oh, dear me, no! It's more like two thousand and eight hundred pieces. Last April we kept track for a whole week, and that is the total we came up with. It's a lot of laundry."

Another girl piped in, "Well, I'm glad they all wash their own socks and underthings. Can you imagine if we had to do those, too? That would give us about ten thousand things to wash."

The girls worked quietly and steadily, and before they knew it, it was time to get ready for lunch. After lunch, the six girls headed back to the laundry. A trainee girl was heading out with her arm full of the neatly folded bunkhouse laundry. She grimaced as she said she wondered what kind of cake the bunkhouse men would have for her, and she tried to get someone to go with her. The others said they couldn't as they all had odd jobs to do for the next half hour before school started. At twenty minutes past one, they stoked the fire and went over to the day school for their afternoon class in home economics.

* * *

As Marjorie worked on her sewing project, she thought about what her cottage mum had told her this morning. She would be one of the two girls they were sending up to the Fairbridge Fintry Training Farm in the Okanagan Valley next week. The other girl's name was Lavinia; she didn't know her very well as she was in a different cottage. Was it good that they picked her to go? Or had she done something wrong? Was this a punishment? She was scared but a little bit excited, too. She would get away from the old battleaxe of a cottage mum. She was going to love that. She hoped Bunny would be okay while she was gone. She would miss her. She knew very little about Fintry, except that it was in the interior of British Columbia. That's what they told her, anyway. She didn't really know what that meant, but her day teacher showed her on the map of Canada. Then she asked him where England was. He laughed and said, "It's not on this map." Then the rest of the classroom laughed. Red-faced, she wondered what happened to England, and it frustrated her that the class laughed at her for asking. It made it hard to ask questions about things if they were just going to laugh at her.

To get to Fintry, the group would have to take the farm truck to Nanaimo and get on the ferry boat back to Vancouver. In Vancouver, they would catch the train to Vernon. The Fintry Farm truck would pick them up in Vernon and drive them the twenty-four miles south to Fintry. It was on the west side of the beautiful Okanagan Lake. At least that was what they told her. Then they told her to watch out for the Ogopogo, the huge lake monster that was supposed to live in this lake. Were they teasing her? Why did all the good things get mixed up with the bad?

Last week was a good week as it was her turn to work with the nurse. Marjorie liked the quiet, calm atmosphere in the hospital, except when someone ran in with an emergency. Last Friday was altogether different. It was a day with no emergencies and a visiting guest. The dentist drove in from Duncan in his old car. He had a strange machine with him. The nurse said it was an ancient foot-powered dental drill.[1] Marjorie watched as the dentist operated the drill by pumping a foot treadle on the side. It was fun to watch him pump the pedal and drill his patient's teeth all at once.

After watching for a few moments, the nurse said, "You do have a knack with this old thing, don't you, doctor?" The nurse seemed delighted to watch him, but she suggested, "Doctor, why don't I pedal for you? It might make it easier. I've got some filling mixture ready."

"Thank you, that would make it a lot easier. This old contraption is a bit awkward, but I suppose that we have to make do with what we've got, don't we?" The dentist chuckled as he moved aside to let the nurse get at the foot pedal.

The nurse pedaled until the doctor needed some more filling mixture prepared, then he went back to doing the pedaling and drilling himself. Marjorie could tell that he had a lot of practice because he was so good at it.

As he drilled, he told them, "I have to visit a lot of remote areas, and many of these places don't have electricity, so this machine serves me well. I find that I can get it in and out of my car easily enough. A standard dentist's drill would be impossible to lug around with me." He looked down at his patient. "Just a bit more drilling, sonny, and we'll be done."

The boy tried to be brave, but he jumped whenever the drill started up. His hands gripped the side of the chair, and Marjorie could see a tear trickle down the side of his face. She was glad it wasn't her turn to be in the chair.

After the midday meal, two cottage mums sat having an afternoon cup of tea. The children would be gone all afternoon with their day school sessions, and then they would begin their afternoon chores after that. They could relax for a bit.

"What do you think of the Fairbridge Farm School?" Miss Bishop asked.

"Well, it's a job. But it's going to take some time to get used to it all." Mrs. Gage, the new mum of a boys' cottage, was surprised at what was expected of her. There were few breaks, and she wondered how she would cope with being at work twenty-four hours a day, seven days a week.

Miss Bishop picked up her tea and sipped at it. She passed the biscuits over.

"Thanks." Mrs. Gage took one. As she bit into it, she looked over at the other mum and smiled.

"How is your group?" Miss Bishop was curious to see how Mrs. Gage was handling the boys. The girls were hard enough, but the boys were worse. She had been the head of a boys' cottage until recently, and she found the boys much more difficult, and they were stronger — something that had frightened her at times.

"Oh, they're fine, I suppose," Mrs. Gage answered. "They're not the happiest group of boys I've ever seen. It can't be easy being an orphan and being sent away to a new country, I suppose." The mum had found her group of boys hard to get to know.

"Oh, most of the children here are not orphans — only a handful. Most of them are from very poor families — bad breeding, you know. So, it's not surprising that the children are difficult."

Miss Bishop was trying to be careful how she worded things. She thought that the program was all wrong. They should have left the little guttersnipes where they belonged. *Canada should be helping its own*, she thought, *not allowing the British trash to be dumped here and saddling the country with the problem. England should take care of her own problems.* Well, that was her opinion, but she usually kept it to herself, as this was not the place to voice it.

"Really!" Mrs. Gage exclaimed. "I assumed they were all poor little orphans." She looked puzzled. What were all these children doing here if they weren't orphans? She went on, trying to clarify. "I didn't mean they were difficult children, just hard to get to know, like they've always got their guard up. The boys don't seem to trust me."

"Well, I certainly wouldn't trust them! You can't trust that sort, you know. You can't turn your back on them. I hope you lock your door at night." Miss Bishop continued on, "Really, I believe anything we give them is probably better than what they left behind. I think they have it too good here most of the time, if you want my opinion. We should be putting this money and effort into helping our own poor children rather than bringing in these English slum children. It just waters down the stock, doesn't it? We have enough of that class in Canada already." Seeing the expression on Mrs. Gage's face, she wondered if she had gone too far.

"But if they're given a chance? Most of my boys seem quite bright and lively. There's no reason they can't be quite successful in their lives, really. That is, as long as they survive their childhoods. They work pretty hard for children." Mrs. Gage was aware that they would not be able to see eye to eye.

"Well, I suppose the boys and girls at Fairbridge do work, but they have lots of time to play, and work is play to them, really."[2]

"You sound as if you think these children are different because they come from poor backgrounds. That they should be treated like little workers, not children."

"Oh, but they are different. You'll see in time. Their expectations about life are different, too. It's just the way they were born. The Fairbridge School is just training them to be farmers and farmers' wives or domestics; that's all their training will give them. They won't be suited for much else, and we don't want them taking our jobs. It's what their class should be doing anyway. Don't you agree?" Miss Bishop was getting riled. She wondered if this young upstart was baiting her. She wanted her to agree.

Deciding that it was best she not pursue the subject further, she asked, "Have you heard of the Fintry Fairbridge Training School?"[3]

"Well, just a little bit. Some of my boys will be going there next week for the summer months," replied Mrs. Gage. She asked for another cup of tea.

As she poured, Miss Bishop explained what Fintry was about: "Well, a couple of years ago a man called Captain Dun-Waters left his entire estate — it's in the interior of the province, right on Okanagan Lake — to the Fairbridge Farm School Society. We're using it as a training centre for the boys. They learn all about the care of orchards — you know, pruning, picking, and packing, that sort of thing. Marjorie, one of my girls, is heading up there next week. She and a girl from another cottage will do the laundry and help with the cooking. She's a handful; I hope they don't send her back early!"

Mrs. Gage didn't want to get into another discussion about the children and what was wrong with them. "If I had a fortune, I would certainly spend it differently, but that's the rich for you. They're different from us, and that's for sure."

"They sure are!" Miss Bishop was beginning to relax. She was happy; she felt that she had begun to sway Mrs. Gage over to her way of thinking.

Mrs. Gage grinned to herself. She knew that her host's ancestors had come from Great Britain, even though she seemed to have forgotten that for the moment.

"More tea?"

Marjorie hurried through her after-school chores. If the weather was warm enough *and* as long as they did a good job with tomorrow morning's chores, they could go to the swimming hole after lunch. They were already on their summer schedule: they divided the girls into two groups and they worked two different shifts. One group worked around the cottage while the other was assigned duties around the farm. The first shift started at 9:00, and then they worked until 10:15. Next came a short break, and then they would work from 10:30 until 11:30. Marjorie wondered which group she would be in tomorrow. She would either be shelling the early peas, weeding the garden, raking the pathways, cleaning the bell, knitting for the Red Cross, picking berries, polishing silver, or chopping wood. The amount of wood they had to chop was a lot less now that they didn't need the furnace on so much, but the big tractors were already hauling in trailer loads of wood for next winter.

She hated chopping wood because it brought back a bad memory from last year. She thought back to that day. She'd finished chopping wood and gone in to change — and that was when she noticed the blood. How could she have cut herself and not know it? She would remember if she'd slipped with the axe. She used rags, but the blood was impossible to stop. She tried to see the cut, but it was too hard to see down there. Asking for help was out of the question. How could she ask someone to look down there for a cut? She found more rags and tossed the old ones in the very back of the cupboard so no one would see them. Fear accompanied her to bed that night. Would she bleed to death in her sleep? When she woke up in the morning, she thought the bleeding had stopped, until she stood up and it started again. Her stomach hurt inside, as if she'd cut herself, but she was alive. She found some more rags, and as she was trying to hide the soiled ones, the cottage mum found her. Marjorie jumped.[4]

"Oh, so you have your visitor, do you?" the cottage mum asked.

"My visitor?" Marjorie whispered.

"Your monthlies. You will be getting them every month now. Here are the supplies you will need." The mum showed her a box of huge thick pads that she kept hidden in the back of the supply closet. The pads had tails on each end. She gave her a belt and showed her how to attach the pads. When Marjorie was done, it felt like she had a huge nappy between her legs. She walked funny, and she was afraid that everyone would know that she was bleeding from her private parts. No one told her why this was happening, just to expect it every month now. What had she done wrong to deserve this horrid punishment?

Marjorie put chopping wood out of her mind and thought about swimming. She loved going down to the Koksilah River swimming hole that ran through the bottom field. When she was down there, it seemed like she was in another world, far away from the farm and all its chores. A raft in the middle of the swimming hole allowed the good swimmers a place to jump and dive.

After dinner, Marjorie and a group of girls were washing up and chatting happily about the prospect of going swimming.

"I'm going to dive off the raft."

"Will you help me swim to the raft?" Bunny asked.

"No. You know the rules. You have to get there on your own or you have to stay on the river's edge."

Marjorie looked at her sister. She was already ten years old. That was how old Marjorie had been when she'd left Whitley Bay. Now she was going to be fourteen after the summer. She would be up at Fintry for her birthday. They told her that the entire group would stay at Fintry until October. She had seen some of the pictures of the farm and the lake. There was a huge manor house and a funny-shaped barn. She hoped she liked it there. She knew there would be no way back if she hated it.

The next afternoon Marjorie stood and watched the group swimming. Bunny's bathing cap was falling off. Why did they make the girls wear these silly caps? They had never worn bathing caps when they swam at the rock pools and beaches at Whitley Bay.

She had had her "visitor" last night, so swimming was out of the question. Of all the rotten luck. *Oh well*, she thought, *at least I'll be able to go swimming when I get to Fintry.*

Marjorie shuddered as she thought of the other unwanted visitor they'd had recently. She thought she was seeing a ghost at first, but it was that horrible man from Newcastle who had been so mean to their mum when he came to their flat in Whitley Bay.[5] Marjorie would never forget his face. When he asked her how things were going, she glared at him.

"What did you do with my sister Joyce? Why didn't she get to come with us?"

Instead of answering her, Malcolm Jackson looked at Kenny and said, "My, my, aren't you a big healthy boy. This fresh air and farm work agrees with you, doesn't it, sonny?" He turned and ruffled Bunny's hair, and then he went to talk with another boy.

Everyone at the farm school was mingling outside of the dining hall. Malcolm Jackson wanted a photograph taken of all the children and all the staff. He said he wanted to take it back to England to show how wonderful the Fairbridge Farm School was doing. Marjorie wanted to shout at him that it was not wonderful, and wanted to ask again about her sister Joyce, but as she tried to find her words, her cottage mum grabbed her arm and dragged her away.

The gnawing frustration that Marjorie had tried to mask for years squirmed around her inner being, threatening to explode. No one ever

Fairbridge Farm School Group. Kenny is in the bottom row, eleven over from the left side, and Marjorie and Audrey are directly above him. Circa 1940.

gave them any answers. Sometimes all they wanted to know was what was going on, yet the grown-ups simply ignored them or seemed frustrated and angered by questions. They had no one to turn to for answers. She just wanted to know what had happened to Joyce. What was he doing here, anyway? Did he come to spy on them? Was he going to go back and tell the king about the good little soldiers that he'd sent out here? Well, if he talked to her cottage mum, he might find out that Marjorie was not such a good little soldier, but what did she care? She hated being here, and she was tired of pretending that she liked it. They made her feel that nothing she did was right, no matter how hard she tried, so what was the point? Sometimes she felt that no one liked her here. She was glad she was going to Fintry. She wanted to get away from them all.

Chapter 9

A BAD HOME IS BETTER THAN ANY INSTITUTION

Most of the children seem to feel cheated, and their
allegiance is still to their own families back in England,
poor though they may be.

— Isobel Harvey Report, August 1944

Home Sweet Home

They say Home Sweet Home
Is the place to be.
Well, I guess
That's just not for me
'Cause my home sweet home
Is across the sea.
Home Sweet Home
Is with my family.

Marjorie thought back to when she was packing her bag to come to
Fintry. She laughed now about how she'd worried she would miss
a lot of good things by having to leave the farm school. For example, they
allowed all the girls who had completed sewing their dresses to model
them in the dress parade when the day school closed for the summer. She
had taken extra care sewing her dress, and she was unhappy at the time
that going to Fintry meant that no one would see what a good job she'd

done. She was proud of her dress, but she no longer minded that she'd missed the dress parade. They were also going to have a session in school on painting fungi. She loved doing that, too. She had already found a great fungus in the woods, almost a foot across. She had planned to paint a beach scene on hers, with a lighthouse just like the St. Mary's Lighthouse at Whitley Bay. She gave the fungus to Bunny before she left. She was a good painter. Marjorie could find another fungus to paint when she returned to Fairbridge.

She would miss swimming in the Koksilah River and the walk to the old Stone Butter Church this summer and to the beach at Cowichan Bay. She thought about those special things. That and hiding. She'd planned to hide so no one could find her, and then the truck would have to leave for Nanaimo without her. She'd had no idea how much better everything was going to be at Fintry. Now she could see that it would have been a disaster if she'd missed the truck.

Shortly after they arrived, they celebrated Dominion Day by going on a picnic to the high farm. The view of the lake was wonderful from the top. Imagine, a walk and a picnic all in one day! Now the group had been at Fintry for almost three weeks. Marjorie thought that it was the best three weeks ever. Once the farm truck pulled out of the farm school's "Pearly Gates," Marjorie began to enjoy herself. She wondered why she'd had such a hard time packing her bag. It may have been the uncertainty of leaving the farm school after being there for almost three years. She might not like it much, but it was also scary leaving it. Would she fit in or stand out and feel judged, just like when she walked into the shops in Duncan?

The carefree feeling as they drove away surprised her. It was as if she had left all her worries and fears back at the farm. She felt relaxed, and it was a wonderful new feeling. The ferry ride was exciting, too. She spent a lot of time outside on the deck, watching the seagulls following the boat. Then, it was magic! They saw some black-and-white whales. Someone called them orca whales. There were about five or six of them travelling together. They kept going down, then surfacing again, spouting large sprays of water into the air as they came up. They looked so unrestricted. There were no gates or rules to stop them. They could travel wherever they wanted.

Marjorie enjoyed seeing Vancouver again. She recognized the ferry dock and the train station. They boarded the train the next morning and settled into their seats. Mrs. Howard, the Fairbridge cottage mother who was travelling to Fintry with them, told them that they would arrive in time for a swim before dinner. She seemed to be as excited as the children in her charge. She had been at Fintry the year before, and during the train ride she told the eighteen boys and the two girls about all the wonderful things they would find at Fintry.

The day seemed to fly by in a haze of rivers, tunnels, trees, and lakes. Before anyone expected it, the train was pulling into Vernon Station. As they scrambled off the train, Mrs. Howard pointed out a rather large open-backed truck. "There is our ride to Fintry."

They travelled the twenty-four bumpy, winding, narrow, and dusty miles down the west side of the lake in tired silence. Parts of the road were scary because the banks down to the lake were so steep. At one point they met a big truck carrying logs, and there was no room to go by, so they had to back up until the road was wide enough for the logging truck to pass by them. It was tricky to back up the old truck, but it was probably a lot easier than backing up the huge logging truck. Marjorie was relieved when they turned off the main road and headed down to Fintry.

The truck pulled over and stopped at the top for a moment so everyone could get a good look at the view. The driver pointed to the fields below. They could see the lake to the north and to the south. "That's Fintry. Beautiful, ain't it? You see that area where the hillside here slopes sharply down to the bottom area? We call that the Fintry Flats."

The driver turned off the road and started down the hillside. The road zigzagged down the steep bank to the bottom. The brakes squealed the entire way. Marjorie prayed for the brakes to hold, as it would be the end of them all if they failed. There was no need for her to worry; they got to the bottom in one piece.

As they passed through the gates, the driver opened the back cab window so the children could hear him, and he explained the layout to them: "There's the ranch manager's house. His name is Mr. Graham. He's been here for ages. He was Captain Dun-Waters' ranch manager, too. There's the house that Captain Dun-Waters lived in after he moved out

The Fintry manor house.

of his manor house. Unfortunately, he died last year. There is the packinghouse. That's where all the fruit is sorted and packed. Look, a boat is at the dock now. The boats travel up and down the lake between Kelowna and Vernon, and they stop in between wherever they're needed."

He stopped the truck so the children could see the boat and the packinghouse.

"Now, did you know that Fintry was once a stopping place on the North West Company's old fur trade route? No? Well, we have to get you up to speed on the local history. The Hudson's Bay Company also used it later on. Yes, the Okanagan Lake is steeped in history. You see, before there were proper roads, the lake was the main travel route, especially for this side of the lake. People still use all kinds of boats, canoes, rowboats, paddle wheelers, you name it; every kind of boat travels this lake. The road we just came in on has only been there since 1909. Before that you could only get here by trail or by boat.

"Over there is the orchard; it is about one hundred acres. Captain Dun-Waters planted about five thousand trees. He planted mainly apple trees, but there are also twenty-two pear trees, over two hundred cherry trees, and over one hundred stone fruit trees, like apricots, peaches, and plums. It looks like we'll have a good crop of cherries this year. The apples are ready to be thinned — so, boys, I guess that will be the first job on your list."

"What kind of apples, sir?"

"Oh, goodness me, all varieties. There are McIntosh, Reds, Rome Beauty, Jonathan, Stayman, Delicious, Wealthy, and Winter Bananas. The farm has averaged between twenty-two thousand and twenty-five thousand boxes every year. Last year we shipped out nine tons of cherries, too. Yes, the trees are in their prime."

The driver pointed and turned to the children. "Now there's a building. That barn was Captain Dun-Waters' pride. Look at the octagonal shape. The cows go in and stand in their stalls all facing the centre. The captain was famous for his herd of purebred Ayrshire cattle. The Fairbridge Farm School inherited those, too, along with the rest of the property. The captain put all modern milking equipment in his barn. His cattle got nothing but the best!"

He drove the truck just a few feet before stopping again. "And up there — you can't see it very well because of the pine trees — but there is a hundred-foot waterfall. We call it Fintry Falls. Shorts Creek flows through the high farm area up above there, on the other side of the road, you know, and comes down here and drops at the Fintry Falls. It is certainly worth a hike up there to see it. The water supply for the entire farm comes from that creek. Captain Dun-Waters put pipes underground to all the buildings so all the houses have a good supply of water. The captain also put in two separate heating systems in the manor house. One is hot water and the other is hot air. The house stays toasty warm even on the cold, snowy, wintry days. The creek drives a large dynamo that generates electricity — you can find it in that building over there — and that gives all the buildings electric light, and there is power to spare for the farm machinery. All the houses have a telephone system, too. He was a smart man, that captain." Again, the driver drove a few feet then stopped.

"Over there, beyond the barn, are the blacksmith and the carpenter shops, some storage sheds, and the stable. And over there, the granary, chicken coop, and pigsties. There's the silo." He put the truck in gear and drove on. A moment later, he drove down a narrow road leading through the trees. They rounded a bend, and the children could see a large stone house with honeysuckle growing up its sides. The ornamental gardens were beautiful, and, best of all, there was a splendid-looking lawn all around the house. Huge pine trees bordered the lawn. Marjorie wondered if this was where they were going to stay. Surely not. It was too posh!

"Okay, here we are then — the manor house." The children craned their necks to get a better look at what was to be their home for the next four or five months. "Don't push. You'll be out in a jiffy, and you can do all the looking you like." The driver pulled the truck close to the house and stopped.

The girls sat there and let everyone else off first; it was safer that way. They could see how anxious the boys were to get off the truck and check out everything. Marjorie looked at Lavinia. "What do you think? I like it so far; do you?"

"I think so. Let's go see the house." Lavinia and Marjorie scrambled off the truck after the boys.

The duty master walked down the manor house stairs to greet the newcomers. He asked for their attention, but it was impossible to be heard over the excited chatter. He let out a loud whistle and yelled, "Boys!" That did the trick. "Okay, now listen. I see some familiar faces, but for those of you who don't know me, I am Mr. Thomas. I will be your duty master for the next few months. I want all you boys to bring your gear up to the porch and find yourselves a bed. You will be sleeping on the porch. The screening keeps the bugs out, and your evenings will be nice and cool. It can be warm up here, and often the temperature stays high, even all night. Once you've done that, you can run down for a quick dip in the lake before our meal." The boys grabbed their gear and charged up to the veranda.

Mrs. Howard stood back. She said, "The children were like this last year as well. They seemed to really like it up here. Marjorie and Lavinia, come with me. I'll show you to your room." The girls followed Mrs. Howard into the manor house.

"What a grand place," Marjorie said as they walked through the large living room. "What a massive fireplace."

"Oh, yes. Can you imagine how wonderful it is to have the fire blazing on the cool September and October evenings? I suppose you would hardly think it now. This has been such a hot day. It must have been in the nineties. It's cooling off a little bit now."

As the girls walked through the dining room and then the kitchen, they looked at each other and gave huge nods of approval.

"Here we are, girls. Your room is through this door off the kitchen. You can put your things down and change for a quick swim if you like. Then I will need your help getting things settled away."

"Thank you, Mrs. Howard. We'll just have a quick swim, and we'll be right back to help you," Marjorie assured her, hardly containing her excitement.

The girls looked at each other. Lavinia was the first to say what was on both their minds. "Marjorie, we get this room all to ourselves! It's lovely." They quickly grabbed their bags and pulled out their swimsuits.

Seconds later they ran through the kitchen. "But, what about the Ogopogo? Won't it get us?" Fear spread across Marjorie's face.

Mrs. Howard laughed. "So, you've heard about the Ogopogo, have you? I dare say it won't come in close to shore. So, as long as you don't go out too far, you should be okay." She winked at the girls.

The girls ran off, and Mrs. Howard smiled as she heard, "Last one in is a rotten egg!" The girls plunged into the cool water, and all the dust and tiredness of the day's travel was quickly washed away.

The lake was divine! It was clearly the best part of being at Fintry. Marjorie could see the lake from the manor house. She and Lavinia had been able to run down the path to have a quick dip and cool off almost whenever they wanted to. It had a beautiful sandy beach that reminded Marjorie of the Whitley Bay sands. It was wonderful, and there were even a few seagulls at the lake.

Marjorie had settled in over the past three weeks and felt she was an important member of the Fintry team. She looked up from her chores in the kitchen. The farm school principal and his wife, Harry and Mrs. Logan, had arrived at the manor house. They had a boy with them, but not one from this year's group of Fintry boys; it was one of the boys from back at the farm school.

As they entered the kitchen, Mrs. Howard greeted them. "How nice to see you. I've put on a pot of tea. Well, Kenny, I hear you're going to take Pat's place. What a shame that he broke his arm. How is he doing? Is he still in the hospital in Vernon?"

"Yes, he is," Harry Logan replied. "He's doing very well. He should be out of the hospital tomorrow."

"Oh, that's good. It really is too bad about his arm. I hear he was working quite well." Mrs. Howard had a soft spot for all the children.

"Yes, yes, he was. It's a shame all right. However, we'll let him stay on here and do whatever he can to help. He will be limited with his arm in a cast, but I'm sure we can find him things to keep him busy.

"Well, how are these two girls doing? Are they good helpers?" Harry Logan walked over in time to watch the girls take a rather large pudding out of the oven.

"As you can see, they are grand workers." Mrs. Howard was rather proud of her two girls. With the pudding cooling, they set to peeling potatoes for the evening meal.

"Marjorie and Lavinia, I'm going to go with the Logans down to the orchard. Are you two okay peeling the potatoes and carrots until I get back?" Mrs. Howard walked toward the door.

"Yes, ma'am. We'll be fine. Don't worry," Lavinia answered for both of them.

The door shut and Lavinia turned to Marjorie. "Isn't she the best? I wish I had her for my cottage mum."

"I do, too. She is the best. She is so nice to us all the time. I think she cares about us. She never yells at us or hits us." Marjorie grabbed some carrots. "I know it's a long time away, but already I'm not looking forward to going back. I hate that old battleaxe of a cottage mother. I think she hates me. She never talks nicely to me. I kept thinking that I must really be a horrible, dumb jerk, and so I deserve all the crap she gives me. Here, Mrs. Howard seems to think that we are okay and not stupid. I feel smarter being here. Is that weird?"

"No, I know what you mean."

"I'm not so jumpy and worried. And I don't think I've had any night-mares here. I guess I feel more relaxed. Mrs. Howard has a different way of talking about mistakes; she says that's how we learn. Where D. Bitch — "

"Marjorie, you'll get into trouble!" Lavinia dropped her potato and laughed.

"Well, she is one. She rubs your face in your mistakes and makes you feel really stupid and that you're garbage. She's such an old hag. I wish I never had to see her again. I wish I could stay here. I miss Bunny, though, and I like to think I can keep track of how Kenny is doing. I wish they could come up here, too. Wouldn't it be lovely to just stay up here all winter and not go back to the farm school?" Marjorie sighed. It was so peaceful here.

The girls set the three long, narrow tables in the dining room. Then they had an inspiration. Because they had special guests, they ran out to gather flowers for the tables. They wanted to surprise Mrs. Howard. Marjorie picked some lavender from around the sundial, and Lavinia clipped some of the honeysuckle that was growing up the walls of the manor house. Marjorie spotted some colour on the edge of the lawn. It was Indian paintbrush. She picked a few of those, too. Before long, they had three beautiful bouquets. When Mrs. Howard returned, the girls had the kitchen chores done, including the three tables set.

"The tables look wonderful, girls. Look at your bouquets! How lovely! Dinner will take a bit to finish cooking, so you have time to run down for a swim if you like." Mrs. Howard smiled after them as they ran off. They were such wonderful girls, so helpful and thoughtful.

The girls quickly changed into their swimsuits. It had been warm working in the kitchen with the stoves going. A swim before dinner would be perfect.

Later that evening, Marjorie curled up with a book in the corner of one of the built-in seats in the trophy room. The bookshelves had dozens of books for the kids to read. She liked this room. Two of the boys were playing a game of ping-pong in the far corner. A couple more were standing by, waiting for their turn. Lavinia, curled up comfortably in the opposite seat, looked up and smiled at Marjorie as she turned a page of her book. The huge fireplace was between them. This room would be cozy in the winter. It would be better than the living room because this room was smaller. The living-room fireplace was huge, but so was the room, so the cozy trophy room would be her first choice on a cold winter evening.

As the sun set, its light shone through the window above Marjorie like a golden fan and touched the wall opposite her, splashing a little on Lavinia's hair. She looked across at the massive Kodiak bear in the man-made cave built into a wall of the room. She'd heard that when Captain Dun-Waters lived here, he had a real stream running through the cave. They said the trickling of the water made it seem very authentic. Marjorie thought the sight of the huge bear peering out at her was almost too realistic. The bear looked like it could jump out at any moment. She realized how huge it was when she was sitting up on it to have her picture taken when she first arrived. Her head had almost touched the ceiling of the cave. The thought of meeting a bear like this walking down the pathway terrified her.

Marjorie read her book for a bit, but soon her mind wandered off. She'd sent letters to both Bunny and Kenny shortly after she arrived at Fintry. She didn't think Kenny was much of a letter writer, but Bunny should have answered her by now. She thought of the lake and what a great place it was for swimming. It was so much better than the Koksilah River. She wondered if Bunny had made it as far as the raft yet. She could do it if she tried. She wished Bunny and Kenny were up here with her. It would be perfect then. They would love the lake.

Later that night, as Marjorie snuggled into her comfortable bed, she asked, "Lavinia, are you asleep?"

"No, not yet," a sleepy voice answered.

"I've been thinking about this place. The Fairbridge Farm School seems like a huge old institution, even though we live in cottages, but this place seems more like a home. It's the first time that I've felt at home since they took me away from my mum. We're treated as if we belong. I remember feeling this way around my mum. You know, as if I was in the right place, as if I was part of a family. I didn't have to think about not belonging. At Fairbridge, my cottage mum once told me to crawl back into the hole I came from. She makes me feel like I don't belong anywhere. I'd rather be with my own family and go hungry than have all the food that the farm grows and live like we have to. It's going to be hard leaving here, isn't it, Lavinia?"

"Yes, it sure will be. Where would you rather be — here or with your mum?" Lavinia propped herself up on her elbow and looked at Marjorie.

"No contest! With my mum, of course. I can hardly remember what she looks like, but I know I would recognize her in a second. Do you ever dream of going home?"

"Yes. Now I have to go to sleep. See you in the morning." Lavinia pulled the covers up over herself.

Marjorie lay quietly. She wanted to share something with Lavinia but she didn't want to spoil how happy she felt. She hid her shock upon seeing the duty master when they first arrived. Kenny told her about him. She didn't need to worry though, as he only liked to mess with the boys. She shuddered and instead, she tried to force a picture of her mother into her mind's eye. The more she tried, the harder it was to see her. She could get little bits. She could see her standing there in the doorway, and she could see her clothes, but when she tried to focus on her face it was just a blur. As she fell asleep, Marjorie wondered if she really would recognize her mother. That was her worst nightmare, forgetting her mother, because then her mother could be forgetting her, too.

Chapter 10

FINTRY OR FAIRBRIDGE?

More than ever the carrying on of our work has become
a matter of Imperial concern, merged in the one great
cause of Empire welfare.

— Principal of the Prince of Wales Fairbridge Farm School,
letter to Mr. Frederick Charles Blair, assistant deputy
minister, Department of Immigration and Colonization,
Ottawa, Ontario, August 23, 1940

Everyone assembled in the manor house living room for evening prayer.
They'd had a lot to be thankful for these past few weeks. It was the
best summer the children could remember. The cherry crop was in and
had yielded over nine tons again this year. Mrs. Howard, Marjorie, and
Lavinia had a marvellous time in the kitchen preparing cherry pies and
tarts, making cherry jam, and canning cherries. But best of all, they got
to eat as many as they liked.

The irrigation system had all its bugs worked out. There were other
bugs (and other animals) that needed attention also. The children had to be
taught to avoid black widow spiders, as they seemed to like the orchard, and
it was important to avoid the rattlesnakes. Many of the boys had encoun-
tered black widow spiders, but only one had heard the unmistakable rattle
of a snake nearby. Despite the presence of these potentially dangerous
animals, the boys felt safe up the ladders as they thinned the apple trees.

There was little to do now but watch the apples grow. The early Macs were almost ready to pick, and that meant they were ready to eat as well. But the very best for eating fresh from the trees were the peaches. Marjorie had never tasted anything like it before. The hot Okanagan sun seemed to lock in the sweetness and the juice. The apricots and the plums were good, too, but nothing compared to the peaches. She loved biting into them, fresh and warm from the tree, and feeling the sticky juice drip down her chin.

Marjorie was thankful for how happy she was at Fintry. She loved the warm, beautiful weather; it was so amazingly hot and dry. She loved swimming in the lake and going for walks. Most of all she loved how relaxed she felt being away from the farm school. This contentment was a new feeling. Well, no, not entirely. It was new for her since she was taken from her family, but not totally new, as this unworried feeling about waking up in the morning was something she'd missed and didn't know it until it returned. When she was with her family, she was always excited about getting up in the morning. In her family, she was an important part of a team, and they all worked together. She felt loved. She didn't know then about worry. She had to be on guard all the time at the farm school, though, and it made her miss her family and that safe feeling all the more. At the farm school she never knew what was coming next or when she would get yelled at or for what, as it was always changing, keeping her constantly on edge. Mrs. Howard appreciated everything the girls did, so it made both her and Lavinia want to complete their chores to the very best of their ability. She did not miss the tension she had learned to live with while at the farm school; still, she was wary about letting her guard down entirely.

The day had been absolutely wonderful. They'd hiked up to the high farm again. They went up by the roadway and came back down by the pathway along the Fintry Falls. On their way up, just across the road, they saw three deer: a mother and two fawns standing in the shade of the pine forest. It was as if they were letting the children have a good look before they turned and dashed off, disappearing right before their eyes. Mr. Thomas said it was called camouflage.

"Nature designed the colour of their coats to protect them from predators," he told them.

"What's a predator? Something that eats the deer? What eats deer?"

"Yes, that's right. Oh, I guess the mountain lions and wolves — and men, of course!"

"Are there any mountain lions and wolves up here now?"

"Probably not; they'll be high up in the hills. They don't like to come around people too much," Mr. Thomas assured them.

"Can we have a campfire for our lunch?" Marjorie wanted to change the subject. She didn't like the idea of the wild animals roaming close to them. She tried not to think about that huge bear in the manor-house cave. No one told her that Kodiak bears didn't live in this area.

"Yes, we can have a campfire. We'll have to put all our boys' scout skills to the test, though. It's extremely dry up here this time of year. We have to be very careful not to start a forest fire. We can make a smallish fire in the firepit. The pit is lined with rocks, so it should be safe, but we'll have to carry buckets of water from Shorts Creek afterward to make sure the fire is completely out."

Later, the children sat around the fire, eating their hot dogs, while Mr. Thomas told some of his fantastic naval battle stories. The children never tired of listening to him.[1]

"Can I have another sausage? We call them sausages, but you call them hot dogs, right?" said a boy. The hike had done wonders for everyone's appetites.

"That's right. The ones we call sausages are the links that we fry up for breakfast," said Mrs. Howard.

"Look!" one of the boys pointed to the top of a nearby tree. "Look at the size of that bird. Is that a bald eagle? Oh, look, there are two of them."

"Yes, it looks like they have a nest up there."

"Why do they call them bald? Don't they have feathers on their head?"

"Well, yes, they have feathers on their head. They have white feathers. At one time, a long time ago, the word *bald* meant *white*, not *hairless*. When they were naming the eagles, the Latin name meant *white head* and because *bald* meant *white* back then, they became known as the *bald eagle*. I know a poem about eagles by Lord Tennyson. Do you want to hear it?"

"Yes!"

"Sure."

"Poetry is dumb," whispered one of the older boys.

"I'd like to hear it." Mrs. Howard frowned at the dissenter.

"Well, okay, it goes like this." Mr. Thomas stood up.

The Eagle
He clasps the crag with crooked hands;
Close to the sun in lonely lands,
Ring'd with the azure world, he stands.

The wrinkled sea beneath him crawls;
He watches from his mountain walls,
And like a thunderbolt he falls.

"Well, I didn't know you could recite poetry!" Mrs. Howard teased him.

"Oh, I am full of surprises."

Marjorie looked back at the eagle. She understood being in a lonely land. Her family was out of reach. She knew what it was like to hold on tight so you won't fall. But unlike her, this bird was free.

The children cleaned up their lunch things. Two of the boys ran to the creek to get water to douse the fire. When they were satisfied that the fire was completely out, they started back down the hillside toward the road. Mr. Thomas was in the lead. He stopped and made sure he had everyone's attention.

"Okay, children, listen up will you? As we head down this trail, we will have to cross over a couple of creeks that have wooden planks for bridges. I want you to go one at a time. Last year three of the children were crossing over at the same time, the plank broke, and they went crashing into the creek.[2] Luckily, no one was hurt, but they all got soaked. So it is to be one at a time, okay?"

"Okay, sir!"

"Good enough. On we go then." He turned and headed down the trail.

Marjorie caught up to him. "What is that tiny house over there?" She pointed off through the trees.

"That's Scotty, the old trapper's, cabin. He's an old hermit who has lived up here for ages. Have you met him? It's quite the experience. He's a very nice man but extremely eccentric. His cabin is as old as he is, I suspect," Mr. Thomas answered.

"Are you joking with me? How could he live there? It's too small." Marjorie found it hard to believe that anyone could live in such a little house.

Just then, the door opened and the old trapper climbed out. "Well, howdy. I thought I heard you all up here. It's a grand day to be out exploring. I have just been smoking some jerky. Would you like to try some?" He reached into his cabin and grabbed a board with strips of dried meat lying on it. The children eagerly surrounded him and helped themselves. They munched and chewed on the tasty salty meat.

One of the boys asked, "Can I have another piece? That was delicious."

"Yes, go ahead. I have lots. I got myself a deer last week. I got it mostly dried now." He held out the wooden board so the boy could grab a piece.

"Is this deer meat?" someone asked.

"Yes. We call it venison. It's the very best, don't you agree, boys?"

"Yes, sir, it's delicious."

Marjorie turned and walked away. She was eating deer meat! She had been enjoying it up until that point, but now it just stuck in her throat. She gagged and spat it out. She tossed her piece into the bushes. She looked back to see if the old man had noticed, but he was busy talking to the boys. She wondered how anyone could eat the little deer.

After their visit, they carried on down the path. Mr. Thomas turned around and said, "I think I hear something. If we walk quietly we might see more deer or some mountain sheep." They walked on, their eyes scanning to the right and left, looking for any signs of wildlife. They could hear an occasional crashing sound through the underbrush. Marjorie hoped it was deer and not a bear or a wolf. When they were almost down to the bottom field of the high farm and close to the road, Mr. Thomas put his hand up for them to stop.

"Shh. Stop for a minute," he whispered. "Look, over there — five or six mountain sheep."

"Oh, they hear us. There they go." Mrs. Howard watched as the sheep bolted off into the woods.

As they got below the road, they could hear the waterfall. "It's not as noisy as it was when we hiked up here last month," one of the boys observed.

"Well, we did have a long dry spell over the past few weeks. The creek slows down a lot during the summer. It's most spectacular when the spring run-off happens." Mr. Thomas motioned the group to follow. "Walk carefully down this part of the path. We don't want anyone to slip over the edge."

They stood for a while and watched the waterfall. It was a long drop to the pool below.

When they got down to the bottom of the cliff, the children dashed out of the pathway.

"I wish I had their energy!" Mrs. Howard said to no one in particular.

"Yes, they are hard to wear out."

As they walked past the octagonal barn, the ranch manager waved to them.

"Mr. Graham, hello. We've been on an adventure," the children shouted out in greeting.

"So, you've been up at the high farm, have you?"

"Yes, and we saw sheep and deer and an eagle's nest, too. And we visited the old trapper, and he gave us some venison jerky."

"Well, you've had quite the day then!" Mr. Graham smiled at the boys.

"Is it time for milking, Mr. Graham?"

"Not quite. I think you have time for a swim first. You all look like you could use one."

Turning to Mr. Thomas, Mr. Graham commented, "You've got a great bunch of kids this year. Mr. Dun-Waters would be happy to know that his wishes have been upheld."

"Run along, boys, and get your swimsuits on." Mr. Thomas did not have to say it twice. With a series of loud "yippees," they were off.

Mrs. Howard walked along with the two girls on either side of her. "Well, girls, I hope we stoked the fires enough so our beans will be baked to perfection."

"We really banked the coals, so it should still be going."

"After your swim, I'll want you to pick some salad greens, and just before dinner I'll need you both to run up and get some milk from the barn. There should be some fresh milk by then. Take a jug each. I'll get the cornbread started. That should make a good meal for us tonight. The cookies that you girls baked yesterday will be perfect for dessert. How does that sound?" Mrs. Howard put her arms around the shoulders of her two helpers. As Marjorie walked along, happiness and contentment filled her.

As they rounded the corner, Mrs. Howard noticed the line full of khaki shirts, all pinned up by their tails. She turned to the girls. "We'll have to get our morning laundry in as well. My, my, look at all the little rips and tears. How do they do it? I guess boys will be boys. We'll have to do some mending and patching, and I have a basket full of socks that need darning as well. That will be a good chore for tomorrow morning."

Marjorie couldn't help but compare Mrs. Howard to her cottage mums back at Fairbridge. Shortly after she'd arrived at the farm school, she tore her dress when she caught it on a piece of wire sticking out from the fence. Her mum had had a fit and slapped her, leaving her ear stinging for ages. She'd tried to tell the mum that it was an accident, but she didn't listen. She'd slapped her again for talking back. It never did any good when she was in one of her moods. Marjorie was careful after that, and when she did have a rip in her clothes, she learned to hide it. You had to get good at hiding things if you wanted to stay out of trouble.

Here she could relax. She started to feel different. A little ray of hope had wormed its way in and changed her, leaving behind a stirring in her where she could dream of a future where she just might belong. Perhaps a future where she wouldn't be so jumpy and afraid would not be too much to ask for. How could anyone relax around people who constantly yelled and struck out when you least expected it? The farm school didn't feel safe most of the time.

It was going to be September soon. Her birthday was less than a month away now. Mrs. Howard had shown the girls how to make special ice cakes for the other children's birthdays. She knew they would make some for her birthday as well. She was excited about turning fourteen, but that also meant that it would be getting close to when they had to go back to the Fairbridge Farm School. Mrs. Howard said they would probably go back in early October, depending on when the apple crop was in. Marjorie was not looking forward to it. It would be difficult going back to the way her cottage mum treated her after feeling so good about herself all summer. Now she knew that not all the mums at Fairbridge were like the mums she had to contend with, because Mrs. Howard was a cottage mum and she was nice. Maybe she could stay with Mrs. Howard when they returned. That would be grand!

The three of them walked up to the veranda just as the last of the boys were running down for their swim. Pat ran past them last, his arm still in a cast. He was not going to miss his swim, so he was very careful to stay on the edge and not get his cast wet. Mrs. Howard looked at the boys' sleeping area. She could see nineteen neatly made little black iron cots. The tops of their grey blankets lay smoothed out and neatly tucked in. In a few of the cots, she could see a small portion of their striped flannelette pajamas peeking out from under their covers. These boys were very tidy, much tidier than her cottage boys back at the Fairbridge Farm School. Maybe it was because their sleeping quarters here were so exposed. Yet, she found herself thinking that it was probably because they were happy here. Everything went smoother when the children were happy. There was definitely a different feeling among the children. Maybe it was just being in a smaller group, and summertime was always easier as well. She knew it wasn't possible, but it would be nice to spend a quiet winter up here with this group of children instead of going back to the farm school.

As Marjorie and Lavinia ran through the house to get their swimsuits, they could smell the delicious aroma of baked beans. "Mrs. Howard, the beans smell great. The stove stayed hot," Marjorie yelled.

Mrs. Howard was still on the porch. "I'll be right in, girls." Mr. Thomas walked up to the porch.

"Well, it was quite a good day, wasn't it?" Mrs. Howard said as he sat beside her.

"Yes, it was. I think I'll just sit here for a bit and enjoy the sun."

"That sounds like an excellent idea. I think I'll get the latest *Fairbridge Gazette* and read it. I haven't had a chance yet." Mrs. Howard disappeared into the house and returned a moment later with two tall glasses of iced tea and the August issue of the *Fairbridge Gazette*.

"Thanks for the iced tea. Anything interesting in this issue?" Mr. Thomas sipped his tea.

"Well, yes. The editorial by Frank Todd is quite good. He's talking about the new arrivals to the school, including the group of Fairbridge children who stopped over on their way to the Molong Fairbridge School in New South Wales, Australia. The Molong group has headed out now. Oh, maybe this war will be over soon after all. The waters must be under British control if they're allowing the transportation of children.

"Listen to this: 'These events show very clearly the confidence of the British Authorities in the safe passage of our merchant marine and passenger ships through the waters which are, according to German sources, absolutely controlled by them. As usual, this German propaganda is proved false. This time it is by the action of the directors of the Fairbridge Society and the British officials, allowing children to travel the sea in time of war. This would never have been done if there had been the slightest doubt as to their safety.' Isn't that wonderful?

"Oh, this is cute; he mentions one of the little girls arriving in the last party. She apparently told the reporters to watch what they say. 'Don't talk,' she said. 'Someone might overhear.'

"Oh, listen to what else he says: 'It is by such willing obedience to authority that Great Britain has been able to achieve the results she has in the short period she has been in the war. With the help of such spirit, we in the Dominions and at home will win the war.'[3]

"That makes me feel good. I feel so confident that we will win the war. We must! Oh, look, the next article says that work on the hospital has finally begun. The society wouldn't start that if they weren't confident about having the funds to finish it. I just have a feeling that things will get back to normal soon. This war can't last."

"That is excellent news. I'll read it later. The girls are heading up. I suppose we should get a few chores done before dinner. I'll give the boys a shout. I swear they would live in the lake if we let them. Morning, noon, and night they are down there. It is so healthy for them." Mr. Thomas stood up and gave a sharp whistle. It wasn't long before the boys headed up the path.

The girls ran up from the beach, refreshed after their swim. They changed and set out for the kitchen garden with a basket to pick greens for a salad. It had been a grand day. The Okanagan sun shone down on them. Marjorie could feel its warmth on her back. They could hear bees droning as they worked to gather pollen in the masses of flowers growing around the manor house. The ever-present hummingbirds were darting here and there, busy collecting nectar from the fragrant honeysuckle vine that covered a good portion of the veranda. They could hear the boys as they ran up the pathway, laughing and singing as they headed up for their late-afternoon chores. Marjorie felt happy, happier than she'd felt in a very long time. She wanted to savour this moment. She wanted to hold on to this feeling forever.

Apple picking at the Fintry Fairbridge Training Farm, Okanagan Valley, British Columbia. In the late 1930s and early 1940s, the Fintry Farm averaged between twenty-two thousand and twenty-five thousand forty-pound boxes of apples every year.

Chapter 11

FOR NOW AND EVERMORE

"Rule, Britannia! rule the waves;
Britons never will be slaves."[1]

— "Rule Britannia," James Thomson

Marjorie tossed in her cot that night. Her world stood still. She tried to understand why the news had affected her so. They were all strangers to her. Perhaps it was because of the secure feeling that had surrounded her throughout the summer. She was sure that nothing bad could happen here. Nothing bad could even reach them here. They were far away from the Fairbridge Farm School, and they were really, really far away from the war. Marjorie remembered that England did not even show up on the big map of Canada hanging in their classroom at Fairbridge. She thought that England must be quite far away from Canada. She remembered that it took many days to get to Canada, almost a fortnight — several days on the ocean and several days on the train to go across the huge country. The war seemed unreal to her simply because it was so far away. How could it touch them here? It was happening in another world. Fintry was like a little Eden, and she felt she had finally gained control over the bad things that had plagued her ever since they had taken her from her mother.

Whenever she heard of the war and the bombing, she prayed that Joyce was safe and her other family, too. She hoped Joyce was being brave. It would be awful to be afraid *and* alone. But these children would have been afraid and alone. Oh, it was too awful to think about. What would it be like? What would she have done? How would she feel if it happened to her? What if it had happened to Bunny's boat? What if Joyce was on that boat? Oh, God, how was she going to find out? She tried to force herself to think about something else. She was making herself sick with worry.

Mr. Thomas and Mrs. Howard had been upset all day. Marjorie could tell that Mrs. Howard had been crying. She could just tell, even though she did not cry in front of the girls. Marjorie and Lavinia went about their chores as quietly as they could. When they went down for their afternoon swim, Marjorie asked Lavinia, "Something is wrong. I can feel it; can you?"

"Yes. I don't have a clue what it is, though. I brought the mail in this morning and there was a telegram from Fairbridge. I just handed it over

Lavinia Anderson and Marjorie Arnison at Fintry Fairbridge, 1940. Marjorie is on the right.

without reading it. It was shortly after that when Mr. Thomas and Mrs. Howard went into the office, and she came out with her face all blotchy as if she had been crying. She hasn't been herself all day." Lavinia gave a shrug. "I don't know what it could be."

"I hope everything is okay at Fairbridge. I hope Bunny and Kenny are okay. Maybe something has happened to them and they don't want to tell me? I wrote to them a few times and they haven't written back, not once." Marjorie was suddenly sure something had happened to Bunny or Kenny.

"No, it can't be that. They would have told you." Lavinia walked into the lake up to her knees. "C'mon, it's lovely."

Mr. Thomas and Mrs. Howard paced in the office. "We have to tell the children something. We should be careful how much we tell them, though." Mr. Thomas looked tense.

"Yes, I think we should be very careful. Oh, God, what a wretched business. Torpedoing children makes no sense whatsoever! What kind of a person does that? I cannot seem to shake the nightmare of it all. What was it like for those poor little children?" Mrs. Howard took out her hanky and wiped her eyes.

"Yes, it's dreadful, isn't it? When I telephoned the farm school, I managed to get a few more details. Not many, as these things are kept hushed up. Apparently the British government finally agreed to organize the transportation of some of the children of the poor. There was quite the clamour from the poor over the fact that wealthy parents are able to ship their children to safe houses in the United States and Canada. The working-class blokes got all up in arms, protesting that it was typical of the government to watch the children of the rich being sent to safe homes and do nothing for the poor. I supposed that Churchill was concerned that if their enemies saw the country evacuating their children they might see that as a sign of fear or weakness. War is just a nasty business, and it is no place for children. How must those parents feel now? I just can't imagine it." Mr. Thomas took his hanky and blew his nose.[2]

"They must be wretched, simply wretched. Who were the children travelling with? I hope it wasn't the Fairbridge Society. How many children were there in all, do you know?" Mrs. Howard picked up the telegram and looked at it again, hoping to find answers that she knew were not there.

"No, I believe that they were coming over with the Children's Overseas Reception Board. There were, I think, about ninety children on the boat. It seems that most of them were lost. Apparently six of the ten escorts travelling with them were lost, too. The ship went down very fast. They said the *City of Benares* sank in thirty-one minutes. Thirty-one minutes! They had no time to prepare." Mr. Thomas paced back and forth.

"Why did they allow it to cross if it was so dangerous? Why didn't they have some kind of flag flying saying they were carrying children?" Mrs. Howard needed to have the details. Too little information left her feeling frustrated.

"I don't have much information, except it was hit on September 17, in the evening."

Mrs. Howard cried, "Oh, those poor little children. Those poor parents. Did they know the dangers? Such a gamble. Who can ever know what is the best thing? To sit still or run?"

"How could they? They wouldn't have sent them if they did. The tragedy for the parents of these lost souls is that they let their children go after being told that if the ship carrying their children was unable to be convoyed the whole way across, then the sailing would be cancelled. But they lied to them, because the convoy turned back earlier that day."

Mr. Thomas banged his fist on the desk. "It's a bloody tragedy. Oh, it is heartbreaking! Mrs. Howard, this whole thing should never have happened. Fairbridge needs more children. The society has really suffered a setback. Now, there will be no more boats crossing with children. It is just too risky. We will have to wait for the war to be over before it will be safe to transport any more children."

"I wish this war would end." Mrs. Howard shook her head slowly.

"Damn, it won't be easy telling the children. Pardon my language, Mrs. Howard, but I have never felt so frustrated."

Mrs. Howard understood. "No, it won't be easy telling them. We should tell them soon, though; Marjorie and Lavinia already know that something is wrong. I think we should tell them tonight at evening prayer. That would be the best time, I think."

"You're right. Evening prayers would be the best time."

"Yes, and we could use the prayer time to pray for the lost ones. It might give the children a positive outlet right away." Mrs. Howard took out her hanky and wiped her eyes. How could this have happened? Those poor innocent children. What a nightmare!

"Well, we'll have to take care how we tell the children. I had better get some chores done or we will never have dinner tonight." She wiped her eyes again before she left the office.

Fairbridge Tears
Lost and alone
On the storm-tossed sea
One by one
Their little souls were gone.

Far from home
With no family
One by one
The little children passed on.

"Marjorie, Marjorie, wake up! You're having a nightmare." Mrs. Howard gave Marjorie a gentle shake. Lavinia was in her cot, looking terrified. Marjorie had been thrashing around and tearing her bed apart, and when Lavinia had no luck waking her, she ran to get Mrs. Howard.

Marjorie finally wrestled free from her nightmare. She looked wild-eyed at Mrs. Howard and then over at Lavinia. She choked out a sob. "It was a dream?"

"Yes, it was a dream. Try to relax now." Mrs. Howard rubbed Marjorie's back, trying to calm her down.

"Oh, Mrs. Howard, it was awful. I tried to swim and it was all black and the waves were huge. They were swallowing me up. I tried to breathe, but I kept swallowing in huge mouthfuls of water. I tried to climb back on the boat, but it kept moving away. There were kids all around me, clawing at the water, trying to get to safety. No one could make it." Marjorie dissolved into sobs.

Mrs. Howard held her; she could feel her heart racing. "There now, Marjorie. There now, take a deep breath. You're safe now. You're going to be all right. You're thinking of those poor children on that boat, aren't you?"

"Yes. I can't get them off my mind. I keep thinking and thinking about them. Why did the Germans do that? Didn't they know all those kids were on the boat?"

"Well, I guess they didn't. I don't know. I'm sure they wouldn't have torpedoed the boat if they knew it was transporting children." Mrs. Howard somehow knew that the best thing for Marjorie would be to talk about the disaster. Keeping it all bottled up inside would do her no good. She had heard that Marjorie suffered from nightmares, and they had almost taken her off the list for Fintry Farm because of that. However, as far as Mrs. Howard knew, this was the first nightmare that Marjorie had had all summer. It was everyone's nightmare, really. She recalled the look on the children's faces when she and Mr. Thomas sat them down for evening prayers. She didn't know how to start, so she let Mr. Thomas begin.

"Children." He cleared his voice and looked at the floor. "I'm afraid I have some rather bad news to tell you. It shows how far-reaching this war is. One of the boats bringing children over to Canada — it was called the *City of Benares* — well, it was torpedoed a few days ago. It sank, and most of the children on board died."

"What children were coming out? Was anyone coming from Middlemore? What if my sister was on that boat?" The sinking horrified Marjorie, but it would be a hundred times worse if her sister or anyone else that she knew was on the boat.

"Marjorie, I'm not really sure, but I don't think there were any Middlemore children. I am quite sure that your sister was not on the boat, though." Mrs. Howard had no idea, really, where the children were from, but she had to do her best to reassure the children here.

"How many children were coming out?" asked one of the boys. They had been awfully quiet up to now.

"Well, there were about four hundred people in all, and about one hundred of them were children. That night seventy-seven children died. Some of the children survived, but only a few, and they took them back to England. I don't think any more children will be coming out until it is absolutely safe." Mr. Thomas hoped that there would not be too many questions; he was simply not up to it tonight.

"It's a great tragedy, and I think we should say a prayer for all the children and the adults who died." Mrs. Howard bowed her head; the others followed.

The children quietly readied themselves for bed. Some had been at Fairbridge for a few years now, but all remembered their boat trip over. For most, the nights were the scariest. It was so dark. Could it have happened to them when they were coming over?

Marjorie fishing off the Fintry packinghouse pier, 1940.

The horror of the sinking of the *City of Benares* spread through the Fintry Farm community. News that the parents had been promised that their children would be convoyed reached them. That promise had been broken with devastating consequences.

Marjorie watched her fishing line bobbing on the surface of the lake. Fishing off the pier gave her time to think about things. She had spent a restless night, full of nightmares. Funny how fishing relaxed her, even though she thought she should be afraid of the water. The lake was a little rough today. If she fell in, she could still swim to shore or climb up the ladder back onto the pier. What had it been like for the children? It was dark and stormy, and they were miles out to sea with someone shooting torpedoes at them. They will remain forevermore in the ocean that must have terrified them in their last minutes on earth. Why is it not safe anywhere?

Chapter 12

I Think I Can ... Make It ...

Charles Buller, member of Parliament in Britain, argued
that some periods of unorganized British emigration to
the colonies entailed "little more than shovelling out your
paupers to where they might die, without shocking their
betters with the sight or sound of their last agony."

— "Systematic Colonization." Speech in the
House of Commons, April 6, 1843

"Marjorie, will you help me? I want to try to win the prize for best
costume." Bunny walked into the playroom carrying an assort-
ment of ribbons and cloth ends left over from the sewing classes. She
dumped them at Marjorie's feet and sat down.

"Well, let me see what you've got." Marjorie reached out for the bigger
bits.

"Are you going to get dressed up?" Bunny asked her sister.

"Nah, I'm getting too old. I'll just help you." Marjorie held up some
pieces. "What did you hope to do with these?"

"I don't know. Can you help me think of something?" The two sisters
worked for a bit, snipping this piece and stitching that piece.

Marjorie pulled out a couple of apples from her locker and passed
one to her sister. The stolen fruit tasted sweet. She and a couple of the
older girls in her cottage made a habit of sneaking down to the apple

A "staged" photograph for publicity purposes. Arnison children at the Prince of Wales Fairbridge Farm School, early 1940s. Left–right: Audrey (Bunny), Marjorie, and Kenny.

orchard below the chapel to pick as many apples as they could hide under their clothing and even in their knickers. They would sneak them into their lockers in the basement of their cottage to eat when their cottage mother wasn't looking. They would devour the core and all to not leave any evidence.

"It's getting close to bedtime. We'll have to work on it tomorrow." Bunny's face fell and she was about to protest, so Marjorie reminded her, "Bunny, it's only Tuesday. Halloween isn't until Friday. We have plenty of time. Maybe I can find a few more odds and ends in the sewing basket tomorrow."

"Well, okay. Remember last Halloween, Marjorie, when we had a huge bonfire, and we roasted those hot dog things and we bobbed for apples and went trick-or-treating to the principal's house? 'Member? Do you think we'll get to do that again this year?" Bunny snuggled next to her sister. "I love Halloween; don't you?"

"I guess so. Go brush your teeth, okay?" Marjorie did remember last Halloween, but for different reasons. They had been back from Fintry for just a couple of weeks. She still remembered how sad she was to leave the lake. It was one of the magical times in her young life. Now she just wondered if she had imagined most of it.

Deep down, she knew that she would find herself back in the same cottage with the same old cranky cottage mum, but she'd hoped and hoped that she would get placed with Mrs. Howard. She wished so hard for it that she had convinced herself that it might come true.

As soon as she was back, she asked Bunny why she hadn't written to her. Bunny was shocked and said that she'd written at least two letters. "I told you that I missed you so much and that I hated being at Fairbridge alone. I asked you about what duty masters the girls should avoid because we had some new girls at the farm school. I was sad when you didn't write back to me. I told Kenny to tell the new boys who to watch out for." Bunny's frustration was all over her face.

"I didn't get any letters from you the whole time I was at Fintry." Marjorie was furious. There was no way to communicate with her sister. *What will it be like,* she wondered, *when I'm sent to Victoria and Bunny is here on her own for four years?* "The old battleaxe probably never sent the letters. What a mean old bag. We should try to figure out a code that we could write in. It will be harder to keep in touch when I'm out at work."

It was difficult to understand why innocent children like the ones on the *City of Benares* had to die last year. Why didn't God take her miserable old cottage mum and leave those children? Wretched old thing, she hardly ever smiled. She was just cruel, and there was nothing Marjorie could do to change that.

Well, she was counting the months now. She would be sixteen in less than a year. She would be out of here then. In the meantime, though, there was a lot to keep her busy.

These past few months she had done very little classroom work; instead, she did a lot of housework and a lot of work on laundry and sewing with their teacher, Tashy. And they had spent a lot of time on cooking and canning. They had been canning plums and making pickles and jams and jellies. The pantry shelves were full. Marjorie had counted 225 jars.[1] They also did what they called household management. At the matron's house, they had learned to handle the fragile china, to polish silver, to dust and polish the woodwork, to care for the carpets and upholstery, and a hundred other little tasks, all to prepare them for when they were sent out to work. They were reminded all the time of the importance of taking care of other people's things and of not ever expecting to have any of them for their own. That was on top of their regular chores.

Marjorie also worked in the hospital. The new hospital had been open for about seven months now. It was a lovely new building designed for looking after patients. It worked so much better than the cottage. Marjorie was one of the first patients, admitted last April when she developed a large carbuncle on her neck. During the Earl of Athlone and Princess Alice's visit to the farm school to open the new hospital, they had visited Marjorie in her hospital bed. A Victoria newspaper had printed a photograph of her with Princess Alice.[2]

Now Marjorie was on morning dining-hall duty. The dining hall got a lot of use with all the kids running in twice a day for breakfast and lunch. It had been rainy lately, and even though there was a big rug at the door, the children tracked mud and dirt right across the room. Marjorie and the girls on dining-hall duty grabbed the big brooms and swept first, then mopped the floor, and finally took the huge heavy bumpers stuck onto long sticks and ran them back and forth until the shine on the linoleum passed inspection.

One morning last week, Marjorie and her companion sat talking during their midmorning break. They knew they would have to hurry to get the floor finished before the noon meal, but they were determined to get their whole break. It seemed hard for the adults to let them rest. "Idle hands, girls, lead to all sorts of trouble. Look busy now," the cottage mothers would say. It seemed that they had to pretend to be busy even when it was break time.

"C'mon, girls. Break's over. I need some help in the kitchen before you go back to your floor." The two girls got up. They were sure they had not been sitting down for more than five minutes.

"Not much of a break," Marjorie whispered.

"Slave drivers!" her friend whispered back.

Next week she would be on chapel duty in the morning. The last time she worked there it seemed to take forever to get everything dusted and polished. The best part of that job was they usually worked in pairs without any adults supervising. The cottage mother came over afterward to inspect their work. Sometimes they would take a break and stand up at the pulpit and pretend to be preaching to their cottage mums. The girls would preach that the mean cottage mums would go to hell unless they started being nice to the kids. Then they would look at each other and chuckle. They were surprised at their own daring, but they were feeling brave because they were sure that they both felt the same way, and besides there was no one around to hear them. They egged each other on.

"God is all-seeing. You cannot hide from him. He will not tolerate mean cottage mothers. You must learn to be nice. He will put you in a pit full of snakes if you continue to be despicable!" The girl held up her arm and pointed at the imaginary cottage mothers sitting in the front pews. Her voice boomed throughout the room. The girls looked at each other and howled with delight.

"That was a good sermon! My turn." Marjorie jumped up to the pulpit. "Okay, listen up all you adults. We've had enough of your wickedness. We will not put up with any more of your evil ways. You are all heading to hell in a handbasket. But you belong there because you are all devils and witches. God will be watching closely to make sure you treat all the children nicely from now on. You will be lined up on Saturday mornings, and we will make you bend over without knickers on, and we will whip you with your own straps and willow switches, so then you will know how it hurts to be hit like that. We will box your ears like you box ours and see how you like the ringing and the bruises. You hit us for no reason, but we have plenty of reasons to hit you. You are mean old witches. You must give all the children more hugs and more allowance and let them have more movie nights, and you must start cleaning your own rooms, and it is your turn to get up early and start the fires so the girls will be warm when they get up, and you must serve the girls their breakfast of bacon and eggs in bed for the next year, and as punishment for your nasty ways you will get lumpy porridge without sugar for breakfast and lunch. And no more screaming at us 'cause we have had enough. Amen."

The two girls looked at each other and shrieked with laughter.

"That will teach the old battleaxes! Shh! What was that?"

They looked toward the entrance and saw someone standing in the shadows. They were having conniption fits until they realized that it was just one of the boys. He poked his head inside and said, "That was good. You should ask if you could give the sermon this Sunday!" His laughter echoed in the empty building.

"What are you doing here?" they yelled at him, but he didn't answer. They heard the door slam shut as he left.

"Well, he won't tell for sure. He hates them as much as we do."

My Memory of Things Gone By

A long time ago in the British Isles, War raged on over
    thousands of miles.

Thousands of children were displaced, separated forever
    in total disgrace.

Their dates of Birth and names were changed, put in
    homes to be rearranged.

Little did they know what horror waited, your turn would
    come and you were gated.

Brothers and Sisters, how would I know, could be in the
    bomb shelter with me below.

Tin dishes and rations on a plate could not match the
    sadness or their fate.

Little faces cold as stone, never knew we would not go
    home.

Discipline was cruel and so unjust, some kids would cry
    till their heart would bust.

A few of us survived this cruel ordeal, there was no love
    and some would steal.

On a great Troop Ship I sailed the North Atlantic, it was
    rough and some were frantic.

It did not bother my little soul; my tiny heart was full
   of holes.
Being shipped alone to a foreign land, I learned survival
   and took a stand.
I did not know the feel or meaning of love, and put my
   faith in the man above.
By the age of ten I became a man, hard outside, but soft
   as a lamb.
I still have trouble with the word called love; the man
   never replied that lives above.
Over sixty years have now gone by, and those awful
   people can't apologize.
I'm not as lonely as I was, I don't look for my mummy
   up in the stars.
The big thought missing in my life is how your own
   people create such strife.
One day these people will be judged as well, and God will
   send them straight to hell.

— Tom Isherwood, former Fairbridge boy

"Did you hear what he did?" Marjorie asked her friend.

"What did he do now?"

"Well, Kenny told me their cottage mum wanted to know where the boys had their forts hidden in the woods, so she demanded that he take her and two other cottage mothers as well. Well, you know, you cannot just say no to a cottage mother, so he had no choice but to agree. Kenny said the big boys were really angry at being betrayed by one of their own, but in the end they didn't have to worry because he really got them good." Marjorie wished she could have seen the cottage mums' faces.

"Spit it out! What did he do?"

"He took them deep into the woods well away from their forts and up and around twisty trails and over logs until they were completely lost, and then he ran like the wind and left them up in the woods. He didn't show them anything. Kenny said that they could hear the cottage mums yelling and screaming for ages before they found their way back." Marjorie giggled at the thought of one of them finally getting back at the mums.

"Did he get it?"

"You bet he did. Kenny said he really got the strap, and then they gated him and he had punishment duties for days. But he told the other boys that it was worth it."

Marjorie loved it when she and Kenny managed to talk. She was able to find out some of what was happening on that side of Fairbridge, and she loved hearing his stories. He didn't say too much about how he was doing, though. He clammed up whenever she asked him. He seemed sad or broken all the time. He told her that his mean old cottage mother informed all the boys in his cottage that they needed whipping because that was the only way to get the bad out of them.

"I'm not bad, Marjorie. I'm not. But when I told her I'm not bad she whooped me, and she said I was bad all the way through and I was lucky to be here as if I stayed in England I would be in jail. Then she made me thank her. Why are we here? What did we do? Sometimes I hate our mum for sending us here. I am not bad."

Marjorie assured him he was not bad, but the cottage mothers were definitely bad. She whispered to him that they were all mean old bitches. Kenny gave a little laugh. She hated that they separated boys and girls. She could not help her brother. It was frustrating. She tried to understand why the boys and girls could not walk on the same pathways. It just didn't make sense to her. Sometimes the new kids would make a mistake, but they learned quickly.

Marjorie knew the Fairbridge routine. More kids arrived, and they sent away the older ones to work, making room for the newcomers. At least that was the plan. The war had stopped England from shipping very many kids to Fairbridge. It was probably still too dangerous, but seven boys had arrived last month, and they were supposed to get another larger group next month. Maybe the war was going to be over soon, and it was getting safe again to bring kids over.

Marjorie was glad that she did not have to travel on the ocean. She still had nightmares about all the children drowning. They would not get her on one of those boats. That was another reason why she tried to be good. She didn't want them to send her back now. What if the Germans torpedoed her ship!

Marjorie and a few of the other fifteen-year-old girls in training worked long, hard hours for their final year at the farm school and were paid a quarter a week. Marjorie made sure the younger girls knew what was coming and often told them about how they were going to really enjoy being slaves to the Fairbridge matron and to the farm school when they turned fifteen.

Training was what Fairbridge called it when they were getting ready to send the girls out into service. They had to do a lot of serving in the dining hall. They served mainly the staff, but they also had to put on their uniforms and serve visiting guests. They were supposed to be pleased about this and were constantly reminded to smile and look happy. However, the only time Marjorie looked happy and could smile a big smile was when she saw one of the kids spit on a cottage mother's plate before placing it on the table.

The trainee girls also took turns being in charge of the matron's house. They had to polish silver, dust, wax floors, clean rugs, and do all her housework. She was not satisfied until her house was sparkling. Marjorie hated it when they had to do something over and over again. The matron would tell them, "You might as well do it right the first time, girls, because it's not done until it's done right!" Then she'd smile that full-of-herself smile, and the girls would have to do it over again. It was impossible to know when it would be good enough. The matron had a magical formula that only she knew. They could polish and polish until they could see their reflections, and she would come along and give one last wipe. She had to show the girls that she could do it better.

Marjorie thought the worst part was when they had to serve her breakfast in bed. She hated going into the matron's dark room. It was creepy, and it smelled funny. Once she almost dropped the breakfast tray because she was in such a hurry to get out. It never helped to show your fears because the cottage mum never understood. She didn't know that you were being clumsy because you were in such a hurry to get out of her room; she thought you just needed more practice.

"Stupid girl!" the matron said to Marjorie. "Why can't you try harder? What placement will we find for you if you cannot do better? What are you going to do if no one wants you? It will never do if you expect to find yourself in the gutters here. Oh, no, British Columbia will not put up with that. You have to earn your keep or they will ship you back. With this war on, who knows what will happen to you or if you'll even make it back."

Marjorie shuddered at the thought of drowning out in the middle of the ocean. She didn't mean to be clumsy, she wanted to explain, but how could she tell the matron that she just didn't like coming into her smelly sleeping chamber?

"I will try harder, mum," she promised the matron on many occasions. She had no other choice but to try harder. Nevertheless, fear was a powerful thing, and no matter how hard she tried, she came down with a case of the nerves as she carried the breakfast tray into the matron's room. The teacup and the teapot always seemed to jangle together, increasing her anxiety.

Her anxiety also had another side to it. Throughout her entire time at Fairbridge, Marjorie was complicit in making the cottage mum's tea with the water that was used to boil her eggs. The thought that this might poison the mum excited Marjorie, but it also frightened her. She couldn't stop; it rattled her composure something awful. Marjorie waited nervously every Sunday afternoon to hear the good news: *The matron is dead. The wicked witch is gone!* Just like the old witch in the *Wizard of Oz*. She loved that film. A group of girls and their cottage mother had walked all the way into Duncan to see it when it came out. Seeing the bad witch get what she deserved gave Marjorie hope.[3]

The matron kept telling the girls that they would be going out to service in Victoria soon, and it was very important to give Fairbridge a good name. "Otherwise, the girls coming along after you won't be wanted. You older girls are the ambassadors for Fairbridge. You need to set a good example. You don't want people to think that we don't train you properly, do you?" Then she would smile that smile.

"No, ma'am" was all that Marjorie would say. But inside she was screaming! She hated serving these people. Couldn't they tell that many of the kids hated them almost as much as they seemed to hate the kids?

At least that's what it felt like most of the time. Some were good to the kids, though, why couldn't they all be?

Marjorie wanted to ruin it for the other girls. She wanted everyone in Victoria to know what a rotten deal they were all getting up at Fairbridge. She didn't know one girl who was happy about having to be someone's serving girl. The girls coming after her would probably be happy if she helped to ruin Fairbridge's name. Then maybe they could choose to do something they wanted to do with their lives.

The thought scared her. What if they kicked her out of Fairbridge? What if no one wanted her in Victoria? Where would she go? Marjorie held on to her hatred of Fairbridge and kept it close to her chest. She was afraid of what they might do to her if she disobeyed. She was afraid of what revenge an unhappy Fairbridge, an unhappy king, and an unhappy England might direct toward her. They might throw her back into the sewers where she came from. And that must have been where she came from, as they told her that over and over again. She didn't remember living in the sewers. All she really remembered was the beautiful sandy beach at Whitley Bay. She didn't remember very much about her life in England anymore. When she yelled back that she would find her mother, she was laughed at and told, "You won't be able to find your mother. We will make sure of that. The sewer we put you back in will not be anywhere near your mother. And besides, your mother doesn't want you. Why do you think she sent you away?" All alone and in the sewers, now that was a nightmare that Marjorie must avoid at all costs. Even though she yelled that her mother did want her and her mother loved her, she worried that was nothing more than a childish dream. She had to hang on to the belief that someone wanted her and loved her. If she didn't have that, she would have nothing.

Last Christmas she'd received a letter from Joyce and her mother. Not two letters, but both writing on the same one. Joyce had been sent home from Middlemore. She was sixteen, and the home didn't keep the children past that time, her mother explained. The pain was so great that Marjorie just had to block it out. She didn't write back. She no longer wrote letters in her head to Joyce, sharing the thoughts and feelings that she dare not write down. It was childish, anyway. She would never write to her mother again. She hated her. She felt so betrayed. She felt so alone. It was as if a big door had slammed shut in front of her. She had always held on to the belief that things would eventually work out and she would find her way home. Now, for the first time, she felt sure that she never would.

Marjorie hated writing letters. All their letters had to pass inspection. It wasn't easy to write how she was feeling. She quickly learned to keep those feelings to herself. She had no way of letting her mum know that she wanted to come home. Maybe when she turned sixteen next year they would send her back to her mum just like they had with Joyce. Then she got mad at herself for having such stupid hopes. It only made the disappointments harder to live with.

And now she wouldn't write to Joyce anymore. Joyce didn't need her. Joyce was back at home, and she had their mother. And she had Phyllis, Jean, and Lawrence. Her mother told her that both her older brothers, Fred and Norman, were fighting in the war. Marjorie choked back a huge sob. And they had a new little brother, Richard. He was almost two and a half years old now. How could her mother have done that? She'd sent Marjorie away and then had another baby!

It all started going wrong last year, right around her birthday. There was the sinking of the *City of Benares*, and then having to come back to the farm, and having to get the same mean old cottage mum, even after all her hoping. It was harder, she thought, because she had become used to the nice treatment over her summer at Fintry.

She'd fought her cottage mum fiercely when she first got back, but she simply got the worst of it. Marjorie tried to keep out of the old battleaxe's way, but living under the same roof made that impossible. Slowly she stopped fighting her and tried her best not to rile her mum. What was the point? She might as well give in. She was no match for any of them.

Then there was the letter from her mother and Joyce.

She had carried the dream that her mother would come for her even though she was so far away. She carried that close to her heart, and in her darkest moments that was what helped her keep hope alive. Now she knew her mother would never come for her. Why should she? She didn't need her; she could just have more children.

It had been a difficult year. She would get out of here one day, and she would never come back. Tears were coming, so she started to hum a few lines from "There'll Always Be an England" to try to hide them. A large sob escaped. What did she care? England didn't want her. There was no England for her, and she felt like a nobody in Canada. Would she ever feel wanted?

Chapter 13

BULLIES! IT'S NOT FAIR!

The tragedy — the absolute tragedy — of childhoods lost.[1]
Without doubt, this is the most catastrophic child sexual
abuse legacy within our living memory.

— Margaret Humphreys, 2017[2]

Down on Misery Farm (boys' version)
Down on Misery
Down on Misery
Down on Misery Farm School
Where you work all day
And get no pay

Down on Misery
Down on Misery
Down on Misery Farm School
When I leave this blasted Fairbridge
Oh, how happy I will be

And gone are the days
When I was young and free
Now are the days
When I work in slavery.[3]

Marjorie had no idea how right she was to worry about the safety of the children at the farm school. The policy of silence was firmly ensconced and the records buried away from the public eye. It wasn't until the 2017 Independent Inquiry into Child Sexual Abuse: Child Migration Programmes released their March 2018 report that some of the accounts of sexual abuse of the children at the Prince of Wales Fairbridge Farm School became public knowledge:

> Fairbridge U.K. thought it was unwise to reinstate Mr. Rogers after he had been found guilty of "immoral relations" with Fairbridge boys. In January 1944, Sir Charles Hambro (Fairbridge U.K.'s chairman) wrote to Mr. Logan, stressing that they "cannot sacrifice the children to some adult who creates suspicion of injurious behaviour." The Bishop of Victoria wrote to Gordon Green (Fairbridge U.K.'s secretary) suggesting that the (unnamed second) duties master accused of sexual misconduct should have been sent to prison, and that Mr. Logan should be replaced, but neither of these events occurred.[4]

From the shadow of the trees, Marjorie kept a close eye on Kenny and his pals as they worked on bringing firewood into their cottage's woodbins. One boy clumsily piled kindling onto another's outstretched arms. It fell for a second time. He quickly scooped it up, looking nervously over his shoulder. She thought of her brothers and sisters at home. It had been over four years since she last saw them. And her new little brother, did he look like Kenny? The boys jumped as an older boy walked past. He did not touch them; he didn't need to. He had firmly established who was boss. The cottage mother poked her head out of the cottage door, her ever-present cigarette hanging from her lips, and asked if she had to wait all day for a bit of kindling. Her cigarette bobbed up and down as she spoke. A long, slender ash flew up into the air before landing at her feet.

Some of the bigger girls in Marjorie's cottage were bossy, especially those assigned to be head cottage girls. They weren't cruel to each other, at least not physically, although their words could cut through your skin no matter how tough you tried to be. The prettier girls were treated better than the plain ones, and they thought they were better than the rest because of this. Funny that they were all in this together, but the meanness around them worked to keep some of them apart. Any girl who had a chance to be in a cottage mother's favour used it to her advantage, and with the support of the cottage mother, the girl could get away with most anything. No one thought twice about pushing aside the weaker ones to get what they wanted.

The best that a girl not in anyone's favour could hope for was to be ignored. Remaining silent was a survival method many used. It was best to look away when things weren't fair, look after yourself, and avoid getting into others' business. It rarely worked out that way for Marjorie, though, as she wasn't quiet when she came to Bunny's rescue and couldn't avoid getting punished if it meant fighting with some of the cottage mother's pets to keep her sister safe.

She couldn't help Kenny, though, even if he needed it, but she kept an eye on him whenever possible. Watching him, remembering his stories, and making a promise to herself not to forget the things he told her were her ways of helping her brother. It was the only power she had. One day she would let the world know what had happened to them at this farm school.

Seeing the boys reminded Marjorie of one of the rare chances she had to speak to Kenny last week. He had talked about the bullies again. Marjorie suspected he was holding something back and not telling her the whole story. Why were the bullies so mean to the younger ones? You would think that the big kids at this farm, many of whom had arrived when they were just little, at five or eight or ten, would know what it was like to be bullied and have some pity on the young ones, especially the newcomers, but instead the bullying just seemed to get worse. Maybe bullying the younger ones was the only way of getting even for the bullying the older ones had endured. There was a lot of anger everywhere. Guarded eyes showed fear and a lot of sadness.

Later that day Marjorie caught a glimpse of Kenny running on the boys' path. She darted out on the girls' path on the opposite side of her cottage and caught up with him where the two pathways joined by the chapel. The two of them sat on the steps. She could see her cottage, which meant her cottage mother could see her if she looked her way. The cottage mum would find some chore for her to do if she saw Marjorie sitting around. Plus, the girls were not supposed to hang out and talk to the boys, but Kenny was her brother so surely this was different. They could go around the back of the chapel where they might not be noticed, but if they were caught "hiding" there, they would be punished. She kept a wary eye on her cottage door and listened while her brother talked about things. He told her that now that he was getting bigger they didn't pick on him nearly as much. His reputation as a fast runner, and the points that winning races brought to his cottage, had gained him the respect of some of the older boys, who were willing to protect him from the bullies in the other cottages when it suited their needs. Kenny punched the air and told her that learning to box helped him, too.

"I'm getting good at it, Marjorie." Kenny punched at the air again to show her. "I'm going to be thirteen soon!" He beamed.

She had almost forgotten. It would be Kenny's birthday on Saturday. He would be a teenager! Now that she was fifteen, she received twenty-five cents a week, and she had been saving her pennies for ages so she could give him something special from the Koksilah Store. She wasn't sure what it would be yet. Maybe she could find a little jackknife. She hoped she could get permission to go, but she would have to find one of the cottage mothers to walk the two miles each way with her; otherwise she would have nothing to give to Kenny. She rarely saw Kenny, though they grabbed a few words together maybe once every two or three weeks. She started to worry about how she could give him his present before she had even picked one out for him. Sometimes she was able to stop him at the chapel, and she did see him in the dining hall, but they weren't allowed to mix. She could try to run his present over to his table before they stopped her, but what if they took it away from him?

"You're going to be a teenager, Kenny!" Marjorie stood up. "Stand up. Hey, you are almost as tall as me now. You'll probably be taller pretty soon."

"I think I will be taller soon." Kenny sat down and sang quietly:

There's a plymmy running back
Down the old Koksilah track
On the way to Fairbridge Farm

There's water in the petrol
The trees are made of wood
The spark plugs are a-missing
And the whole darn thing's no good.[5]

"I think this whole place is no darn good. I can't wait to be old enough to get out of here. Can you? Do you like it here?"

"I hate it here, Kenny, and I dream of getting away every day. Do you want to try to go home? We would have to wait for Bunny. She will be twelve in January, so we would have to wait another four years. Or maybe we can go and send for her once we find our mum."

"Maybe. But I still have a long time before I can get away. It all seems so impossible at times. Sometimes I can see us looking for our family, but now I mostly think, what is the use? How can we? Where do we start? How do we even get back to England? Where would we find the money? What if they didn't want to see us?"

They sat quietly for a bit, and then Kenny whispered about one of the boys in his cottage.

"Marjorie, it's awful. I don't know what to do. He is really little, and he has no one to protect him. He cries himself to sleep every night. And it's not only the bullies; the cottage mother doesn't like him, either. I don't know why; he's just a little guy."

"Why do they have to do that? Why do they have to be so mean?" Marjorie's frustration grew, and with no way to get rid of it, it was overwhelming at times. She could just imagine what it must be like for that little boy all alone at night. She knew first-hand, as she'd felt it herself when she'd risked a thrashing many times after leaving her bed to comfort Bunny. If she didn't quiet Bunny, the cottage mother would be in, flashing her belt. But if she got caught out of her bed, she would be the one to get a thrashing. They couldn't win.

How could anyone think this was a good place? But how could she let the outside people know? No one would listen to her. The trouble was, every time visitors came to the farm, they never left the kids alone with them. And when the visitors asked questions, the mums and the principal listened carefully to the children's answers, so they all had to say that they loved it here, even though they certainly did not. They lined the children up beforehand and warned them what would happen if they were not on their very best behaviour and reinforced the way any questions must be answered.

"I don't want to hear that any of you have been whining and snivelling to our guests. Have I made myself clear?"

It would have been too difficult for the children to tell total strangers anything. Most had their feelings stomped on so effectively that they had buried them deep inside long ago and now they were impossible to find. Over the years their mistrust for adults grew, especially where their emotions were concerned.

Marjorie sighed as she looked at Kenny. She tried to piece together what he told her about the goings-on in his cottage. She thought it must be harder for the boys than for the girls. Kenny admitted that he once prayed to God for help, but it didn't work. She wondered if there really was a God, and if there was, then it was obvious to her that he certainly did not care for all the little children.

When Marjorie told Kenny that one of the girls in her cottage wet her bed again the other night and the cottage mother went mental, Kenny wasn't surprised — not even when she told him that the cottage mother had strapped the mattress to the girl's back and made her carry it around for ages. He told her that his cottage mother went mental also and boxed kids' ears if they wet the bed and that sometimes the little kids just cried all night and the cottage mother didn't seem to care.

"She just ignores them, Marjorie, and all they probably need is a hug. We get smacked if we help the little ones, and the bullies tease us. It's not right, is it?" Kenny looked to his sister for confirmation. "What did we do to deserve this? And another thing." Kenny lowered his voice and looked around. "I'm not sure what it is, but this big boy in our cottage, when the lights are out and he thinks everyone is sleeping, he creeps across the dorm and climbs into this other kid's bed. At first I thought they were brothers and he was helping him, but then I could hear the little kid crying, and ... and I hear odd noises and the crying getting worse. I think he makes him do things."

"Like sex things?" Marjorie, horrified by this, looked at her brother. "He doesn't do it to you, does he?

"No! No way! But that's wrong, isn't it?"

Marjorie didn't have time to answer before she heard her cottage mother yell, "Marjorie, get over here! You have chores to do. Stop wasting time. And, Kenny, get going or I'll report you." Miss Bishop was surprised how close those two were, even though the staff did their best to keep them apart.

"Who can we tell? Bye, Kenny," Marjorie said quickly and scampered off.

No one here, not even his big sister, could help him or anyone else.

* * *

In a lonely cot in a lonely cottage, Kenny closed his eyes and prayed to find himself back in Whitley Bay with his family. He wiped the tears from his eyes. He knew that he must not let anyone hear him crying. If the bigger boys heard, he would be in trouble. He shoved the coarse grey wool blanket into his mouth to muffle his sobs. He hated this place. He didn't feel safe anywhere. His cottage mother was cruel to him, and the bigger boys bullied him. He didn't know what he'd done wrong. He tried to make friends with the bigger boys, and he tried and tried to get his cottage mother to like him, but it seemed that the harder he tried, the worse it got. He would be thirteen soon. He was growing up. He needed to survive. He wouldn't let them break him. He would run away from this place as soon as he could.

He shuddered at how the day had begun. Right after breakfast, his mum shouted for all the boys to line up.

"Okay, boys!" Miss Brown had a peculiar look on her face as she looked them up and down. "One of you has taken a tin of milk from my pantry. Who took it?" She lunged out with her strap, threatening the line of boys. The big boys didn't flinch, but the little ones nearly peed their pants. Kenny felt safe this time because he had been nowhere near the cottage all morning. "No one will move until the culprit confesses. You can stand there all day." Her voice was getting higher and higher. She pointed to one of the older boys. "Was it you?"

Kenny was surprised because he thought that this boy was one of her favourites.

"No, ma'am. I saw Kenny in the pantry." The boy grinned as he watched Kenny react with terror.

Miss Brown turned to Kenny.

"I knew it! You stay put. The rest of you can go. Get off with you and start your chores." The group ran off; the older boys snickered at Kenny and poked at him as they hurried past.

Kenny knew which boy had taken the tin of milk from the cottage mum's pantry because he had overheard him bragging about it. It wasn't just any tin, it was the special tin of milk that the mum ordered in for her tea, and she had warned the boys never to touch it. Kenny had tasted the open tin once when she left it on the table. It was thick and sweet. But he would never take a whole tin. At first he had smiled to himself, wanting to see this big bully finally get it. Now, looking back, it only reinforced in his young mind that it was dangerous to have a sense of security at any time. It put you off your guard.

"It, it …" Kenny's mind was screaming, *It wasn't me! I didn't steal that tin of milk from the pantry. I don't even know how to get the door unlocked.*

Miss Brown turned to him and shrieked, "Well, out with it!"

"It wasn't me, mum." He finally choked the words out.

"You little liar!" she snarled at him. "I can spot a thief a mile away! The first time I laid eyes on you I knew you were no good, you little guttersnipe. Get over here."

Kenny knew the drill. His eyes were huge. Fat tears wormed their way out. He took off his shirt.

"Bend over." Miss Brown took her strap and laid three good whacks across his back: *whack! whack! whack!* "Maybe that will teach you not to steal." She gave him one more whack across his legs as he stood up.

"Why do you hate me?" he sobbed. "Why do you hate me?" he yelled this time.

"Because you are no good." She slapped his back and boxed his ears. "Don't you ever yell at me, do you hear me?" She laid the strap across the back of his legs again. "You little slum child, you waif, you street urchin, get out of my sight."

Kenny grabbed his shirt and ran. He felt like he was going to fall over — but not here; he had to get away.

Miss Brown clung to her strap. She hated it when the boys yelled at her. How dare that little street rat! She hung the strap up in her favourite place: on the kitchen wall where they could all see it. She always felt better after she used it. These little ragamuffins didn't deserve to live in this decent cottage. They should be back on the street where they belonged. She hated this job. She especially hated boys who yelled at her. Well, she hated them all, but she was secretly afraid of the older boys; that was why she let them get away with everything. She was afraid that they would gang up on her, and then what would she be able to do? She was alone every night with these little hooligans. Who knew what these boys were capable of doing, with the lack of breeding and horrible backgrounds they had? They were probably all from the criminal class. She had to take her frustrations out on the younger ones. They deserved it, too, looking up at her with those innocent little eyes. Innocent, ha! These slum children were born with bad tendencies, and it was her job to beat the bad out of them. She was doing them a favour. But this one needed a lesson. She tracked him to his hiding place and sent him to the principal's office.

Later Kenny whispered to the others, "I had to go to the office, and when I walked in I could see the slipper, the strap, and the willow stick hanging on the wall. I didn't know which one I would get. I closed my eyes as I bent over."[6] Kenny tried to stifle a sob.

"Well, out with it. What did you get?"

"The willow stick. I wouldn't cry, though. I ran off afterward. I hate our horrible cottage mother. I got blamed and it wasn't even me, but she never listens. I was nowhere near the cottage mum's stuff!"

"You know how it is; she always blames us for everything. She hates us. And so do the big boys. They always get us."

"It was awful," piped up Kenny's pal. "After you ran off, I tried to tell her that it was one of the big boys, and then she really got mad." He shuddered and went on, "She said she was going to teach me for lying, and she thrashed me across the legs and called me a liar and a thief just like you."

If any of the boys had had anywhere to run, they would have gone. But there was nowhere to go, no one to turn to for help.

It just didn't seem fair, but then nothing had seemed fair to Kenny since he'd arrived. He had only one person he could talk to: his sister Marjorie.[7]

Kenny never stopped trying to gain the affection of his cottage mother. It was survival. The boys worked hard to do their chores right, hoping to break down the wall that stood between them and a peaceful day.

Now that the winter weather had settled in, bringing in and stacking firewood was a relentless chore for the young ones. Kenny and his cottage mates had painstakingly carried in what they hoped was a full week's supply of wood into the basement for their furnace, the cookstove, and for their cottage mother's sitting room fireplace. Their cottage mother wanted nothing less than perfection. They tried hard to avoid her anger. They stood back and admired how high their woodpile was. As they stacked, they sang a song that they heard the older boys singing. They made sure their mum didn't hear them. It might make her mad.

> There is a mouldy home,
> Far far away,
> Where I get bread and jam
> Three times a day
> Eggs and bacon
> We don't see
> Moth balls we get in our tea

"Is that right? How does it go again? I can never remember it."

"I think it goes 'There is a mouldy old home, far away — we never see eggs and bacon.' No. I can't remember."

"How come we never get bacon and eggs, just the cottage mum?"

"That's just the way it is."

"It's not fair. We do all the work. Slop out the pigpen and feed and care for the pigs. Feed the chickens, clean out their cage, and collect the eggs, too."

The boys continued to work hard on the woodpile, always with the hope that this would get their cottage mum's approval. As they worked, the boys sang another song. They had to be careful not to sing this one too loud when the adults were around.

Down on Misery Farm School
Where you work all day
And get no pay
I slave and slave and slave away
And there is no tea
For you and me
I must be a fool
To be at this wretched old school.

"Look at our woodpile. It's huge. It should last all week. Should we show the mum?" The boys stood back and surveyed their work. They were feeling pleased. "Okay, let's call her."

They excitedly called to their mum, secure in the knowledge of a job well done.

"What is all this yelling about? Why are you disturbing me?" The boys' smiles disappeared. Miss Brown seemed angry.

"Mum, we just wanted to show you the woodpile. We got all the wood stacked." Kenny barely spoke above a whisper.

"Speak up, boy! I can't understand you when you mumble." She walked down the stairs toward the boys. "What do you want?"

"The wood, ma'am. Look, we got the wood all stacked and the kindling, too." Kenny was beaming with the pride of a job well done.

"You disturbed my peace and quiet to show me this? Look at that pile. It's crooked!" She reached out and pushed on the woodpile until it fell over. All their hard work lay in a heap. "A two-year-old could have done a better job. They should have left you on the streets where you belong. You will never amount to anything! You won't live to see twenty-one. Do you hear me? You are nothing! Pick up that wood and do it properly this time." She curled her upper lip, baring her teeth, and her cigarette nearly fell out of her mouth. She looked like a trapped animal. "And don't expect your supper until it's perfect. Am I understood?"

"Yes, ma'am," their terrified voices answered in unison. She stomped up the stairs and yelled for them to do a better job or else.

The boys bent down to rebuild their pile. They had it about half done when they noticed two of the older boys staring at them. These were the meanest bullies in their cottage. Everyone jumped to get out of their way.

"I see you babies have been crying." The taller of the two bullies walked closer and shoved one of the boys. He tripped over the fallen firewood and landed on his backside. He sat there and looked up at the older boy, trying to anticipate what he might do next, his young mind searching for a way out. "Get outside. It's time to teach you a lesson."

The bully pushed Kenny through the doorway. He fell and stayed where he was. The others followed. They could see the cottage mum peering out the window, but she quickly stood back. They knew there would be no help from her.

"Well, you cry babies. I think we need to toughen you up. You, what's your name again?"

The boy was too terrified to answer.

"Well, stupid, we want you and that little wimp Kenny there to run to the gate and back. I will personally thrash the loser. Go!"

The two little boys knew tears wouldn't help, but they came running down anyway. "Stop that snivelling. Wipe the tears off your gobs or I'll smack you now. Run! And don't look back!"

The two bullies stood with their arms crossed, pleased smirks spread across their faces. For a fleeting moment it crossed Kenny's mind that maybe the four of them would be able to tackle these two bullies. But he knew that they were no match, even with four against two, and if they were able to get them down, then what? The rest of their lives would be made miserable. The bullies would follow them and one by one get even with them, over and over again, and that was something they could count on.

The boys had no choice. Doing the bullies' bidding had become routine for them. They ran off. When they returned a few minutes later, running neck and neck, wondering how to avoid a beating, the bullies were gone, but that didn't stop them from looking over their shoulders for the rest of the day.

Kenny wondered what he had done wrong and why he had to come to this horrible place. Some of the cottages had nice cottage mothers — he knew because one of the boys that he came from England with had told him so. He tried to understand why he couldn't have a nice cottage mother, too.[8]

On another day, the little band of four- and five-year-olds were happily climbing a fence. They were known as the Baldy Bean Gang because they all had ringworm and had to have their heads shaved. They wore matching bandanas. A nearby duty master called to them. He gave the first boy to reach him a jackknife and told him to cut one of the thin willow branches. Puzzled, the little boy obeyed. He had never held a jackknife before.

As he walked away the duty master yelled, "Be careful. The knife is sharp."

It only took a couple of cuts to free a long, slender piece of the willow. Pleased with himself, the boy quickly ran back to show his companions.

"Okay, you boys. Pants down and stand facing the fence with your hands on the railing."

Whack! Whack! Whack!

"Now you know better than to climb these fences. Get along to wherever you're supposed to be."[9] The bruises on the boys' buttocks and legs were felt for days.

Mr. Sampson, a boys' duty master, briefly watched from the shadows of the cottage doorway as two lads pummelled each other in front of the cottage. The match was uneven; an older boy was pounding on the face of a younger boy. Blood mingled with the dirt and the tears of anger and frustration on the younger boy's face. He kept yelling, "I'll squeal on you! I'll squeal on you!"

Mr. Sampson shouted for the boys to stop fighting and to get inside. He quickly got to the bottom of the fight. The older boy had been forcing the younger boy to have sex with him. Recently they had been put in the same cottage and the younger boy had had enough, as now his abuser expected to do it to him more often. Mr. Sampson was shocked. He sat the boys down and gave them a talk on the "harmfulness of sexual perversion." Satisfied with the boys' promises not to carry on this practice, he let them go without a whipping and without reporting them. *Of course, reporting on any of this would be pointless,* the duty master thought. *The principal would only say that the British are oversexed. What rubbish! The young victims have no one to turn to, and they suffer because of that attitude.* As he went over the incident in his mind, the duty master thought about his recent diary entry: "Had I known what I was letting myself in for, I probably wouldn't have taken the job as duty master." The job left him emotionally drained.[10]

Once out of sight, the older boy threatened the younger one with silence or else. He had every intention of carrying on the practice, leaving the young boy with little or no recourse. A strict talking-to didn't worry the older boy in the least and certainly would not have taken the little boy out of harm's way or this bigger boy's reach.

Marjorie heaved a sigh as she filled the basement tub with water. She knew Kenny was telling her the truth when he told her stories about what went on in the boys' cottages. She dumped the socks in and grabbed the washboard. She always got the worst of the chores. The longer she was at the farm school, the greater her frustration grew. She scrubbed vigorously, taking her exasperation out on the socks. She knew that she could not change any of the bad things that went on here, and her powerlessness ate away at her.

Her big sister Phyllis had told her what the Fairbridge man in Whitley Bay had said to their mum when he came calling for them to sign the papers. Funny, sometimes she couldn't remember anything about her family, then clear memories came out of nowhere and flooded her. The man had said, "You'll be giving the children a better chance, a better life. You owe it to them. You'll be doing them a favour, and one day they'll thank you for it. Mark my words; they will grow to hate you if you leave them here in this squalor."

How could any parent fall for such lies? Marjorie wished she could write to her mum and tell her to warn other mums. Do not send your children here, not if you care about them. It's not a land of milk and honey. A better life? What nonsense! Far from it! We are slaves, and we have no rights, and no one loves us. We have no one to turn to. The kids know what punishment to expect if they dare to break any of the rules. And the most important rule: don't talk about what goes on here. It didn't matter anyway, as there was no one she could trust to tell. Everything had to be held in. At times she felt close to bursting as she tried to push

away the fury that bubbled up whenever she thought too long about what
had happened to them. It was not right. She was trapped here until she
was old enough to get out. It was not fair! Their cottage mothers told
them over and over again to be obedient and to be thankful for what the
Fairbridge Farm School gave them. She wanted to scream that it gave her
nothing but grief, and furthermore it was not what the farm gave her; it
was what it took away. Her cottage mum said that it was about time that
she forgot her family. Never! She never would, and they couldn't make her.

Marjorie's talks with Kenny worried her for days afterward. She wished
she could just forget all the badness that he told her about. Sometimes she
could, then at other times, like when she saw the fear on Kenny's and the
other boys' faces, it made all the bad stuff about the farm school come right
back to her. She knew she would be leaving soon and she was glad, but
there was something about seeing more little children arrive that haunted
her; some of these little ones would be here for almost ten years. Well,
what could she do about it? She couldn't help them.

She sighed again and looked out the window. As she scrubbed the
crusty socks, she hummed to herself.

Cheerio!
Here we are
Working hard
On our Fairbridge Farm …
Our Empire home
For we love our Island home
Our Empire home in Canada.

Fury filled Marjorie. They made everyone sing these songs until they
were firmly stuck. She didn't love her home here. She didn't want to be in
Canada. It wasn't *her* Fairbridge Farm.

Snow was falling. Large light flakes drifted down, quickly covering the
ground. If the snow continued all afternoon, they could go sledding up
behind the barn. Last year they went sledding in the moonlight. It was

Gathering, chopping, and stacking firewood was a chore that all Fairbridge children knew well because all the buildings were heated by a wood furnace and the kitchens all used wood cookstoves.

wonderful being out in that special light. The snow made everything so bright, just like daytime but softer.

After dinner the farm school children ran out to play in the snow. Kenny ran up to his sisters, ready to launch a snowball. The girls ducked, and it missed both of them. Marjorie ran after him and threw one back. It missed Kenny but hit one of the little boys who had recently arrived at the farm. Marjorie dusted the snow off his head and said she was sorry. He just stood there. He said he didn't mind.

Marjorie said goodbye and ran off to help Bunny. A group of girls had ambushed her. She gathered up a handful of snow and rubbed it into the face of one of the girls. They all collapsed in a heap of snow and laughter. They lay on their backs making snow angels, looking up at the sky. For a moment, they were quiet. Just then, a large owl flew over them. The girls watched. The owl didn't make a sound, as if it was never there.

Chapter 14

CHRISTMAS EVE: SURVIVAL IS THE MOST IMPORTANT THING[1]

We believe that this is called a Christian country — from the Queen to the beggar we all lay claim to the character of Christians — we boast that our property and persons are free — and yet the most outrageously tyrannical, unnatural, and un-Christian practices are tolerated, or cloaked under a sympathetic regard for the poor and their offspring.... There is a callous indifference to the feelings of the poor ... which outrages belief.

— "Transportation of Children by Parish Officers,"
The Operative (London), February 3, 1839

Lost Love
As you celebrate your Christmas Eve
In the traditions of your own way,
Take a moment to pause and remember
How sad it was for a home child that day.

A hundred thousand British children
Set sail toward Canada's shore,
To be tagged and shipped to farmers
Seeing their Moms and Dads no more.

To a land called milk and honey
These children went to live.
Their little hands became calloused
From the hard work they had to give.

How sad a Christmas Eve would be
To a home child so far from home and family.
As the carollers sang "Silent Night,"
Tears fell as he cried with fright.

At Christmastime a child should be
Gathered around his Christmas tree,
Not way off in a distant land
Made to live and work like a man.

Christmas bells are ringing
Around this time of year.
Families gather merrily
To spread their Christmas cheer.

Take time out this Christmas
To think back on the past.
And remember all the home children
Whose lives were shattered like broken glass.[2]

Marjorie sat on the edge of the bed and looked around her beautiful bedroom. Her quarters came with her own sitting room and her own bathroom, too. It was absolutely grand, yet she was absolutely miserable. She put her head on the fancy pillows of her bed and cried and cried. It was a trick of fate that she found herself in a room that most girls could only dream of, only to find that it meant nothing to her. She would much rather be back in their crowded little Whitley Bay flat, sleeping on the floor with all her family around her, than be in this luxurious room all alone. *I have all this comfort but no one to comfort me.*

Marjorie had become used to her life during her five years at the Fairbridge Farm School. She was never alone. She always had the companionship of the other girls, especially her sister and, to a lesser degree, her brother. It took a long while before Marjorie realized that they actually had each other's backs and that most of the girls in her cottage had become her "family." Over the years, trust had built up between many of them, and even the mums' pets would stand together with the other girls against the adults when necessary. She may have longed for a smaller group or a quieter life such as she had experienced during the summer of 1940 while at the Fairbridge Fintry Training Farm, but the loneliness here swallowed her up, and it was more than she could take.

Marjorie lacked the skills to cope with this. All the training and preparation Fairbridge put into getting her ready to be a servant girl in Victoria had not prepared her for the tremendous feeling of isolation that she found in the midst of one of the busiest cities in British Columbia. Fairbridge was isolated from the larger outside community. But here in Victoria, Marjorie was isolated from everything that was familiar to her. She found herself in a situation where she felt stranded all day, every day, with a woman who was confined to a wheelchair. It was just the two of them. A nurse came in occasionally to help with things like baths, so Marjorie didn't have to do that, but she was the main companion, plus she was responsible for all the cleaning and the cooking. The lonely evenings stretched out, never-ending like the garden rows she had to weed at the farm school. She woke up in the mornings to such quietness. She had never slept in a room all by herself before. She missed the chatter of her roommates.

They sent Marjorie out to work on September 11, 1942, ten days before her sixteenth birthday. At the farm school, being one of the senior girls, she felt so grown up and her confidence grew. Here in Victoria, she was unsure of herself. Her employer was a lovely person, but it wasn't enough. Marjorie didn't feel prepared or trained for the task at hand. She had plenty of training in the Fairbridge Hospital, but no one had trained her to care for an elderly wheelchair-bound patient all on her own. The new hospital was a busy place. Here it was lonely.

Marjorie fell back on her bed and hummed a tune, trying to control her tears. It was funny how songs came into her head and brought memories with them. She recalled working in the hospital after the Pearl Harbor attack last year. Sometimes they could pretend that the war would not touch them, but after the attack, the whole school had a blackout enforced on them. The new hospital didn't have any blinds, so on a cloudy dark day in the winter, when normally they'd put the lights on as early as three o'clock, they had to do everything in semidarkness. It was much too early to put the patients to bed, and it was too dark for Marjorie to read to them. The nurse made it easier for the patients by leaving the ward doors open so the children could talk to each other. Then it started. One child began to sing "There'll Always Be an England." Before long, they had all joined in. It was eerie working in the hospital on those dark evenings, jumping at every unexplained noise, waiting for the bombs to fall on them. Singing seemed to help make their fears disappear for a while.

Marjorie sat on the edge of her bed. The responsibilities coupled with the loneliness were too much for her. She wanted to go back to her real home and be with her own mum. She couldn't stay here.

She stood up and paced about her room, feeling desperate. Like a trapped animal, she surveyed her cage. She looked at the things in her room but felt no comfort in seeing them. Mrs. Kent had put a little radio in her room. She said it was to keep her company. It was such a luxury, a radio just for herself, but she had not turned it on yet. It seemed too out of the ordinary, and, besides, it reminded her of other hopes and dreams dashed last spring. She hated thinking about the radio program they had broadcast from the farm. The radio people had come to Fairbridge to interview the principal and the kids. When it was her turn, the radioman asked for her name and what she did at the school. She didn't like speaking into the microphone. She felt shy, but part of her wanted to yell out for someone to help her find her mum so she could get out of this place. She remembered that her mother had a radio once. She had to pawn that one, but maybe she'd gotten another one. She remembered the voices coming out of her mother's old radio. She prayed that her mother would be listening. She tried to yell for help, but everyone was looking at her, and so she simply said, "My name is Marjorie. I work in the laundry."[3]

And that was it; her chance at rescue was over. She should have yelled out. She didn't know what happened to her voice; it just got stuck. She had forgotten how to ask for help.

If only she had yelled into the radio that day. Maybe she would not be here now, in this desperate situation. She wished she were dead. Then, with a shudder, she remembered the girl who died last summer. She was only fifteen. They were the same age. No one talked about her. The cottage mother wouldn't tell them anything. One day she was just gone, and they were supposed to forget about her.[4] Marjorie thought about all the kids on the torpedoed boat. Then she remembered the little boy who died just before they'd brought her to the farm school. Kenny told her about it. Why was she thinking about all these dead kids? It was giving her the creeps. She had it better than they did, didn't she? She was alive.

A week or so after she arrived in Victoria, Marjorie was surprised by a letter from her sister Bunny. She turned it over a few times, wondering why it looked different, and then she realized that it was still sealed. She had never had a sealed letter before. She went into her room and ripped open the envelope.

Dear Marjorie,

How are you? I miss you so much. I never see Kenny. I hope this letter gets to you. I sent a letter in code, but maybe my code wasn't good enough because your last letter said that you hadn't heard anything from me, so I guess my letter didn't make it. One of the girls from our cottage who is working in Victoria now was visiting for a couple of days, and I asked her to smuggle this letter out to you, and she said she would. It is going to be such a long time before I get to leave here. I don't know if I can stand it. Four more years is forever. This place is awful without you. I have no one to protect me. My new cottage mother is an old hag. One of the girls went into *his* cottage, and you know who I mean. I don't know what happened but something not good. She cried a long time, and no one could get her to stop. Sometimes it is hard, though, because they act so nice and offer you sweets and things, but don't worry, nothing will get me to go into his cottage. I wish I was with you or that you were still here. I am all alone. I miss you so much.

Love from your sister, Bunny

Bunny's letter added to Marjorie's distress. She felt a powerlessness that nearly overwhelmed her. She couldn't help her sister, and her sister couldn't help her. But an even more pressing issue for her was that she needed to change her placement and was afraid to even ask.

She wanted to scream, but her training at the Fairbridge Farm School compelled her to suffer in silence. So she tried to settle in, like they told her, but it was in vain. She could no longer willingly accept the things that didn't seem right. She had to find some courage to tell Mrs. Williams, the after-care mum, to find her another placement. For days now she had been picking up the phone and starting to dial the number, but then she would panic and quickly replace the phone on its cradle. She felt certain that she could talk to Mrs. Williams; she knew she would listen to her, but she was afraid to try. Several times a day she would rehearse what she would say, but it never sounded proper. She had to find the right words. She might have only one shot. She needed to be taken seriously.

She smiled as she thought about Mrs. Williams. In her final few months at the farm school, the girls in her cottage got a very pleasant surprise in the way of this new cottage mum. Mrs. Williams was just an acting cottage mum, but it was a blessing for everyone to have her there. The girls were apprehensive at first. They had grown to mistrust all cottage mothers, but they soon realized that they had a real gem; she was an angel in disguise. Mrs. Williams was one of the best things that happened for Marjorie during all her Fairbridge years. She needed her now, if she could find the courage to approach her. But it was too bad she wasn't Bunny's cottage mum, as then she wouldn't have to worry so much about her little sister.

Under the guidance of Mrs. Williams, Marjorie began to relax a little and gain more confidence. Mrs. Williams was her cottage mum when they had the day school closing ceremonies in June. The day was so lovely they held the ceremonies on the lawn. Before that, they were always in the auditorium. Marjorie felt so proud showing off her dress in the dress parade. When they passed the prizes out, Marjorie was shocked to hear her name called, and when she was handed the home economics prize for industry and initiative, she could hardly believe it. She knew it was the encouragement and help from Mrs. Williams that had enabled her to win the prize.[5] That was a grand day. They ended it with folk dancing and singing. Marjorie felt so smart dancing in her new dress. This would be her last day school closing ceremony. After the summer, it was her turn to go to Victoria. She had dreamed of that day, and now, here she was in Victoria, and her newfound confidence was in danger of being shattered.

Mrs. Williams had left Fairbridge in early September to go back to Victoria and then was appointed the after-care provider for the girls who were working in service. Marjorie kept telling herself that Mrs. Williams was there for the girls to call. Her words were still fresh in her mind: "Now, Marjorie, you have my telephone number in case you need anything. You can call me any time; that is what I'm here for."

After several failed attempts, Marjorie got her nerve up on the morning of Christmas Eve. Perhaps it was the thought of spending Christmas Eve without her Fairbridge family or waking up Christmas morning all alone that prompted her. Her employer was napping. She picked up the telephone, and this time she dialled the number right through without hanging up. Mrs. Williams answered. At the sound of her voice, Marjorie fell to pieces. Her carefully rehearsed speech came out all wrong. She tried to tell her how she was feeling, but it was difficult to find the right words. She had grown so used to hiding her feelings that she didn't know how to tell Mrs. Williams what she was feeling.

"Mrs. Williams, I just can't stay here!" Marjorie cried, the tears rolling down her face.

"Dear, calm down, calm down. You haven't even identified yourself. With whom am I speaking?" Mrs. Williams's voice was reassuring. She didn't sound angry with Marjorie for calling.

"It's Marjorie. Marjorie from the farm school. I'm over at Mrs. Kent's." Marjorie's words came out choked.

"Speak up, Marjorie. I can hardly hear you. Tell me what's wrong. Has anyone hurt you?" Mrs. Williams knew she needed to calm this girl down before she could get to the bottom of this.

"No. No, nothing like that. Mrs. Kent is a very nice woman. She's having a nap right now. I didn't want to wake her. It's just that I'm so alone. I can't do this." The tears were streaming now, and the sobs were making her more difficult to understand.

"Marjorie, listen to me! Can you get away for a few hours this afternoon?"

"I think so. I have my half day today."

"Well, can you come to my house for tea, say around three o'clock?"

"Okay." Marjorie was getting quieter.

"Do you know which bus to take?"

"No."

"Okay, write this down. You walk down to the Oak Bay Village and take the Oak Bay bus. You get off at the crossroads of Fort Street and Oak Bay Avenue. Tell the bus driver. I will meet you there at three. Can you do that?"

"Okay."

"Try to be a brave girl, and I'll see you this afternoon. In the meantime I'll start looking into other possibilities for you, okay?"

"Yes, thank you." Marjorie hung up the phone. She felt much better. She wiped the tears and smiled at how hard it had been for her to call. In the end, it was not so bad. She was going to see Mrs. Williams that very afternoon. She would help her; she just knew it.

She planned to leave a little earlier this afternoon and walk. She only had enough money to take the bus one way. When she started her job, her mum had told her the farm school would put half of her wages in the Fairbridge savings account. When Marjorie began to protest, her mum assured her that a trust fund would be set up for her, and she would get it all back when she turned twenty-one. She was not happy with that idea. But she was happy at the thought of her freedom and no longer being under the control of Fairbridge. Nevertheless, it was hard to make seven dollars and fifty cents last the whole month. She supposed the policy might be a good one, though; she would have a nice little nest egg to fall back on when she turned twenty-one. But she didn't trust the Fairbridge people. They probably wouldn't give it back to her.

Marjorie walked down Oak Bay Avenue. As she walked along, she practised what she was going to say. It was important. Mrs. Williams had to listen to her, so she knew she must find just the right words. She needed her to understand that she could not stay another day.

The walk was taking longer than she expected, so Marjorie ran to the next block. A feeling of panic came over her and she wondered whether she had passed the intersection. Just as she was about to turn around and retrace her steps, she saw Mrs. Williams waving to her. Relief nearly brought her to tears, but she squared her shoulders, forced out a smile and waved back.

Marjorie sat in Mrs. Williams' living room. It was a pleasant room, very cozy but crowded. The Christmas tree was the focal point. It towered over one end of the room. Marjorie had never seen anything so prettily decorated. There was so much tinsel that you could hardly see the tree! Mrs. Williams came in with a tray of tea things and saw Marjorie looking at her tree.

"It's quite pretty, isn't it? My sister and I always decorate it together."

"It is very pretty."

"Let's have a nice cuppa, and then we'll talk about things, shall we?" Mrs. Williams set the tray on the coffee table and sat down. "Would you like to pour, dear?"

Marjorie picked up the teapot. It was a delicate china teapot with a rose pattern on it. She poured two cups and passed one over to Mrs. Williams. They sat quietly, sipping their tea. Marjorie was enjoying the peaceful atmosphere of the room. Then she had a great idea; maybe she could come here. But she was too afraid to ask, so she didn't say anything. She just waited patiently until Mrs. Williams spoke.

"Now, Marjorie, as I told you, it is not that easy finding a new placement. We cannot leave Mrs. Kent in the lurch, and especially not at Christmastime, can we? That would not be fair."

Marjorie looked at Mrs. Williams, but she didn't trust her own voice, so she just shook her head.

"I have started to make some inquiries, but it may take a little while to find something else for you. Can you try extra hard to make it work until I come up with something?"

"I guess so." Marjorie's voice came out in a whisper; she cleared her throat and tried to be brave. "I'm just not suited for it. The loneliness just wraps itself around me, especially in the evenings, and I feel like I can't breathe. I wake up every night having nightmares. Sometimes my heart is pounding so hard I think I'm going to have a heart attack. I can't relax. I'm all alone." Marjorie's voice was getting higher, and the tears were making their way down her face. "It's too quiet. I'm not used to so much quiet." She sobbed.

Marjorie was trying her best to tell Mrs. Williams how she was feeling, but she didn't think her words really conveyed how desperately alone she felt. She had spent the last several years at Fairbridge hiding her real feelings. It wasn't easy for her to understand her feelings now, except that she knew she would have to run away somewhere if Mrs. Williams forced her to stay. But where would she go?

Mrs. Williams could see that this was not a case of the girl trying to get out of her work. She was desperate. "Marjorie, here's a tissue. It may take me a little while, but I promise I will do my best. Because it is Christmastime, I may not be able to do anything until after the new year. Can you try to make it until then?" Mrs. Williams reached over and patted Marjorie's arm.

A look of alarm spread across Marjorie's face.

"Marjorie, try to make the best of it for now."

"Can't I go back to the farm for Christmas? I miss my sister and my brother, and we have never been apart at Christmas. I've always had some of my family around."[6] Marjorie thought that she couldn't go back to Mrs. Kent's even for a moment. She had been full of hope that Mrs. Williams would understand that she needed to get away, now, today. She had even started to pack up her few belongings. She'd stopped, though, because she didn't want to jinx her chances.

"I'm afraid that wouldn't work. Mrs. Kent is counting on you. You must try to be a brave girl and stay there for now. Please give it a try, Marjorie."

"Okay, I'll try. But do you promise me that you'll find me another place?"

"Yes. I will do my best." Mrs. Williams stood up and hugged Marjorie.

Marjorie knew she would have a hard time being brave. All she could think of was sitting alone in her room on Christmas Eve and waking up all alone on Christmas morning. She was surprised that she missed the farm school so much. She wished that Bunny and Kenny could be here with her.

On the bus ride back, Marjorie went over the afternoon again. She thought about the promises that she'd made to herself on the walk up Oak Bay Avenue, that if Mrs. Williams didn't help her get away today, she would just run away. It was funny how childish that sounded now. Where would she go, anyway? She smiled to herself. She felt so much better now that she had talked to Mrs. Williams. Mrs. Williams didn't call her names and tell her that she was ungrateful, like her old cottage mum always did. Having this little bit of control helped Marjorie to hope she might be able to change the direction of her life. It felt good, even if she would have to wait it out a bit. Maybe it would not be so bad working in service if she could have a little say over some of the things that affected her life. She knew that the most important thing was that she had to survive. She must not let them break her, because one day she would not have to answer to them any longer. She would truly be on her own and be her own person. Then she could start saving up and go back and find her family. Yes, she needed to survive so she could go find her family.

Marjorie got ready for bed that evening feeling more positive about things. She trusted Mrs. Williams to help her. After she returned, it surprised her when Mrs. Kent put the phone down and said that she had been talking to Mrs. Williams, and it was all arranged for her to go visit her sister and brother at the school right after Christmas. The phone call was a sign that Mrs. Williams really cared. Marjorie knew she would find another placement for her. She looked around. She would miss her lovely room, but instead of being a haven for her over the past few weeks, it was more like a prison.

It was Christmas Eve. Her very first one all on her own. Getting away was all she had thought about for so long, and now that she was away, it wasn't at all like she'd thought it would be. She still longed to go back home, however unrealistic that had become. Last fall one of the little girls received a letter from her mother, asking her daughter what she wanted for Christmas. She showed Marjorie her letter before she sent it to her mum: "Dear Mum, All I want is to see you."[7] That is all she said. Those few words said it all. Marjorie had thought of that letter many times since then, wishing and hoping for a day when that might come true for both of them.

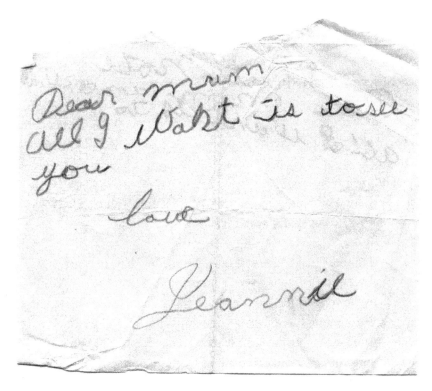

Jeannie's Christmas letter to her mother.

A tear struggled down Marjorie's cheek, but she brushed it away. She could make it a special Christmas Eve, one to remember, or she could just mope and wish for things that were not meant to be. She decided to write a letter in her head to her mum. She had given that up ages ago, when she lost hope, but she felt different tonight. Writing a letter would make the time pass pleasantly and ease her loneliness. She hummed to herself as she tidied up a few things. She sat back on her bed, feeling stunned. Where did that song suddenly come from? It was her mum's favourite song, "Red Sails in the Sunset." She used to sing it all the time. She hummed a little more and then tried to remember the words: *Carry my loved one home safely to me.*[8]

She couldn't remember all the words, but she suddenly had such a clear picture of her mum as she used to sing the song to her and her brothers and sisters. Her heart was filled with joy at this memory. What a special Christmas Eve. She curled up in her chair and began her letter.

Dear Mum. No, she would write to Joyce, too. *Dear Mum and Joyce.* No! She would include everyone. No wait! She excitedly jumped up and opened her drawer. She had not touched last year's Christmas present. It was some stationery. She no longer had to worry about hiding her letters from her cottage mother, so she took her pen, sat down at her table, and wrote.

> Dear Mum and Joyce and Phyllis, Jean, Lawrence, Fred and Norman, and even the new baby, Richard,
>
> I'm sorry that I haven't written for so long. It's Christmas Eve, and I'm feeling pretty lonely, so I thought I would write you a letter. I'm working here in Victoria for a nice lady, but it's too lonely for me. I miss Bunny and Kenny, and I even miss the farm school. I'm not happy right now, but I have a wonderful friend who is going to help me find another place to work. I trust she will do this.
>
> I will tell you about some of the Christmases at Fairbridge. Every Christmas they allowed all the kids to pick out a gift worth one dollar from the Sears catalogue. (Oh, did you know that Fairbridge, and I guess Canada, has dollars and cents and not pounds and pence and ha'pennies and farthings?) Anyway, we picked out the present we wanted quite a long time before Christmas, so when Christmas came most of us had forgotten what we had picked out and it came as a big surprise. Last year I picked stationery, and I just found it, so I am writing my letter to you on it.
>
> Maybe I should start at the beginning. On Christmas morning when the bell chimed, we would all wake up and get our stockings from the fireplace. We always had a lot of things in there, such as nuts and oranges and candy and small things, like jacks or marbles. I always

saved my orange for Kenny because one of the bigger boys always took his. He never wanted to take mine, but I told him a white lie and said that I didn't like oranges. Usually we had breakfast in the dining hall but not on holidays and weekends. So for Christmas morning we had a bowl of porridge or a bowl of puffed wheat, and some kids had toast and peanut butter. We always had more choices on Christmas. The cottages get huge bags of puffed wheat all the time and enormous thirty-pound pails of peanut butter. But I should tell you that the night before Christmas we sang carols. Then we had a special Christmas Day communion service first thing in the morning before breakfast, and it was special because we decorated the whole chapel with cedar boughs and wreaths, and we put holly on the font. It was very lovely, and all the kids were really excited about the whole day. Then the trainee girls helped with the Christmas dinner, and last year we cooked twenty turkeys! We all took turns stirring the Christmas puddings, and most of us tossed in a wish. I hope I get my wish because I am still waiting and it has almost been a year, but I can't tell you my wish because it might not come true, and I really, really want it to come true. Then we decorated the tables. First we covered the centre with red, green, or white paper, and then we put Yule logs with candles stuck in them on each end. We put some moss around the logs and then sprinkled imitation snow around the logs. To top it off, we put a few cedar branches in the centre of the table. There are loads of cedar trees around here, and it gives off such a lovely smell.

On Christmas Eve, we all went to the big dining hall. They put up a huge Christmas tree, and all the kids helped decorate it. We put paper chains and strings of dried berries and popcorn all around it. Then after we finished dinner, a telegram from Santa was read, which meant he was on his way. While we waited we all sang carols at the top of our lungs, even me, and when Santa finally arrived everyone cheered so loud. Then Santa removed the presents from his sack and put them under the tree. It looked so grand to see the mountain of presents. Then he called out the names one at a time until all the presents were given out. After that, the little kids had to go back to their cottages and get ready for bed, but they allowed the older kids to stay up. We cleared the tables, and then we had a dance in the dining hall. Sometimes they allowed us to stay up until midnight. Those were the best nights. Even the cranky cottage mums were usually nice to everyone on Christmas. Oh yeah, on New Year's Eve we would have a dance, too. Those were fun times, and now that I'm not there anymore, I really miss them.

I'm trying to understand everything, like why I had to go away and why I have a new brother and why Joyce is back home and I'm not and why you never came and got me, and I will have to just keep trying to understand, I guess. Right now I have to work on my problems here so that I can work on these other things later. I have to go now. I hope you are having a merry Christmas Eve.

I love you, Mum, and Joyce, Fred, Norman, Phyllis, Lawrence, Jean, and the baby ... wherever you are.
Your daughter always, Marjorie

P.S. I almost forgot to tell you about the last cross-country race. Kenny came in first, and he had the best time ever at thirty-one minutes and five seconds. It was in the *Fairbridge Gazette* from June 1942. I will try to get a copy and mail it to you.

Marjorie folded her letter and sealed it in an envelope. She wiped away a tear. She held her letter up and looked at it. Her letter! She thought this was the best letter she had ever written. No one could tear it open and read it. It was just for her family. She would get a stamp and put it in the mailbox herself.

She went to touch her radio but hesitated. Every Christmas Day at noon, the farm school would sit quietly and listen to the king's Christmas speech. Last year's speech was about family, and it had stuck in her mind. The king said we should remember those who must spend Christmas away from home. *What about me?* she had wanted to scream. *Do you mean me? Do you care? He said we all belong to each other. What rot! I don't belong to anyone.* The speech had distressed her, so she'd put her head on the table and her hands over her ears.

She wouldn't listen tomorrow. He was not her king anymore. She was truly on her own and must make her way somehow. She pulled out her nightdress and got ready for bed. She brushed her hair and, almost without realizing it, she was humming again. "There'll be bluebirds over the white cliffs of Dover …" Marjorie could hear the tune in her head, but she couldn't remember the words. *Hmmm, hmmm, hmmm, hmmm,* "and peace ever after when the world is free."[9]

That night she made a promise to herself that one day she would see those famous white cliffs of Dover. One day, she, too, would be free. She just knew it.

Chapter 15

WHY WOULD I GO BACK?
MY COUNTRY DIDN'T WANT ME

Did we not know that justice, when employed in the cause of the poor, is always a one-sided hobbling beldame.... We are well aware that many of the supporters of this society [Children's Friend Society] would willingly transport all the children and half the adult population of the land to the most unhealthy portion of the globe, if by so doing they could increase their own security and get rid of what they impiously term the "surplus population" of the country.

— "Transportation and Sale of Children of the Poor,
Defence of the Children's Friend Society,"
The Operative (London), May 5, 1839

"I never dared to dream that I would actually be standing on the Whitley Bay sands with you," I said, and turned to my mother with a smile.

"I never ever thought I would see Whitley Bay again." She grinned back at me. "I never wanted to come back to England. Why would I? No one wanted me here."

"But it's different now, isn't it? Are you glad you came back?" I asked.

"Yes, I think so," Mum answered with a slight hesitation in her voice. "It will take a while to process it all. Imagine! I played on these sands so

Sisters Joyce and Marjorie at Whitley Bay, 2007. Joyce is pointing to the periwinkles that they used to pick for their dinner. St. Mary's Lighthouse is in the background. Memories flooded back as the two sisters walked around Whitley Bay for the first time since leaving in 1937.

very long ago. I lived here with my family. *My family!* I went to school here. I liked the Rockcliffe School because it was so close to the sands. How could we resist skipping school to play on the sands when we could see the beach from the school playground? Once we were taken away, I lost everything that defined my life up to that point. We didn't have much, but we had each other. I was loved. It took me forever to get over losing my family. Well, maybe I never got over it. I don't think the people who were shipping kids out to the colonies realized just how much they were taking away from us. Perhaps they didn't care. We were just 'material' to distribute around the colonies. Just numbers to them."

"You children were an Imperial investment. It was important to keep a steady flow of white stock to the colonies. Unemployment made England feel crowded with needy people, while the colonies were 'man-hungry'[1] by comparison and desperate for settlers. Children would not find it easy to come back. They gave you a one-way ticket. I really can't imagine what it was like living in poverty in England in the 1930s, but you had each other and, really, it wasn't much better in Canada at that time."

"I was born at the wrong time. If I was one of the older ones in our family or one of the younger ones, I would have stayed home." Mum sighed. She was quiet for a long time. We stood on the beach, her beach. "As we left Liverpool, I wondered why we were going," she began again. "I remember covering myself up emotionally; it was almost a physical feeling, heavy, like whatever I covered myself with had a lot of weight to it. Eventually, we were told we were going to Canada, and we were told that was where the Indians fought the white man.[2] The boys were frightened, but the girls weren't as frightened because we didn't think they went after little girls. I was frightened for Kenny, though. It nearly drove me to distraction that I couldn't protect him."

"He was kept from you?"

"Yes. I will never understand why we weren't allowed to look after the little family that we had left. They took so much." Marjorie's voice trailed off. "It became too heavy to carry, so I had to try to chop that part of my life away and just look ahead. I needed to go into the unknown as light as possible. My future was so uncertain. While living with my family in Whitley Bay, I had no worries. In my heart, I knew when I left England that I wouldn't see my family again. My time at Middlemore Emigration Homes in Birmingham assured me of that. I hadn't heard a word from my mother. She just disappeared as if the past ten years of my life meant nothing to her. I had no way of telling her that she meant the world to me. I held up hope that she would come for me, for us. I hated her for letting us go like that. I knew if I let my fear and despair have its way, it would take over. I needed to have my wits about me. I needed to take care of me now, and Kenny. He had no one else. I had to be the one. Then later, I needed to look after Audrey when she arrived."

"And at first you didn't know whether Audrey or Joyce would follow you out to Canada, did you?" I asked.

"No, I couldn't count on ever seeing them again. I checked every busload of kids landing at the school, hoping to see them again. But at the same time, I also hoped that somehow they got away. Nevertheless, it was a happy day for me when Audrey arrived. But then I felt guilty because I was being selfish, and I knew it wasn't the best day for her." Mum picked up a rock and tossed it into the North Sea. "Thinking of my family just drove me crazy, so by chopping that part away, I could survive. What I didn't realize at first was how much I actually lost. Really, I lost so much. I lost my stories. You lose part of who you are when you lose your stories. I didn't like the story I was given at the farm school. I fought it, and they labelled me as rebellious and uncooperative. Imagine that! You get a new identity crammed down your throat, and when you resist and fight back you get called names and are treated like you are the problem."

"Children don't have the experience to separate themselves from that type of abuse." I suggested, "They internalize that they are a problem, that they are bad, and they have no other stick to measure themselves by, especially on your isolated farm."

"Oh, we couldn't fight back. Our voices had no power. We had no power. We were taught early on that if we complained it could get a lot worse. And believe me, they used sticks and straps to hit us, and they made certain we knew to follow their rules."

"I guess that was important to instil in you right away. After all, the children outnumbered the adults. Control of you children would have been a high priority. A child who feels powerless is less likely to fight back. Children who fear those who have power over them fight back in other ways, which is probably why the bully system was so firmly entrenched in institutions like the Prince of Wales Fairbridge Farm School."

"Bullies, yes. The boys could be mean to each other. Some of the older boys from the first group were the biggest bullies. They were a-holes, and they thought they were King Shit. Everything had to be done around them. They were pushy, and for some reason they were favoured."

"I guess Kenny didn't avoid being bullied," I said.

"No, he couldn't avoid it. I know that for a fact." Mum tossed another rock into the sea. I sensed she was hoping I would let this go, toss it away like her rock, leave her be, and find something else to write about, to worry about.

"I wish I had been able to spend more time with my mother as an adult. I wish I'd had a chance to tell her that I mostly forgive her and that I understand better now. I still have a feeling, though, that she didn't fight hard enough for us. But maybe she had little choice. Maybe she didn't just toss us aside."

"I don't think she did. Remember the letter we were given that stated that it was to your mother's 'eternal distress'[3] that she had lost her children to Canada. I am quite sure she never got over losing you." We continued to walk down the beach, lost in our own thoughts for a moment.

"By the time I was out on my own, and then married with you children, my past was firmly set behind me. By the time I was in my midthirties, it was just a dim memory. That is why when you started asking me about my English family, I couldn't really answer. What I had lost was still too painful to look at. I didn't know how to tell you this. You were such an angry child, and I suspected you were looking for answers, for good stories about where I came from, and I had none to give."

"I hadn't thought of it that way. I probably was looking for good stories. Perhaps hoping for a surprise, something showing that we weren't such an isolated family all alone in the world. I needed an anchor, some roots, and I didn't have any." I wondered how to tell my own mother that I was sorry or that I forgave her before it was too late. Forgave her for what, though? She had hung on to us. She had never tossed us away. Perhaps I should ask her to forgive me for being such a difficult daughter.

"You had me. Wasn't I anchor enough?"

"But I didn't realize that. And so, no, it wasn't enough back then."

"Is it enough now?"

"Yes, I believe it is."

"Coming back here to where you were born completes the circle, at least for me," I mused. "Imagine, you played on this beach as a little girl. You searched for treasure and for periwinkles. This was your home. This is what they took from you. I have heard it said that the first few years of a child's life are the most formative. Perhaps your strength came from your time here, growing up in these beautiful surroundings. It sounds like you had a lot of freedom."

"We did. There were days when we felt free as the birds. I wonder what my life would have been like if I'd stayed here, with my family. If I grew up in England, where would I be now?" Mum looked out to sea. The wind blew through her hair.

"Well, we wouldn't be standing here together. I would not have been born. And I guess I wouldn't have spent the last several years researching your past and the ins and outs of British child migration."

"No, I guess not. But it makes me wonder, you know, to look back and see how it all could have been so different." Mum looked at her sister Joyce, who was walking ahead, lost in her own thoughts. "I missed Joyce for years and years. I would have liked to have had my family around me."

"Life can take so many turns. Some we take, some are taken for us, and some are taken from us. I think it's easier to go with the flow, but that's not always the path that gives us what we want or need."

My sister, Joan, and our mother's youngest brother, David, and his wife, Marion, walked ahead of Joyce. This visit to Whitley Bay was a family adventure. David was the last of Winifred's children, Marjorie's youngest brother. He was born near London in 1943, six years after my mother was sent away. It was a blow to her when she first learned of her brother Richard's birth in 1939, then of David's birth, but those were the days when she buried everything, so she had no real emotional investment in either of them. She didn't meet David until 1986; they were both nervous about the initial meeting, but it was love at first sight. There was an instant bond with her brother, and getting to know the members of our English family has enriched our lives.

"What do you think, Aunt Joyce?" I asked as we caught up with her.

"Think?" Joyce turned to me.

"About being here?" I said. "Being back in Whitley Bay."

"Well, I never thought I'd see the day when I would be back standing on the sands at Whitley Bay with Marjorie. It was seventy-odd years ago that we played on this beach and ran through those streets."

"So much has changed, but so much has stayed the same." Mum looked out to sea, then along the beach. Her eyes stopped on the light-house — St. Mary's Lighthouse. "We weren't allowed to go past St. Mary's Lighthouse, but we ended up going so much farther. We were so far from Whitley Bay."

"I was so mad at you for leaving me at Middlemore. My heart nearly broke when I heard you and Kenny were gone. They didn't tell me you were going. I watched you go down the path, and we waved to each other, remember? And you didn't come back that night. You and Kenny just vanished." Joyce stared out to sea, her eyes moist at the edges.

"They didn't let me say goodbye. I didn't know I wasn't coming back. I thought we were going on a day trip somewhere." Mum looked at her sister.

"Well, we are here together now." Joyce smiled. She grabbed her scarf as the wind whipped around her.

"They say you can't go back, but we have, haven't we, Joyce? And we have found something to take back with us. Memories to always keep with us, and no one can take them away," said Mum.

"Yes, our shared memories can keep us close to each other even when we live so far apart." Joyce looked out to sea.

"I was so mad at you for getting to stay," Mum said so softly that I didn't think Joyce could hear her.

A pair of seagulls swooped by, their raucous calls, not to be ignored, forced a change in the conversation.

"Look. They're still nesting up on those cliffs." Joyce laughed. "We tried to get their eggs, but the cliff was too steep."

"Are those the cliffs that Uncle Kenny fell from?" I asked.

"No," both sisters answered and both pointed south. "It was those rocks just past the walkway there." Marjorie and Joyce laughed at each other.

"There was a lot of blood. I remember that," Mum said.

"Yes, and our mum nearly had a fit when you brought Kenny home. She blamed me, and I wasn't even there." Joyce laughed at the memory as she watched the waves touch the toes of her shoes.

The sisters stood for a moment, watching the waves.

Joyce turned away from her sister. "Look, you can see the Spanish City Dome from here. It's a shame that they're tearing it down. It was the life of the town." Joyce pointed north up the beach. "Shall we drive up to the lighthouse tomorrow?"

"I hated you for staying because I missed you so much and I needed you." Mum didn't turn or answer Joyce. She continued to stare at the waves, absorbed in this past hurt that she carried for so long.

"I needed you more," Joyce said simply.

"After a while I stopped needing you. I had to forget. I forgot until you came over for a visit in 1977. Can you forgive me for forgetting you?" Mum grabbed at Joyce's sleeve.

"I hadn't seen you for forty years. It was a lifetime."

I stood back, listening quietly, making mental notes.

"It was hard for me. In the end, I was left all alone in the Middlemore Emigration Home. I had no one. You had Bunny and Kenny. I hated that. It hurt so much that I had to forget about being left behind." Joyce looked at me and said, "I lost everyone."

"Funny, huh? And I was so mad about you staying." Mum looked at her sister.

"Sometimes I get so damn mad when I think how they broke up this family. We all lost so much. Our roots were severed. Brothers and sisters were torn apart. I was denied my grandparents, aunts, uncles, and cousins," I said angrily. I grew up with a mother who didn't understand why she was sent away. It made me angry but mostly scared because I, too, could not understand.

The two sisters walked on, ignoring my outburst. Mum always avoided conflict. Her childhood anger at the betrayal she felt from her family and her country had quickly turned to fear as she traversed first through the Middlemore Emigration Home and then the Prince of Wales Fairbridge Farm School. She had carried that fear all her life. I quickly realized that it was not fair for me to drag up those emotions now. The two sisters, separated for so long, had found a bit of peace and comfort in each other's company while travelling down memory lane, back to their once carefree childhood.

But I am angry, and I am no longer afraid.

"Oh, I wish Kenny was with us today. I have always missed him." Joyce sighed.

"When Bunny arrived they put her in my cottage. Kenny had no one at Fairbridge. He was one of the younger boys, and I know many were picked on." Mum looked at Joyce. "I wish he was here with us, too."

"He died so young, just like Jean."

"I think he is here in spirit with us. And we are back now. Together." Mum touched Joyce's back, softly, hesitantly, unsure of herself.

"Yes, we are. I dreamed about coming to Canada to be with you. I had no home. I was going to save up my money, but the time went by and it never amounted to enough." Joyce turned away. "We have to make the best of things, don't we?"

"Oh, Joyce, you are right. And what do we really have but the here and now! I can hardly find the words to describe how it feels to be here. I never thought I'd be here again. I think it's a dream that I'm standing on the sands at Whitley Bay. I don't remember a lot about living here as a kid, but I never forgot the sands."

The two sisters stood still, watching the waves crash onto the sand.

"Ouch!" Mum jumped. "What did you pinch me for?"

"To show you that you're not dreaming!" Joyce laughed.

The sisters linked arms as they continued their walk. This simple gesture was so foreign to them. Physical and emotional distance had kept them from this basic intimacy of sisterhood. As they walked arm in arm up the beach, I heard the sisters softly singing "Red Sails in the Sunset."

The next tide would wash away their footsteps, but nothing could wash this away, not from them, and not from me.

Full Circle
Here we stand
Heart in hand
Arm in arm, and
Cry — Oh, the Whitley Bay sand.

Seventy long years
All kinds of tears
And the toil it took
To get back to this nook.

Here we stand
Tears in our eyes, as
We peer over the land
Oh — our Whitley Bay sand.

Seventy long years if a day
Innocent issue at play
Searching this land
For treasure in the sand.

Now — full circle at last
Searching for our past
Our lives not so bleak
New treasure we seek.

Here we stand
Hand in hand.
And survey the land
Of our Whitley Bay sand.

Afterword (Afterward):

PEACE IN MARJORIE'S SENIOR YEARS

The child migration scheme is now universally recognised as having been fundamentally flawed with tragic consequences. Indeed, Barnardos Australia stated 'We have no hesitation in saying that it was a shameful practice, that it was barbaric, and that it was completely against any practices that we would currently uphold'; and the NCH [National Children's Home] 'is firmly of the view that child migration was a major mistake and we now deeply regret having taken part in it'. Many of the sending and receiving agencies now recognise that the effects of the Scheme were profoundly damaging to many of the children involved and that they now share a continuing moral responsibility to the well-being of the former migrant children affected by their experience in the agencies' care.

— Inquiry into child migration, Parliament of Australia, 2001

Today, when I look at photographs of my mother, Marjorie, smiling, I try to imagine what the long road to that smile was really like. Over the past few years, I have attempted to travel back in time, often with her by my side, searching for pieces of her in an effort to re-create her lost childhood, her 1937 journey as a British child migrant, and the five years she spent at the Prince of Wales Fairbridge Farm School. I needed to know what British child migration was all about, why it happened, and especially why it happened to my family. I needed to ensure that our family's stories would no longer be broken by the vast expanse of the Atlantic Ocean. I needed to make peace with my mother's past so that our family's future stories would be more complete and no longer severed.

It was sometime in 1999 that I started pestering my mother in earnest for information. The wall of silence that I found as a child was too great for me to penetrate. I gave up for years, and then I just needed to know. It didn't take me long to realize that my mother wasn't hiding her past from me — she had lost it, burying it so deep that she could no longer find her own way back.

Marjorie kept in touch with her family, but she was never able to talk with them about the circumstances around her being sent to Canada. She found out that her English siblings knew nothing as well, as her parents had refused to talk about how three of their eleven children were sent to Canada.

We had little information, so I had to get out and find what I could. When I started I had only two photographs — one of my mother and her brother arriving at the farm school in the Cowichan Valley on September 22, 1937, and one of her sister Joyce, taken while she was at the Birmingham Middlemore Emigration Home after Marjorie was sent to Canada.[1] I had no documentation about my mother's 1937 journey to Canada or of her five years at the farm school; however, I had a small handful of her memories from the time when she was with her family in Whitley Bay: playing on the sands, St. Mary's Lighthouse, and the strongest memory and the one my mother mentioned the most often, of her swinging on a rusty gate and yelling to her mother for a "ha'penny" on her tenth birthday.

My mother could not recall when she was removed from her family in Whitley Bay or how long she stayed first in Newcastle, then Birmingham, where the Middlemore Emigration Home was located, before heading to the Fairbridge Hostel, Creagh House, in Kensington, London, then up to Liverpool and finally across the Atlantic on the *Duchess of Atholl* on her way to Canada. For me these were just names, and as such, they held little meaning.

I didn't know where to start, so I started at the beginning: Whitley Bay. Marjorie Arnison's birth certificate showed that she was born in Whitley Bay, just east of Newcastle, in the Tyneside area of northern England, on September 21, 1926. I found out that she was the fifth child of Thomas Frederick and Winifred Arnison. I read that this area of England had experienced years of crippling unemployment. Sometime in the summer of 1933, Marjorie's father left Whitley Bay to look for work in London, unaware that Winifred was pregnant with their ninth child. Baby Lawrence was born in February 1934.

Winifred and her nine children received little money from her husband and not much in the way of social support. The two older boys, Norman and Fred, did what they could to help out, but they took it a step too far in the fall of 1935, when they broke into a home. The boys were caught, and Fred was sent to a borstal, a boys' juvenile detention home, and Norman was sent to the Castle Howard Reformatory in York. I have been unable to find any records of Fred's incarceration, but the records show that Norman was at the reformatory for three years.

Many reformatories in England at that time had the authority to transport children in their care to the colonies, but many first taught their inmates skills that they would need, mainly farming. Norman told me that he was taught farming at Castle Howard. However, I can find no record of boys being sent to the colonies from this particular reformatory. If they had, Norman might have been lost to the family for years after, if not forever.

By early 1937, the family had not seen Thomas for almost four years, and with her two older boys gone, Winifred and her children — Phyllis, Joyce, Marjorie, Kenny, Audrey, Jean, and baby Lawrence — were having a difficult time living on the money Thomas was sending. The Fairbridge Society was actively recruiting for children in the Tyneside area and had approached the local schools and sent home handbills, searching out children who would be bright enough to pass the Canadian immigration officials' stringent regulations.[2] I believe that their school attendance officer flagged the Arnison children as potential candidates for immigration with the Fairbridge Society.

I did not have the actual date when the children were removed, so I started by contacting the Whitley Bay School District. Much to my delight, the school district's archive had records of the Arnison children, and this included addresses and dates of where the family lived and, most importantly, I could see where Marjorie's school records ended. I began to get a clearer picture of what it must have been like for my grandmother, as I located fourteen different addresses that the family lived at in Whitley Bay between the years 1923, when their third child, Norman, was born, and 1937, when Marjorie and her siblings were removed.

The eldest, Fred, was born in Gourock, Scotland, and their second child, Phyllis, was born in Alston in northern England about sixty miles west of Whitley Bay. The next seven children were born in Whitley Bay, and the last two sons were born in the London area.

Next I contacted the University of Liverpool Library, Special Collections and Archives Department, as that is where the Fairbridge Archive from the London Fairbridge Society (today the Fairbridge Society is amalgamated with The Prince's Trust) is currently held. One thing led to the next, and in time I located many bits and pieces, including important dates in Marjorie's young life. I continued my search in Birmingham; the Library and Archives Canada in Ottawa, Ontario; the B.C. Archives in Victoria, British Columbia; the Cowichan Valley Museum and Archives in Duncan, British Columbia; the UBC Archives in Vancouver, British Columbia; and finally the Vernon and District Museum and Archives in the interior of British Columbia. The pieces to the puzzle of Marjorie's early childhood were starting to fill in.

By a stroke of luck, I also got in contact with local Whitley Bay resident and historian Morag Horseman, who told me to send her the addresses I had been given by the school district, and she would take photographs of the Whitley Bay homes and email them to me. I forwarded her all the addresses, and I had an immediate response. She said that I would not believe this, but she was living in the house right next door to one of the houses my mother and her family lived in in 1936. Seeing where my mother lived, and having a photograph of the last flat that my mother lived in with her family on Whitley Road in 1937, gave me hope that I could bring back some of my mother's childhood. Morag's photographs made me determined to one day take my mother back to Whitley Bay.

I shared each little finding with my mother, including the photos of her former homes in Whitley Bay. Every little bit that I found contributed to drawing out more of her memories. I told myself that I would stop if this process distressed her, but in my heart I knew that I would not, as it wasn't just her past that I was finding, *it was mine, too.* I had hoped for a positive outcome, of course, but I tried to prepare myself for the possibility that she might shut down and continue to keep her past hidden. However, after I shared the findings from Whitley Bay and showed her the Fairbridge file sent from the University of Liverpool Library Archives and her Middlemore file from the Birmingham Archives, my mother said to me with a smile, "Well, they didn't just throw me away, then; they kept records of me." I took this as a sign that I could continue this research with her blessing.

As mentioned earlier, the Fairbridge Society actively recruited children from the Newcastle Tyneside area. "The Commissioner for Special Areas saw in the Fairbridge Society a means of saving some, at least, of the children [of the Tyneside], where there is relentless squalor, where there is relentless injury to body and soul.... A friend came forward with a sum of money in her hand. 'It is obvious,' she said, 'that the children on the Tyneside must be shewn the way to Fairbridge.'"[3]

Marjorie's father, Thomas, was contacted while he was working in London and asked for his permission to take four of his children for the Fairbridge Farm School scheme. Thomas responded, saying he was agreeable to what they proposed as long as his wife and children were willing. Thomas was the head of the household, so that was all the consent required. It did not matter that his wife was not willing and that his children did not want to go.[4]

In February 1937 four Arnison children — Joyce, age twelve; Marjorie, age ten; Kenny, age eight; and Audrey, age seven — were removed from their mother's care. Their older sister Phyllis recalled helping her mother put the four children on the Whitley Bay train bound for Newcastle. The children were told to get off at Newcastle's Central Station and wait under the main clock. Someone would meet them there. They were in Newcastle for a brief period, perhaps only one or two nights, before being taken to the Middlemore Emigration Home in Birmingham. At the home they were prepped for emigration and groomed to pass the medical and mental testing given by Canadian officials before their approval to sail to Canada could be granted.

In September 1937 Marjorie and her younger brother Kenny were sent to Canada. Audrey (a.k.a. Bunny) did not go at that time because she was quarantined in the home's sick bay. Joyce also stayed at the home for reasons unknown at that time. In early 1995, I wrote to Aunt Joyce, asking her to tell me anything that she would be willing to share from her Middlemore years. Joyce wrote a letter back to me on February 13, 1995: "The last time I saw Ken [and] your mum ... I was looking out the window seeing them go down the garden path with all the other children off to Canada, but at the time I did not know where they were going, that was the last time I saw them. I was ill in Sick Bay a long time, they said I was ill with a broken heart, because they had taken them away and left me." Eight-year-old Audrey was sent over to Canada in August 1938.

In 2006 we accessed Joyce's Middlemore Emigration Home file. Her papers show that she was not sent with Marjorie and Kenny because the records listed her as being thirteen and not twelve years old when she arrived at the Middlemore Emigration Home; thus she was considered too old for the Fairbridge Farm School program. It took another year before the Middlemore Home discovered the mistake. By that time Joyce was well into her thirteenth year and definitely too old for the program, so they kept her at the home to work in the kitchen until she was sixteen. Was she the lucky one to have stayed in England? Or had the four siblings sent to Middlemore become a little family, and did Joyce lose her sense of family all over again when her siblings were torn from her a second and then a third time?

Part of the selection process entailed a rigid screening by Canadian officials based at Canada House, Trafalgar Square, in London. This team travelled to the Middlemore Emigration Home to test prospective children. Of the first 170 to 175 children brought together for the 1935 opening of the Prince of Wales Fairbridge Farm School, Canadian officials rejected 75 percent.[5] This was a blow to the Fairbridge Society and caused tension between the society and the Canadian officials. The firm restrictions placed by the Canadian Immigration Department may have been the reason why few orphans were sent to the Prince of Wales Fairbridge Farm School on Vancouver Island, British Columbia, and instead, children were recruited from families, as 95 percent of the 329 children sent to this farm school were not orphans.

As mentioned earlier, this last wave of British child migration to Canada was allowed after the 1929 ban on bringing in unaccompanied children under the age of fourteen in part because the Fairbridge Society promised the Canadian government that they would be responsible for the children they brought into Canada until they reached twenty-one years of age. When Fairbridge children reached the age of sixteen, they were usually placed out to work on local B.C. farms for the boys and in homes in Victoria and Vancouver for the girls. The job placements were organized by the Fairbridge Farm School. The children placed to work from the age of sixteen to twenty-one had half their wages taken from them and kept by the Fairbridge Society. The children were told that this would give them a nest egg to start their independent lives. However, I have only heard of one person who had her money returned; many never saw a penny of their savings, including Marjorie.

In September 1942 Marjorie was first placed temporarily in a home in Victoria where another Fairbridge girl worked until a full-time placement could be found for her. On November 1 she was placed to work in a lovely home looking after an elderly woman who was confined to a wheelchair. The shock at finding herself so alone and untrained in this field of care was overwhelming for Marjorie, and she reached out to her after-care worker, Mrs. Williams, to find her another placement. Mrs. Williams was one of the few good people who treated Marjorie well during her years at Fairbridge, and so she was able to find the courage to ask for a change rather than make both her life and her employer's miserable.

It took until March 1, 1943, for another placement to be found for Marjorie with the Wheaton family in Victoria. The young family had a son, and a daughter soon arrived. Marjorie quickly settled in and made herself at home. She worked for the family for the next two years and then continued to live with them for two more years while she worked at Spencer's Department Store in downtown Victoria. When I asked my mother what it was like being placed with the Wheaton family, she replied, "They were a lifesaver." For the first time since leaving Whitley Bay, she was with a real family. Although they weren't related, she felt that she was an important member of this family. And as she found at Fintry Farm in the summer of 1940, life was so much easier when she felt appreciated and accepted as she was. She no longer had to worry about horrid cottage mothers with their sharp tongues and quick slaps or about unwanted advances from the wretched men hired at the Fairbridge Farm School. She did constantly worry about her sister Bunny, though, and Kenny, too, but there was little she could do for them. She told me she worked hard for the Wheaton family, but her work was valued and she was safe. They were very kind to her. We have remained in touch with this family.

In the spring of 1947 Marjorie moved to Vancouver with a group of Fairbridge girls. She would turn twenty-one in a few months, and it was time to seek her independence.

Marjorie and Clifford, circa 1948.

Marjorie married Clifford Scott Skidmore from Truro, Nova Scotia, on May 22, 1948. She met him while she was working and living with the Wheaton family in Victoria. Like many girls in Victoria at the time, Marjorie had set her sights on one of the handsome navy boys who came into town from the local naval base in Esquimalt.

Their marriage lasted only a few years. It was a troubled one, as my father was suffering from a mental illness that was not fully diagnosed until his files were reviewed in 2000, when it was determined that he'd had post-traumatic stress disorder as a result of his experiences during the war. But this disorder was not named until the 1980s, and so he was sent to Riverview/Essondale, a mental institution in Coquitlam, just outside of Vancouver, British Columbia. He was in and out of care throughout the early 1950s and received shock therapy and other treatments that did not give him any relief.

The next procedure the doctors suggested was a lobotomy, which was popular if controversial at that time and has since fallen into disrepute and is no longer performed. My mother's signature was required for the operation; she was reluctant, but the doctors and my father pressured her until she relented.

Cliff was never the same afterward, and he immediately began to suffer from debilitating headaches. In the fall of 1957 he ran away from Riverview, crossed the nearby Lougheed Highway, and hopped on a train. He got off in Calgary, Alberta, and started to look for a job but was unsuccessful. He was soon picked up and put in an institution there. He escaped and found his way to the nearby Bow River. His suicide note simply stated: "I cannot take the headaches any longer. Kiss the baby's head for me."

That was on November 5, 1957. The "baby" was just three weeks old. Marjorie and Cliff had five children under the age of eight. Cliff's parents lived near Montreal, too far away to help out, so Marjorie was faced with raising five young children on her own. Being raised in an institution did not leave Marjorie with any positive parenting skills. Her four years as a teenager working and living with the Wheaton family in Victoria likely saved her, as it gave her some experience and insight into how to raise children, how to be a parent, and how to be a family. The Wheaton family were always there for support if our family needed them. It was not easy for Marjorie, of that I am certain, but she kept our family together, telling us often, "We may not have much, but we have each other."

Cliff was buried in Calgary in the veterans' section of the Burnsland Cemetery. We don't know who identified him or if anyone attended his burial. How alone he must have been. Eight years later, in 1965, when my older brother turned sixteen and had a licence and a car, he took our mother to Calgary to see where her beloved Cliff was buried. It was 1986 before I stood by his grave for the first time.

Kenny turned sixteen in the fall of 1944 and was placed out to work on a farm outside of Victoria. Disillusioned with farming life, and enamoured by the stories of adventure on the high seas during the Second World War, he ran away within two weeks of being placed on the farm, lied about his age, and joined the merchant navy. His older "English" brother, Norman, also enamoured with life at sea, had joined the DEMS, or Defensibly Equipped Merchant Ship. DEMS was a division of the Royal Navy. Norman was trained to man the machine guns on the merchant ships.

Kenny located his sister Marjorie, told her that he had run away from the farm and joined the merchant navy, and swore her to secrecy. He didn't want her worrying about him if anyone from Fairbridge came looking for him. He gave the name of the ship he was on and when he was leaving port. Marjorie sent a letter to their mother in England and told her what Kenny had done, so she, too, would know that he was okay. Winifred must have been able to get word to her son Norman that his younger brother Kenny was on a merchant navy ship, along with the name of the vessel and the few details she had. It seems to me that it was an amazing feat of communication for the times, considering letters or even telegrams were not that easy to send during the war.

At some point in 1945, a few months before the war ended, Norman's ship pulled into an Australian harbour. It was crowded, and their ship had to tie alongside another ship. Once the ship was secure and permission was granted, Norman began to ready himself to go ashore. As he asked permission to cross the ship they were tied to, the name of the vessel, which was flying a Canadian flag, caught his attention. Well, it couldn't be, but it was! This was the ship that his younger, "Canadian" brother Kenny was supposed to be on. Norman, now twenty-two, hadn't seen

Marjorie and Patricia Skidmore at Clifford Skidmore's grave in Calgary, 2014.

Ogden Hostel.
Calgary
Sat. Nov 2 1957

Dear Marge
Hi honey Ive been busy trying to get a job here in Calgary as your probally well aware. I just had a little thought I heard that the baby had an accident. Hope its not true. Marge I dont know how you feel. But I do love you
Love Cliff

The last letter, besides the suicide note, that Marjorie received from Cliff.

his sixteen-year-old brother for almost ten years. What were the chances that he might actually be on the ship they had just tied up to? Would he still be on board? What if he was transferred? Or gone home on leave? Excitedly, Norman asked for permission to go aboard, and he quickly made enquiries as to whether there was a Kenny Arnison with the crew.

There was! Both brothers were granted shore leave, and they spent the next several hours catching up on each other's lives. They ended up sobering up in a jail cell for the night, but they were no worse for wear! Norman told me that he always wondered about the odds of that happening and was thankful for the chance to have spent a memorable evening in an Aussie pub with his younger brother.

Kenny's love of boats stayed with him throughout his life. He worked toward and finally obtained his sea captain's licence and spent his working life on the tugboats on the B.C. coast. Kenny married and had five children, one of whom was adopted. In 1975, Captain Kenneth Arnison, S.C., and

Arnison brothers Kenny, left, and Norman, right, met by chance in Australia, circa 1945.

three others were awarded the Star of Courage, a decoration for bravery in recognition for a heroic act, for towing a burning barge to a place of safety away from the other ships where it could be beached and the hulk abandoned to burn itself out.

During the 1970s Kenny fought a federal regulation that the maximum age that one could begin training to become a Fraser River pilot was fifty, "although once on the job, he could stay until the age of sixty-five, or even sixty-eight." He enlisted in the Canadian Human Rights Commission and fought against the Pacific Pilotage Authority's ruling. A decision was rendered in his favour on July 28, 1980. However, as one newspaper reported at the time, "after a seven-year struggle, Arnison has been told there is no vacancy at the Pacific Pilotage Authority."[6]

Kenny never realized his dream of becoming a Fraser River pilot. He was on his tugboat at the bottom end of the Sechelt Inlet when he suffered a fatal heart attack. He was just fifty-four. It was April 9, 1983, his big brother Norman's sixtieth birthday.

Audrey (a.k.a. Bunny) left the farm school in early 1946. She had to endure four years there without her sister Marjorie. Audrey's available Fairbridge Farm School records show that she had at least eight different cottage mothers between 1938 and 1946 and was placed in four different cottages during her eight years at this institution. These records are incomplete, so there may have been other cottages and cottage mothers.

Audrey was placed out to work as a domestic servant in Victoria in the summer of 1946. Previously her half-yearly progress reports at the farm school had noted that she was too dependent on her sister Marjorie; however, when she was placed out as a domestic servant, her March 1946 half-yearly progress report stated, "Her older sister should have a good influence on her." When Audrey was sent to Victoria, Marjorie had been working there for almost four years. In the spring of 1947, Marjorie moved to Vancouver with two other Fairbridge girls, so she was not in Victoria to have a good influence on her younger sister.

Audrey married a Fairbridge boy, Robert Duncan, in the fall of 1947. She was not yet eighteen. Once Fairbridge girls married, they appeared to be no longer under the guardianship of the Fairbridge Society; thus Audrey attained her "freedom" before the age of twenty-one through marriage. The couple did, however, need the Fairbridge Society's permission to marry as they were both under the age of twenty-one.

Audrey and Robert had five children, and Robert passed away in 1976. Audrey remarried in 1992 to a second Fairbridge boy, Eric Lewis, who passed away in 2012. When her big sister Marjorie was nearing the end of her life in January 2017, Audrey's childhood stresses began to surface. The sisters had remained close during their adult lives, even though they lived miles apart. Their bond became stronger after losing their brother, Kenny, in the 1980s, and even though they came from a large family, they saw each other as their only real source of "family" support. She told me that she was left alone at the Middlemore Emigration Home as well as the Fairbridge Farm School when Marjorie was sent away to work, and now she was left alone again. Her children and grandchildren and Marjorie's family rallied around her, but she found it difficult to face the memories and anxiety of a childhood racked with loss and separation.

Joyce was left behind at the Middlemore Emigration Home in Birmingham due to an incorrect birthdate. The birthdates noted on Joyce, Marjorie, and Kenny's Fairbridge Farm School immigration forms listed them as a year older than they were, causing all sorts of grief throughout the years because the children did not come to Canada with birth certificates. It was very difficult for Joyce to be left behind *yet again* when Audrey was sent to Canada in August 1938. Joyce ran away a few times, and each time when she reached the train station near Selly Oaks in Birmingham with no money and not a clue where to go, she just sat on the bench and cried until someone from the home was contacted to come and get her. Joyce remained in the care of the home until she turned sixteen, and in the winter of 1940, she was sent back to her mother. Unfortunately, there was no room for Joyce, so she found a job working for a family, looking after their children.

Joyce married her husband, Dennis, in 1952. Den passed away in 1976, and Joyce's only son, Raymond, passed away in 2001. Joyce has made a number of trips to Canada, beginning in 1977. And during our many visits to London since 2001, we have had some memorable times with Joyce, including a 2001 trip back to Birmingham to see the Middlemore Emigration Home (demolished circa 2005), a trip back to Whitley Bay in 2007, many visits around London, and two trips to Scotland. It was rewarding for Marjorie to develop strong family relationships with some of her siblings in her senior years, and most especially with her sister Joyce, whom she missed so terribly when she was sent to Canada.

Marjorie's mother, Winifred Arnison, moved to the London area shortly after the four children were taken from her care. During the war she was evacuated out of the city to a home in the country east of London. She had her twelfth and final child in May 1943 at the age of forty-three. After the war the family regrouped, and because the two older sons, Frederick and Norman, had been in service, they were eligible for a council house. The parents, Winifred and Thomas, lived in that house until they passed away, Winifred in 1972 and Thomas in 1977. Winifred made a trip to Canada in 1969 on her own. It was Marjorie's first time seeing her mother since waving goodbye at the Whitley Bay train station in early February 1937, but it was not a very satisfactory visit as Marjorie wanted answers and her mother could not give any.

Today the Child Migrants Trust recognizes this as a barrier when reuniting families affected by child migration, and they help to bridge the gap for former child migrants and their families before they meet. Unfortunately, this was not available to our family in 1969. The removal of children from their families for British child migration had a tremendous effect throughout the generations, as is so evident in our family. So many, like my grandparents, went to their graves without any resolution or real understanding of why their family had been torn apart.

Marjorie's father, Thomas Arnison, made a trip to Canada in 1972. I believe that he alone carried the blame for the children being sent to Canada. Marjorie's visit with her father was also unsuccessful. She said to me in August 2014, "I didn't get along with either of them. I didn't try. My mother gave me the brooch she was wearing. I don't know why; perhaps it was to make me feel better. I gave it away to your sister right away. I didn't want it. Why would I?"

I told my mother, "I was there in 1986 when you met your youngest brother, David, for the first time, then again in 2011 when you met your brother Richard for the first time. To me it looked like there was an instant bond on both occasions. But this didn't appear to be the case when you saw your parents." I wasn't certain why my mother didn't feel an attachment to her parents. I met my grandmother in 1969 but did not make the effort to meet my grandfather when he came to Canada in 1972. I found it interesting that my mother basically rejected her parents but bonded immediately with brothers who were born after she was sent to Canada and whom she had never met. Perhaps her anger at her parents ran too deep.

"It wasn't my brothers' fault, was it? I guess I had a chip on my shoulder, and I resented my parents. I just couldn't feel close to either of them. I guess I still carried a grudge. I didn't know the circumstances then, like I do now. I didn't realize that my mother missed me as much as I missed her. How could I know?"

"I suppose your rejection of your mother during her 1969 visit reopened her wounds. Likely for you and your mother, you both carried wounds that you both had been trying to heal since 1937. She was unable to talk about the circumstances of the loss of her children to Canada just like you were unable to talk to me about the loss of your family."

This loss, and the removal and dispersal of our family, is an ongoing generational issue. I gave up asking as a teenager and left home at eighteen, and I carried my anger with me. I had minimal contact with my mother for the next eight years.

It wasn't until my first son was born in 1976 that I once again began to seek answers because I didn't know what to tell my children about their grandmother and why she was in Canada while her family was in England. I vividly recall my son's first illness. We were living on a small sailboat at the time, and I was so overwhelmed by lack of sleep and the demands of a sick baby that I worried about being able to cope with raising this child. It was then that I thought about my mother growing up without her parents and then being left to raise her five children on her own after my father's suicide. It hit me like a ton of bricks, as I always thought I was stronger than my mother, but here I was, undone by my baby's first illness. Who was this woman who kept her little family together against all odds? Social welfare swooped in after my father's death, but she fought like a mother bear to keep all five of her children. It was then that I realized that I had something that she did not, and I had so casually tossed it aside. I had *my mother*.

During Marjorie's first trip back to England in 2001, she was reunited with her older brother Fred (1919–2006), whom she hadn't seen since

1935; her older sister Phyllis (1920–2007), whom she had last seen in February 1937, when she and their mother put the four children on the train at Whitley Bay bound for Birmingham's Middlemore Emigration Home; her brother Norman (1923–2012), whom she had met once when he and his wife, Marion, made a trip to Canada in 1973; her sister Joyce, who had been out to Canada a number of times; and her younger brother Lawrence, whom she hadn't seen since February 1937. Lawrence has not been to Canada, but visits to Lawrence and his wife, Pam, were high on the priority list whenever Marjorie travelled to London.

During our 2010 visit to witness the British government's apology, Lawrence very gently took Marjorie's hand and said, "It didn't just affect you, Marjorie; it affected the whole family."

And there is Marjorie's youngest brother, David, who was born in 1943, six years after Marjorie was sent to Canada. David made his first trip to Canada in 1986. Joyce accompanied him, but he did not bring his family because he wanted to see if he was welcomed and accepted. For his big sister Marjorie's eulogy, he wrote: "I will always remember having this frightening thought on the plane going over [in 1986], what if Margie doesn't take to me? Suppose we don't get on. I can't turn back now. Well, when I met my sister at the airport for the very first time, she gave me the biggest smile and the biggest hug I had ever had. You could say we clicked right away. So the fear of meeting her for the first time vanished completely." The bond was instant and strong. Two years later he brought out his wife, Marion, and three daughters, Katie, Jennifer, and Julie.

During the formal February 2010 "Apology to All British Child Migrants," Prime Minister Gordon Brown made provisions for a Family Restoration Fund, which was to be administered by the Child Migrants Trust (CMT) to allow former child migrants sent to Canada, Australia, New Zealand, and Rhodesia (now Zimbabwe) to return to England to be reunited with their families. The CMT has helped many former migrants access their files from their sending agencies in order to locate their families, as so many had lost touch. Marjorie and her brother Richard accessed the fund, and a representative of the CMT met with Richard beforehand to answer his questions and to prepare him to meet his sister for the first time. Richard flew in from Cyprus, and Marjorie flew from Vancouver, and they met at Richard's daughter Jackie's home in Ashford, east of London. Richard made a trip to Canada the following summer. Sadly, he passed away in 2013, but getting to know him, even for a brief time, enriched all our lives.

A number of things came together to enable the Arnison family on either side of the Atlantic to feel a sense of family again. Even though the visit from Marjorie's mother was strained, it started a web that continued to be woven next by Marjorie's father in his attempt to find a way to right the wrongs of the past, and then by Marjorie's siblings, who needed to know how it came about that two sisters and a brother were sent to Canada as children. Their visits continued, and letters, exchanges of photographs, and sharing of family events on both sides served to strengthen the bond.

Marjorie maintained that she had no desire to go back to England, saying they did not want her, so why should she want them? (With this comment she meant both family *and* country.) But her siblings' persistence won her over, and her four adventures (2001, 2007, 2010, and 2011) to see her family and her country of birth were tremendously healing.

Attending the February 2010 apology was an important milestone, as she finally heard what she had been waiting to hear for so long — a formal recognition that it had been wrong to take her from her family and deport her, sending her thousands of miles away. With Britain's formal public apology, with Prime Minister Gordon Brown's hand in hers, and hearing him say directly to her, "I am truly sorry," Marjorie could finally shed the shame so firmly placed on her by her caregivers at the farm school when they called her a British guttersnipe and a worthless orphan and told her she was undeserving of their kindness and caring. Marjorie carried this dishonour with her for over seventy-three years. Finally, she could hold her head high with the knowledge that she was strong, she was a survivor, she was special, and she was right.

I had such a difficult time loving her throughout my younger years. She would not let me in, not let me be close, and would not share her stories, so I pushed her away, like I thought she was pushing me away. And that is precisely what she thought her mother, family, and country had done to her. We broke this cycle by finally talking and then writing about her life. It was better late than never.

The Final Word

Marjorie passed away on January 18, 2017. She had celebrated her nineti-eth birthday the previous September. Her birthday was a grand affair, with many little celebrations over several days leading up to the actual day. She fared well and loved all the attention from her family and friends. However, in the few months leading up to her death, her family felt helpless as we watched her health decline at a rapid pace. She lived in her own home until she was eighty-eight, and then she moved into a basement suite in her daughter Joan's home and lived there relatively independently. During the last few months it was obvious that she needed more care than any one person could give her. A couple of options were discussed — getting in-home care to give Joan a break and putting her in a seniors' assisted-living residence.

Marjorie became agitated whenever a seniors' home was discussed, so the subject was usually dropped, but it was brought up again during those moments when respiratory distress took her breath away, indicating that professional care would be a better option.

At times Marjorie would reply, "I looked after you, now it is your turn to look after me." She was unable to see the strain that her failing health was putting on her daughter. At one point, when the subject of a home was brought up again, Marjorie cried out, the desperation clear in her voice, "If you put me in a home, I will jump off a bridge."

Her beloved Cliff had jumped off a bridge, and the devastation of his loss reverberates to this day. I believe that my mother wanted to ensure that her children knew what going into a home would do to her. "Don't," she pleaded, the fear in her eyes as clear as her mind. "It will be like going back to Fairbridge. I cannot end my days in Canada like I started them."

Marjorie did not go into assisted living. Once we fully understood that her fear stemmed from finding herself back in an institution, we vowed to keep her at home. We did not want to bring back the stressful memories of her incarceration in the farm school, which had turned her life into an unacceptable mess.

Acknowledgements

I would like to acknowledge the following for their support, kind words, and contributions to this book.

My mother, Marjorie (née Arnison) Skidmore, whose steadfastness and quiet strength should have been bottled and passed around. She had enough for an entire community.

To my uncle Kenny, whose stories were carried by his sister for nearly a lifetime before she shared them, and to my aunt Bunny (a.k.a. Audrey) and her husband, Eric Lewis, for sharing their stories.

To my sister, Joan, and my brothers Frederic and Rick, whom I corner to share my growing knowledge of child migration, especially as it pertains to our family, whether they want to hear it or not. And to my brother Lloyd, who was lost in Okanagan Lake in 2007 and never found. When I see the photograph of my thirteen-year-old mother fishing off the Fintry packing-house pier in Okanagan Lake in 1940, I feel they are connected somehow, which indeed they are now as some of Marjorie's ashes were scattered on the lake on August 2, 2017, the ten-year anniversary of the loss of my brother.

To Gordon Brown, former prime minister of Britain, for taking the time out of his busy schedule to provide a foreword for my book. It is so very greatly appreciated. Witnessing his 2010 "Apology to All British Child Migrants" allowed not for closure but for a new beginning and, with his backing, a platform to speak from; our voices are no longer silenced.

To Margaret Humphreys, Ian Thwaite, and the Child Migrants Trust; their work has changed my family's world in so many ways.

242 Her War Years

To Rex Weyler for his ongoing support and important words for the back of this book.

To Sally Campbell for her support and encouragement.

To Judith Rassenti for her support and wise words.

To the members of the former Prince of Wales Fairbridge Farm School. They are too numerous for me to acknowledge them all, but I would like to thank the many who shared their experiences and their friendship and contributed to my knowledge and understanding of this unique place and period in Canadian and British history.

To Sheila, Barbara, and Susan for the use of their dining-room table to work on my manuscript.

To the libraries and archives that are such a rich source of information. Most especially to the University of Liverpool Library and Special Collections, where the Fairbridge Archive is located. The support from the staff there has enabled me to unravel many important points of my mother's story. I thank them for their assistance and patience.

To the best professor ever, Christine St. Peter; among many other things, she introduced me to the magic of the archives and, in doing so, unlocked doors that I never dreamed even existed.

To Gil Woods, a contact person for the former Fairbridge Society, and John Anderson, head of legal, The Prince's Trust; both have helped to keep the doors open to family members looking for information stored in the Fairbridge Archive at the University of Liverpool. Seeking information that is stored six thousand miles away is an arduous task, and having their support has helped in so many ways.

And to Morag Horseman, a Whitley Bay, England, resident who granted the request of a total stranger. With the addresses I located from the Whitley Bay School records and from my mother and her siblings' birth certificates, she went out and photographed the various houses that my family lived in, bringing Whitley Bay alive and allowing me to see that the past was waiting to be discovered. It also spurred me on to take my mother back to her place of birth in 2007.

And last but not least, to my son Joshua Havelaar and his wife, Jenny; my grandsons, Jaden and Rylan; my son Fletcher Havelaar and his wife, Aleksa; and my son Jack Weyler. It is through you, my sons, that I was able to see my family moving forward, and it helped me to realize the importance of finding my past so that I could give you the gift of our family history to carry with you into the future.

Appendix:

"Fairbridge the Founder"

Fairbridge the Founder

We are Fairbridge folk, all as good as e'er
English, Welsh, and Scottish, we have come from
    everywhere;
Boys to be farmers and girls for farmers' wives,
We follow Fairbridge the Founder.

Chorus

Hurrah, hurrah, we're Fairbridge through and through;
Hurrah, hurrah, we try to show we're true.
Do as Kingsley Fairbridge did, before him evil flew —
"Follow Fairbridge, the Founder."

We have a resolution, and we'll never let it down,
With honour we'll be faithful to our God, our Queen,
    and Crown,
We keep away from evil, thus we try to stamp it down.
And "Follow Fairbridge, the Founder."

Chorus

We try to learn the bushcraft, so keep open eye and ear;
We try to show our courage and so restrain our fear.
We have a splendid motto, to which we all adhere;
"Follow Fairbridge, the Founder."

Chorus

— Written by Neil Morrison (age twelve).
Sung to the tune of "Marching Through Georgia."

Notes

Author's Note

1. In 1956, a fact-finding mission was sent to Australia to evaluate the institutions housing the child migrants. The resulting *Ross Report* placed both Fairbridge schools on a blacklist. The Fairbridge Society's president, the Duke of Gloucester, was the Queen's uncle and the former governor general of Australia. The blacklist was quickly lifted and the British government allowed children to be sent to the Fairbridge farms in NSW and WA. See abc.net.au/news/2017-02-27/british-government-knew-fairbridge-farms-were-unfit-for-children/8306144.

Introduction

1. Harry Morris Cassidy to George Weir, February 14, 1935. PABC, GR 496, vol. 58, file 1. See Dunae, "Waifs: The Fairbridge Society in B.C., 1931–1951," 240.
2. *The Guardian*, U.K., July 12, 2015.
3. "Transportation and Sale of the Children of the Poor. Defence of the Children's Friend Society," *The Operative* (London), May 5, 1839, 1.
4. Andrew Doyle Report.
5. For an in-depth look at British child migration to Canada, see Kohli, *The Golden Bridge: Young Immigrants to Canada, 1833–1938.*
6. "Our Gutter Children," published in 1869. Cruikshank opposed child migration: "If such a transportation of innocent children ... should take

place, it will not only be a *degradation* and a *disgrace* to this nation, but also a disgrace to the Christian world, for I consider such a proceeding would be contrary to the laws of nature, and also Christian civilization." © Victoria and Albert Museum, London.

7. Minister of immigration and colonization, Ottawa, Canada, letter regarding Premier Pattullo's support for a farm school in British Columbia, to L.R. Lumley, Esq., MP, chairman, Executive Committee, The Child Emigration Society, Inc. (later renamed the Fairbridge Society), March 12, 1934, Savoy House, Strand, London, University of Liverpool Archives, Special Collections Branch, Fairbridge Fonds, D296/K/1/1/1, 89.

8. Harry T. Logan Fonds, UBC Library Archives, Vancouver, British Columbia, box 10, file 10-3. A-Z 1940–48. 1946/47 memo, 5. See also "Train Them Young Is Fairbridge Plan. Age Surprises Even Matrons. School Is Thousand-Acre Farm; Children Paddle in Koksilah River," *Victoria Daily Times* (B.C.), October 5, 1935.

9. "House of Commons Apology, Feb. 16/2017," British Home Child Group International, accessed March 19, 2017, britishhomechild.com/apology-petition.

10. Fairbridge U.K. said in February 1943 that Mr. Rogers' reappointment was unwise, but that it could not be involved because Duties Master appointments were a matter for the Principal and local Committee. This is another example of the inherent difficulties in an organisation in one country obtaining reassurance that the children in another country were being properly cared for, when the sending institution did not have authority to change the practice of the receiving institution. (Independent Inquiry Child Sexual Abuse: Child Migration Programmes. Investigation Report March 2018, 80.)

11. "Farm Schools for the Empire," *The Times* (London), June 21, 1934.

CHAPTER 1: WINIFRED'S CHILDREN

1. See Skidmore, *Marjorie Too Afraid to Cry*, 47, for a copy of this letter.

2. Brown, "Apology to Britain's Child Migrants." See Skidmore, *Marjorie Too Afraid to Cry*, 243–54.

3. The Évian Conference was convened by U.S. president Franklin D. Roosevelt in July 1938 to respond to the increasing numbers of Jewish refugees fleeing Nazi persecution. It was believed that Roosevelt desired to deflect attention and criticism from his country's national policy that limited the quota of Jewish refugees admitted to the United States. Wells, *Tropical Zion: General Trujillo, FDR, and the Jews of Sosua*, 6–8. "Évian Conference," *Wikipedia*, accessed July 7, 2017, en.wikipedia. org/wiki/%C3%89vian_Conference.

4. W. R. Little, director of Department of Immigration and Colonization, Canada House, Trafalgar Square, London, letter to Mr. Frederick Charles Blair, assistant deputy minister, Department of Immigration and Colonization, Ottawa, Ontario, Library and Archives Canada, Prince of Wales Fairbridge Farm School Files, 1936–1942.

5. In spring 2018, research found that two former Fairbridge men had siblings living. One had been told as a child that he was an orphan, and the other vaguely knew of a long lost sister, but not his other three siblings. These men lived a lifetime separated from their families because of a bureaucratic decision that claimed their family was not important to them. It is likely that many former child migrants had siblings they were separated from and lived their lives without any knowledge of them. When told at a very early age that you have no family and that you are alone, there is little reason to disbelieve.

6. The names of the school staff, with the exception of the school principal, Harry Logan, have been changed in order to avoid potential conflicts with any still living.

7. Stated by Marjorie's cottage mother, in a school report dated March 1940. See image (bottom) on page 44.

CHAPTER 2: A DIFFICULT YEAR

1. Images of Marjorie carrying the little box of cake can be seen in Skidmore, *Marjorie Too Afraid to Cry*, front cover, top image; on page 160 (morning in Vancouver); and on page 172 (afternoon at the Prince of Wales Fairbridge Farm School).

2. The official name was the Kenilworth Dining Hall, but in this book, it will simply be called the dining hall.

3. Many former Fairbridgians have stated that the quality of life there depended heavily on the cottage mother that you were assigned. Joe Jessop: "If you were not liked by your cottage mother your life was hell," in Bean and Melville, *Lost Children of the Empire*, 17.

4. Herb Moore (son of a home child sent to Canada in 1888 at the age of eight), interview with the author, 2007. His father was called a "spawn of the Devil" by the local community and was not counted in the census because, as a home child, he was not considered to be a "person."

5. Harry T. Logan, letter regarding the request for a Fairbridge girl to be returned to her mother in England, September 28, 1944. Ellen Preece, (girl's mother), letter requesting her daughter be sent back, undated. Fairbridge Society, letter denying request, November 8, 1944. University of Liverpool Archives, Special Collections Branch, Fairbridge Fonds, Mollie Preece files.

6. The old Stone Butter Church was the mission church for the Cowichan First Nations. It was built in 1870 but abandoned in 1880 in favour of nearby Saint Ann's Church. It has remained a haunted structure on the hill, abandoned and deconsecrated. For a more detailed history, see "Old Stone Butter Church — Duncan, B.C. — This Old Church on Waymarking.com," *Waymarking*, accessed July 7, 2017, waymarking. com/waymarks/WM699H_Old_Stone_Butter_Church__Duncan_BC.

CHAPTER 3: BUNNY'S BIRTHDAY

1. Marjorie and Bunny's school reports show they were housed in Attwood Cottage on March 31, 1939. They were placed in Pennant Cottage in 1940.

2. Marjorie Skidmore: "My letters from my mother were already opened, and large sections were often blacked out or cut out completely. They were impossible to read." It was common practice among the sending agencies to black out sections of the children's letters, and they often kept letters and did not pass them on to the children. See Bean and Melville, *Lost Children of the Empire*, 47.

CHAPTER 4: EXILED

1. Sexual abuse has been documented, but few former Fairbridgians are willing to speak about it. Two former Fairbridge men have told me about attempts from their duty master to sexually molest them. One said he was able get away, and that was as much as he was willing to say. Another said that he was sent to see a duty master after dinner for punishment. The duty master told the eight-year-old boy he wouldn't punish him. He lifted the boy on his knee and then put his hand up the leg of the boy's short pants. Shocked, the boy grabbed the duty master's nose, dug his nails in, and squeezed, and then he ran. See also Dunae, "Waifs: The Fairbridge Society in B.C., 1931–1951," 224–50, especially sexual misconduct charges against staff member in 1944, 244. Some of this abuse has been made public in the March 2018 Report from the Independent Inquiry into Child Sexual Abuse with regard to British Child Migration Programmes. Also see Patricia Skidmore, Witness Statement, "IICSA Inquiry — Child Migration Programmes Case Study Public Hearing Transcript," iicsa.org.uk/cy/key-documents/1160/view/Public%20hearing%20 transcript%209th%20March%202017.pdf.

2. Humphreys, *Empty Cradles*, 282. "Like all child migrants, he had left Britain with no return ticket. It was a one-way journey."

CHAPTER 5: I AIN'T GONNA BE A FARMER'S WIFE

1. Marjorie Skidmore: "Children who wet their beds in my cottage were treated very badly at Fairbridge. We tried to help each other, but we had to do it behind the cottage mother's back. She encouraged us to be cruel to each other. But all we had was each other." See also, Parr, *Labouring Children. British Immigrant Apprentices to Canada, 1869-1924*," 103–04, 107; Humphreys, *Empty Cradles*, 94; and Hill, *The Forgotten Children: Fairbridge Farm School and Its Betrayal of Australia's Child Migrants*, 157–58.

2. "Fairbridge the Founder" was written by Neil Morrison (age twelve) while he was at the Molong Fairbridge Farm School, New South Wales,

Australia. Rutherford, "Follow the Founder: An Account of the Fairbridge Society at Molong," 43. See the appendix for the complete song.

3. "Anonymous Friend Gives Funds to Provide Chapel at Duncan," *Daily Province* (Vancouver), March 22, 1939.

4. Fairbridge Alumni Association, Fairbridge newspaper clippings. Correspondence of Katie O'Neill, 1936, 1941, 1960, PABC Add. MSS, 2465, box 1, file 6. A letter dated October 27, 1936, offering O'Neill the appointment as a cottage mother with the starting wage of $32.50/month. The maximum cottage mother's wage at that time was $52.50.

5. Marjorie told of many instances of cruelty at the hands of the various cottage mothers. Other accounts of the cruelty by the cottage mothers can be found in Humphreys, *Empty Cradles*, 128–29; Bean and Melville, *Lost Children of the Empire*, 17, 119; PABC Add. MSS 2121, box 1, file 5, Fairbridge Farm School, Roll of Farm School Staff, 1935, 1950. This file contains a book that lists the name, date of appointment, occupation, and date of leaving for the Fairbridge staff members. Approximately 155 cottage mothers are listed; this includes relief and temporary cottage mothers. Dunae, "Waifs: The Fairbridge Society in B.C., 1931–1951," 243. By comparison, principal Harry Logan's salary was $400.00/month. Logan Fonds, UBC Archives, letter dated July 3, 1936.

Chapter 6: A Partial Eclipse

1. "Victorians See Partial Eclipse," *Victoria Daily Times*, April 19, 1939, 11. "Nanaimo Sees Partial Eclipse," *Nanaimo Free Press* (B.C.), April 19, 1939, 1.

2. Eric Broderick, "Tillicum Traveller Visits Fairbridge Farm," *Daily Province* (Vancouver), September 16, 1939, magazine section, 6.

3. "Fairbridge Glimpses," 53.

Chapter 7: Little Farmers

1. Marjorie recalled that the children used to sing songs like this one as they worked in the gardens and fields. Author unknown.

2. Nurse King discusses this fluffy phenomenon in her journal, PABC Add. MSS 2121, box 1, file 6; I also experienced it while driving in the Cowichan Valley area one May.

3. "They hate her with a vehemence which is heart-breaking. They feel she is not fair; she shouts at them, orders them around and has no understanding. One girl of superior intelligence was so infuriated when interviewed that the Principal was warned by me that Mrs. ___ had better be careful." Isobel Harvey Report. Also note, the Independent Inquiry into Child Sexual Abuse: Child Migration Programmes, Investigation Report in March 2018, stated that in December 1949, Ms. Carberry, Fairbridge U.K.'s psychiatric social worker, provided a damning report in which she stated that generally the school *"does not fit into child welfare pattern of B.C."* She again suggested that *"unsatisfactory staff are largely to blame for the present state of affairs."*

4. *Fairbridge Gazette* 1, no. 3 (May 1939): 3.

5. Bean and Melville, *Lost Children of the Empire*, 20. Australian lad said, "I felt like running away, but where would I go?"

6. Fairbridge Farm School Punishment Book 1944, PABC Add. MSS, file 2/2.

7. Kenny Arnison did eventually run away, but not while he was at the farm school. He was placed on a farm in Saanich outside of Victoria, British Columbia, when he turned sixteen in 1944. He hated it and ran away within two weeks of being placed there and joined the merchant navy. He lied about his age. He didn't have a birth certificate.

8. Sager, *It's in the Book: Notes of a Naïve Young Man*, 172–74.

9. "The Fairbridge March." Words and music by John Rowland, Victoria, British Columbia. This song was copyrighted in the name of the Fairbridge Farm School. A copy of this song was accepted by His Majesty the King. See also Skidmore, *Marjorie Too Afraid to Cry*, 225–26.

10. Marjorie Skidmore, 2016 interview with author. See also Broderick, "Tillicum Traveller Visits Fairbridge Farm," *Daily Province* (Vancouver), September 16, 1939, magazine section, 6.

11. Gating was a form of punishment. When gated, the children were not allowed to leave the immediate vicinity of their cottage except for

meals at the dining hall and to go to school and church. An imaginary line was drawn, and most children did not dare cross it.

12. Lucky tatties are still available in some candy stores in the United Kingdom.

13. "There'll Always Be an England" is an English patriotic song, written and distributed in the summer of 1939. It was composed and written by Ross Parker and Hughie Charles.

14. *Fairbridge Gazette*, Autumn 1946, by Leon Mendoza, a Fairbridge boy.

CHAPTER 8: OFF TO FINTRY

1. Nurse King's scrapbook, 1940–1942, Fairbridge Farm School, PABC Add. MSS 2121, box 1, file 6.

2. Broderick, "Tillicum Traveller Visits Fairbridge Farm," *Daily Province* (Vancouver), September 16, 1939, magazine section, 6.

3. "What Manner of Man Is This Laird of Fintry?" *Country Life in B.C.*, Golden Jubilee ed., 1939. "Fintry Laird Tells of Hopes in Farm School," *Nanaimo Free Press* (B.C.), March 22, 1939. "Presented to Fairbridge Schools. 2,500 Acre Property To Be Used to Train Youths for Life on Canadian Farms," *Vernon News* (B.C.), July 7, 1938, 1, 6.

4. Marjorie, in an interview in 2010, said that she was terrified when she started menstruating, as she had no knowledge of how her body worked. See the Independent Inquiry Child Sexual Abuse: Child Migration Programmes. Investigation Report in March 2018: In December 1949, Ms Carberry, Fairbridge U.K.'s psychiatric social worker, provided a damning report in which she stated that the high pregnancy rate was *"The actual result of life at Fairbridge with its failure to satisfy emotional needs and the repressive attitude of bad Cottage Mothers, together with an inadequate knowledge of sex or in some cases of knowledge gained in the wrong way at Fairbridge or earlier still in life."*

5. Malcolm Jackson, letter to Winifred Arnison, June 11, 1940. See also "Impressed by Island School. Malcolm H. Jackson Arrives from England with Party for Fairbridge Farm," *Daily Colonist* (Victoria), May 12, 1940, 2.

Chapter 10: Fintry or Fairbridge

1. See *Fairbridge Gazette*, Summer 2000, 16.
2. *Fairbridge Gazette*, July 1939, 4.
3. *Fairbridge Gazette*, August 1940; "Children Come to Fairbridge," *Daily Colonist* (Victoria), May 8, 1940, 8; "Tyneside Lad Seeking Roving Buffalo on Way to Fairbridge," *Daily Province* (Vancouver), May 8, 1940, 9.

Chapter 11: For Now and Evermore

1. "Britons will never be slaves," yet for 350 years the children of Britain were shipped away to the colonies to be slaves to their new masters. "Rule, Britannia!" originates from the poem "Rule, Britannia" by James Thomson.
2. For more information, see Barker, *Children of the Benares. A War Crime and Its Victims*, 29 and 157–58. See also "Three-Fold British Blow Again. Children's Terrible Sea Adventure," *Vancouver Sun*, September 23, 1940, 1; "Sinking of Mercy Ship Won't Halt Refugee Exodus. 87 Children Drowned as Sub Blasts Vessel in Midatlantic — Down in 20 Minutes," *Daily Province* (Vancouver), September 23, 1940, 1; "Nazis' Sinking of Ship with 87 Children and 206 Grown-Ups Steels Britain," *Victoria Daily Times*, September 23, 1940, 3; "293 Perish, 113 Rescued in Nazi Outrage at Sea. Passenger Ship Sunk Deliberately in Heavy Storm 600 Miles Off Coast; Many Die of Exposure," *The Vancouver Sun*, September 28, 1940, 1.

Chapter 12: I Think I Can ... Make It ...

1. *Fairbridge Gazette* 1, no. 6 (December 1939): 3.
2. "Governor-General Opens New Fairbridge Hospital," *Cowichan Leader* (B.C.), April 3, 1941, 1. "Earl of Athlone at Fairbridge Farm," *Daily Colonist* (Victoria), April 3, 1941, 10.
3. Marjorie Skidmore, 2016 interview with the author: "One of us had to walk up the stairs with the tray and say, 'Good morning, here's your

breakfast.' Then we waited down in the kitchen for sounds that she was dying. When she rang her bell, we knew it didn't work. She had no kindness to anyone. She was simply a bitch, and she made our lives a living hell. She was a bitch. I am sorry, but that is what she was."

CHAPTER 13: BULLIES! IT'S NOT FAIR!

1. Kevin Rudd, "Apology to Forgotten Australians and Former Child Migrants," *The Australian*, accessed July 7, 2017, theaustralian.com.au/archive/politics/apology-by-prime-minister-kevin-rudd-to-the-forgotten-australians-and-child-migrants/news-story/7197a8b7e8026d2d8e04abb7dfbba025. See also Gordon Brown, "Apology to Britain's Child Migrants," parliament.uk. The full transcript of Brown's apology can be found in Skidmore, *Marjorie Too Afraid to Cry*, 244.

2. Margaret Humphreys, witness statement, Independent Inquiry into Child Sexual Abuse with regard to British Child Migration Programmes, accessed April 4, 2017, iicsa.org.uk/cy/key-documents/1160/view/Public%20hearing%20transcript%209th%20March%202017.pdf; iicsa.org.uk. Nigel Haynes said that when he was director of the Fairbridge charity from 1993 until 2008 he had been too busy with the charity's work to research the archives, where there was ample evidence of child sex abuse "U.K. Charity Dodged Child Sex Abuse Blame," 9 *News*, accessed July 24, 2017, 9news.com.au/world/2017/07/20/00/07/uk-charity-dodged-child-sex-abuse-blame#tCdg5Z7LDjTJlxID.99.

3. Marjorie Skidmore recalled that the children used to sing songs like this one as they worked in the gardens and fields. Author unknown.

4. Independent Inquiry Child Sexual Abuse: Child Migration Programmes. Investigation Report, March 2018.

5. The song was brought to the farm school by games master Tony Branson. The original came from Australia — *There's a flivver running back down the old Pinjarra track …* — and was changed to suit the Prince of Wales Fairbridge Farm School.

6. Ron Smith, *Fairbridge Gazette*, Spring 2004, 10. "As one recalled, 'You lined up face to the ground, bent over and just prayed it wasn't the willow stick.'"

7. Kenny's stories were passed to his sister Marjorie during their time at the farm school and as young adults when they both lived in Vancouver. She vowed to remember them, even though she could do little to help him. Marjorie carried a lifelong burden of shame because she could not protect her brother Kenny at the farm school. See also John Jones's account in Humphreys, *Empty Cradles*, 160–61.
8. Peter Conlon, *Fairbridge Gazette*, Summer 2000, 12. Mike Nevard (Pownall), *Fairbridge Gazette*, Summer 2000, 6; Joe Jessop, in Bean and Melville, *Lost Children of the Empire*, 17.
9. From a 2013 interview with a Fairbridge boy who wishes to remain anonymous. He wears his bitterness and a sense of loss that is heartbreaking. The stories portrayed here are not necessarily in chronological order, but they are a compilation of stories and memories told to me by various Fairbridgians who were at the farm school between 1935 and the late 1940s, including my mother, Marjorie.
10. Sager, *It's In the Book: Notes of a Naïve Young Man*, 167–77.

CHAPTER 14: CHRISTMAS EVE

1. Survival is a common theme. Humphreys, *Empty Cradles*, 160. Bean and Melville, *Lost Children of the Empire*, 17.
2. Grace MacCollum, reproduced with permission.
3. "B.C. School Broadcast. Fairbridge Farm School," CBC Radio, May 22, 1942, B.C. Archives, T4216:0001 – 0002 of description AAAB6101.
4. There are four Fairbridge Farm School children buried in the Mountain View Cemetery just to the north of Duncan. John Reid Taylor, died October 27, 1937, age twelve; Dorothy Meta Philips, died July 22, 1942, age fifteen; Ethel Anderson, died May 1, 1944, age sixteen; Elizabeth Lenton, died March 24, 1945, age twenty.
5. *Fairbridge Gazette* 2, no. 3 (July 1941).
6. Marjorie Skidmore, 2016 interview with author: "I was so lonely then. I was placed with a nice family in the new year, and I got to go back to the farm for a few days. Imagine wanting to go back to the farm school! But I didn't know anything else, did I?"

7. Jean (née Hanson) Conlon, letter to her mother, n.d. Her letters were returned to her when her mother passed away. Printed with permission from Jean Conlon, who sadly passed away in November 2014. This is not in chronological order, as Jean Hanson did not arrive until 1948. Letters home to parents may not have been as closely vetted by 1948.
8. "Red Sails in the Sunset," 1935, lyrics by Jimmy Kennedy.
9. "White Cliffs of Dover," words by Nat Burton. It took until 2001 for Marjorie to return to England for the first time, and during that trip, she did see the white cliffs of Dover.

CHAPTER 15: WHY WOULD I GO BACK?

1. Fairbridge said, "I saw great Colleges of Agriculture (not workhouses) springing up in every man-hungry corner of the Empire." Fairbridge, *Kingsley Fairbridge. His Life and Verse*, 159.
2. "Are There Really Indians Here?" "Upon arriving in Vancouver, the newcomers were told, 'You'll have to watch out for the Indians on Vancouver Island.' ... There was an uneasy silence. 'Are there really Indians here then?' asked a wide-eyed lad. 'Sure,' returned the man, and turning toward a boy who ... claimed Irish parentage, 'you will have to be careful, the Indians over there love Irish stew.'" September 25, 1935. *Daily Province*, (Vancouver) "Fairbridge Children Decide B.C. Rain Just Usual Kind. Weather Doesn't Worry Them But Kenneth Dobbs, 6, Not So Sure About Indians." "Dobbs climbed off the train with his toy gun cocked. 'Why the gun laddie?' he was asked. The boy murmured something about the Indians and the bad men." November 10, 1937. *Daily Province* (Vancouver).
3. Barbara Arnison, Marjorie (Arnison) Skidmore's cousin, letter to Marjorie Skidmore.

AFTERWORD (AFTERWARD)

1. See Skidmore, *Marjorie Too Afraid to Cry*, cover, 172, 191.
2. Canada House, memo to the Department of Immigration and Colonization, September 6, 1935, Library and Archives Canada,

Prince of Wales Fairbridge Farm School Files, 1936–1942.

3. Fairbridge Farm School, "Fairbridge Farm Schools Twenty-Sixth Year, 1935," *Annual Report*, 3.

4. Skidmore, *Marjorie Too Afraid to Cry*, 47.

5. Letters between the Department of Immigration and Colonization, Canada House, Trafalgar Square, London; Mr. Frederick Charles Blair, assistant deputy minister, Department of Immigration and Colonization, Ottawa, Ontario; the Canadian Pacific Railway Company; and the Fairbridge Farm School, 1935, Library and Archives Canada, Prince of Wales Fairbridge Farm School Files, 1936–1942.

6. "Skipper Wins Fight Over Age Rule," unidentified and undated newspaper article, Global Case Law, accessed July 7, 2017, canlii. org/en/ca/fca/doc/1980/1980canlii2563/1980canlii2563.html? autocompleteStr=arnison-v-pacific-pilotage-authority-1980& autocompletePos=1.

Bibliography

ARCHIVES

Birmingham Archives and Heritage, England
Sir John Middlemore Charitable Trust, Middlemore Fonds, MS 517/25.

British Columbia Archives
Prince of Wales Fairbridge Farm School Records, PABC Add. MSS 2121, box 1, file 5–6, file 2/2; Add. MSS 2465, box 1, file 6; PABC GR496, vol. 58, file 1.

Library and Archives Canada
Prince of Wales Fairbridge Farm School Files, 1936–1942, Immigration Branch Central Registry Files (RG 76, vol. 375, file 510340, pt. 2–4), microfilm reel C-10273.
Middlemore Homes Records (MG 28, I 492), Papers of the Middlemore Children's Emigration Home, Birmingham Archives Service, Birmingham, England, 1914–1937, vol. 248 A-2079, Reference MS 517/248, Application Book No. 4.

University of British Columbia Library/Archives
Logan Family Fonds, Fairbridge Farm School series, 1910–1971.

University of Liverpool, Special Collections Branch, Archives
Fairbridge Society (now under The Prince's Trust) Archives: D.296.E1, Children's Records, Case Files; D.296.F1, 1912–1982, Publicity and

Fundraising—Appeal Leaflets, 1914–c1975; D296.F4, Publicity and Fundraising Photographs, 1912–1982. D715 contains committee minute books, 1873–1933; *Annual Reports*, 1873–1907; and letters.

ARTICLES, BOOKLETS, PAMPHLETS, REPORTS

Bondfield, Margaret. "Report to the Secretary of State for the Colonies, President of the Overseas Settlement Committee, from the Delegation Appointed to Obtain Information Regarding the System of Child Migration and Settlement in Canada, 1924–1925." *Parliamentary Papers*, XV, CMD, 2285, 1–20.

Buller, Charles. "Systematic Colonization." Speech in the House of Commons, April 6, 1843. Earl Grey Pamphlets Collection, 1843.

Child Emigration Society Pamphlet (ca. 1912). "Train them in the Countries where they are wanted … The object of the Child Emigration Society is to emigrate these children, and to educate them in Farm-Schools in Over-Seas Dominions."

Doyle, Andrew. "Doyle Report. Pauper Children. Canada. Report to the Right Honourable the President of the Local Government Board, as to the Emigration of Pauper Children to Canada." Ordered by the House of Commons. February 8, 1875.

Dunae, Patrick. "Waifs: The Fairbridge Society in B.C., 1931–1951." *Social History* 219, no. 42 (November 1988): 224–50.

Earl of Athlone. "Address by His Excellency, the Governor General of Canada at the Opening of the Prince of Wales Fairbridge Farm School Hospital, April 1, 1941." *Cowichan Leader* (B.C.), 1941.

Fairbridge Farm School. "Fairbridge Farm School's Twenty-Sixth Year, 1935." London: Baynard Press, 1935.

_____. "Fairbridge Farm School's Twenty-Seventh Year, 1936." London: Baynard Press, 1936.

_____. "Fairbridge Farm School's Now at a Crossroads." London: Baynard Press, undated ca. 1949.

"Fairbridge Glimpses." Prince of Wales Fairbridge Farm School Fiftieth Anniversary, 1935–1985, booklet of the Old Fairbridge Alumni Committee.

Hansard Parliament of Australia. "2001 Inquiry into Child Migration: Chapter 1. Perspectives of Child Migration." Item 1.25. Barnardo reference: Committee Hansard, 22.3.01, p. 467. Barnardos Australia and the National Children's Home reference: Submission no. 98, p. 2 NCH.

Harvey, Isobel. "Report on Study Made of Fairbridge Farm School during the Month of August 1944." PABC Add. MSS 2045, vol. 1, file 14.

Independent Inquiry into Child Sexual Abuse with Regard to British Child Migration Programmes Report. Published on March 1, 2018. Assessed March 1, 2018. iicsa.org.uk/key-documents/4265/view/Child%20Migration%20Programmes%20Investigation%20Report%20March%202018.pdf.

Rashid, Abdul. "Seven Decades of Wage Changes." *Perspectives on Labour and Income* 5, no. 2 (Summer 1993): article no. 1. (Statistics Canada, Catalogue 75-001E.)Ward, Rebecca Rose. "An Alternative Approach to Child Rescue: Child Emigration Societies in Birmingham and Manchester, 1870–1914." Thesis, Durham University, 2010, accessed July 8, 2017, etheses.dur.ac.uk/611.

BOOKS

Barker, Ralph. *Children of the Benares. A War Crime and Its Victims.* Trowbridge, England: Redwood Burn, 1987.

Bean, Philip, and Joy Melville. *Lost Children of the Empire.* London: Unwin Hyman, 1989.

Blackburn, Geoff. *The Children's Friend Society: Juvenile Emigrants to Western Australia, South Africa and Canada, 1834–1842.* Northbridge, Western Australia: Access Press, 1993.

Boucher, Ellen. *Empire's Children. Child Emigration, Welfare, and the Decline of the British World, 1869–1967.* Cambridge, England: University Printing House, 2014.

Buchanan-Brown, John. *The Book Illustrations of George Cruikshank.* North Pomfret, VT: David and Charles, 1980.

Corbett, Gail H. *Barnardo Children in Canada.* Woodview, ON: Homestead Studios, 1981.

Fairbridge, Kingsley Ogilvie. *The Autobiography of Kingsley Fairbridge*. London: Oxford University Press, 1927.

_____. *Kingsley Fairbridge. His Life and Verse*. Bulawayo, Rhodesia: Mardon Printers, 1974.

_____. *The Story of Kingsley Fairbridge, by Himself*. Illustrated ed. London: Oxford University Press, 1936.

Hill, David. *The Forgotten Children: Fairbridge Farm School and Its Betrayal of Australia's Child Migrants*. Sydney: Random House, Australia, 2007.

Humphreys, Margaret. *Empty Cradles*. London: Doubleday, 1994.

Johnson, Stanley C. *A History of Emigration from the United Kingdom to North America, 1763–1912*. London: George Routledge & Sons, 1913.

Kershaw, Roger, and Janet Sacks. *New Lives for Old: The Story of Britain's Child Migrants*. Surrey, England: National Archives, 2008.

Kohli, Marjorie. *The Golden Bridge: Young Immigrants to Canada, 1833–1938*. Toronto: Natural Heritage Books, 2003.

Marriot, Sir John A.R. *Empire Settlement*. London: Oxford University Press, 1927.

Parr, Joy. *Labouring Children. British Immigrant Apprentices to Canada, 1869–1924*. London: McGill University Press, 1980.

Rooke, Patricia T., and R.L. Schnell. *Discarding the Asylum: From Child Rescue to the Welfare State in English-Canada (1800–1950)*. Lanham, MD: University Press of America, 1983.

Rutherford, David A., and the Molong Historical Society. *Follow Fairbridge the Founder: An Account of the Fairbridge Farm School at Molong, NSW*. Forster, Australia: 1983.

Sager, Arthur. *It's in the Book: Notes of a Naïve Young Man*. Victoria, BC: Trafford Publishing, 2003.

Sherington, Geoffrey, and Chris Jeffery. *Fairbridge. Empire and Child Migration*. Portland, OR: Woburn Press, 1998.

Skidmore, Patricia. *Marjorie Too Afraid to Cry: A Home Child Experience*. Toronto: Dundurn, 2013.

Waugh, Father N. *These, My Little Ones*. London: Sands and Co., 1911.

Wells, Allen. *Tropical Zion: General Trujillo, FDR, and the Jews of Sosua*. Durham, NC: Duke University Press, 2009.

West, Arthur George Bainbridge. *Fairbridge Farm School in B.C.* London: A.R. Mowbray, 1936.

MAGAZINES

Fairbridge Gazette. Magazine of the Prince of Wales Fairbridge Farm School, now published by the Fairbridge Canada Association, February 1939 to mid-1950s and 1980 to present day.
Illustrated London News, Coronation Ceremony Number, May 15, 1937.

NEWSPAPER ARTICLES

"18 [*sic* 28] Youngsters for Fairbridge School." *Vancouver Sun,* August 23, 1938.

"293 Perish, 113 Rescued in Nazi Outrage at Sea. Passenger Ship Sunk Deliberately in Heavy Storm 600 Miles Off Coast; Many Die of Exposure." *Vancouver Sun,* September 28, 1940.

"£40,000 for Fairbridge Farm School." *Morning Post* (London), February 26, 1937.

"Australia Day. Prince of Wales on Empire Settlement. Appeal for Closer Cooperation. The Prince's Service." *The Times* (London), January 27, 1926.

Broderick, Eric. "Tillicum Traveller Visits Fairbridge Farm." *Daily Province* (Vancouver), September 16, 1939.

Brown, Edgar. "New Canadians at Fairbridge." *Daily Province* (Vancouver), December 18, 1937.

Bullock-Webster, B.H. "The Girls of Fairbridge." *Daily Colonist* (Victoria), April 14, 1940.

"Child Farmers to Meet Gov. General. Lord and Lady Tweedsmuir Paying Visit to Fairbridge Farm School Today." *Victoria Daily Times,* August 22, 1936.

"Child Settlers." *The Times* (London), June 14, 1934.

"Children Come to Fairbridge." *Daily Colonist* (Victoria), May 8, 1940.

"Church Plan for Fairbridge School." *Daily Province* (Vancouver), December 3, 1938.

"Earl of Athlone at Fairbridge Farm." *Daily Colonist* (Victoria), April 3, 1941.

"Fairbridge Farm School." *The Times* (London), July 25, 1934.

"Fairbridge Farm School Scheme to Open Three More … The Prince's £1,000 gift." *The Times* (London), June 15, 1934.

"Fairbridge School for Island." *Daily Colonist* (Victoria), March 9, 1935.

"Farm School Plan Is British-Backed." *Gazette* (Montreal), February 14, 1935.

"Farm Schools for the Empire." *The Times* (London), June 21, 1934.

"Fintry Laird Tells of Hopes in Farm School." *Nanaimo Free Press* (B.C.), March 22, 1939.

The Flying Post or Post-Master (London), August 30–September 1, 1698, no. 526.

"Gift for Fairbridge Farm Schools. £100,000 from Sir John Siddeley." *The Times* (London), May 8, 1937.

"Governor-General Opens New Fairbridge Hospital." *Cowichan Leader* (B.C.), April 3, 1941.

"Happy British Children Here to Start New Life in Canada." *Daily Province* (Vancouver), August 23, 1938.

Lawley, Sir Arthur, G.C.S.I. K.C.M.G. "Fairbridge Farm School: Realization of an Ideal. From Slum to Sunshine." *The Times* (London), May 9, 1927.

"Little Empire Migrants." *London Spectator.* Reprinted in the *Evening Journal* (Ottawa), February 23, 1939.

Logan, Harry. "The Fairbridge Farm School, an Imperial Venture." *The Times* (London), May 13, 1939.

"Lord Kenilworth, Gives a $500,000 Donation to Aid Farm in B.C." *Gazette* (Montreal), August 30, 1937.

"May Select Island for Farm School." *Daily Colonist* (Victoria), October 5, 1934.

"Mr. Kingsley Fairbridge." *The Times* (London), July 26, 1924.

"Mr. Kipling Leaves £155,228." *Morning Post* (London), April 7, 1936.

"Nanaimo Sees Partial Eclipse." *Nanaimo Free Press* (B.C.), April 19, 1939.

"Nazis' Sinking of Ship with 87 Children and 206 Grown-Ups Steels Britain." *Victoria Daily Times*, September 23, 1940.

"New Canadians at Fairbridge." *Daily Province* (Vancouver), December 18, 1937.

"New Fairbridge Girls Declare They Won't Be Farmer's Wives." *Daily Province* (Vancouver), September 21, 1938.

"North-East Children in British Columbia." *Evening Chronicle* (Newcastle-on-Tyne), December 8, 1938.

"Presented to Fairbridge Schools. 2,500 Acre Property To Be Used to Train Youths for Life on Canadian Farms." *Vernon News* (B.C.), July 7, 1938.

Rye, Maria. "Our Gutter Children." *The Times* (London), March 29, 1869.

Scott, Cecil. "More Children for B.C." *Daily Province* (Vancouver), September 21, 1935.

"Sinking of Mercy Ship Won't Halt Refugee Exodus. 87 Children Drowned as Sub Blasts Vessel in Midatlantic — Down in 20 Minutes." *Daily Province* (Vancouver), September 23, 1940.

"Sir John Siddeley Gives Coronation Gift of $493,000." *Journal* (Montreal), May 8, 1937.

"Tells Great Experiment. Major C. Holmes Describes Struggle of Kingsley Fairbridge to Gyros." *Victoria Daily Times*, December 10, 1935.

"Those Empty Spaces." *Morning Post* (London), May 10, 1935.

"Train Them Young Is Fairbridge Plan. Age Surprises Even Matrons. School Is Thousand-Acre Farm; Children Paddle in Koksilah River." *Victoria Daily Times*, October 5, 1935.

"Transportation and Sale of Children of the Poor: Defence of the Children's Friend Society." *The Operative* (London), May 5, 1839.

"Transportation of Children by Parish Officers." *The Operative* (London), February 3, 1839.

"Tyneside Lad Seeking Roving Buffalo on Way to Fairbridge." *Daily Province* (Vancouver), May 8, 1940.

"Victorians See Partial Eclipse. Clear Sky Gives Splendid View of Sun Being Blotted Out." *Victoria Daily Times*, April 19, 1939.

"The Voyage of 28 Children. New Opportunities at Fairbridge." *The Times* (London), August 11, 1938.

"What Manner of Man Is This Laird of Fintry?" *Country Life in B.C.*, Golden Jubilee ed., 1939.

PERSONAL LETTERS, PERSONAL STORIES, PERSONAL FILES, AND INTERVIEWS

Anonymous. Interview with a former Fairbridge student, 2013.

Arnison, David (Marjorie's youngest brother, born after she left for Canada). Personal letters and interviews, 1995–2015.

Arnison, Frederick (Marjorie's oldest brother). Interviews, 2001 and 2005.

Arnison, Josephine (Marjorie's aunt). Diary. "Recollections," 1911–1988.

Arnison, Lawrence (Marjorie's younger brother; he was four years old when she left for Canada). Conversations 2001–2018.

Arnison, Norman (Marjorie's older brother). Personal letters and interviews, 1999–2007.

Arnison, Richard (Marjorie's younger brother, born after she left for Canada). Conversations 2011–2013.

Bennett, John (Jock; a former Fairbridgian). Fairbridge Canada Association Reunion, Duncan, British Columbia, September 2013.

Conlon, Jean (a former Fairbridgian). Conversations, 2005–2014, and Prince of Wales Fairbridge Farm School records.

Conlon, Peter (a former Fairbridgian). *Fairbridge Gazette*, Summer 2000, 12.

Earl, Joyce (Arnison; Marjorie's older sister). Personal letters and interviews, 1995–2014.

Lewis, Audrey (Arnison; Marjorie's younger sister). Fairbridge Farm School personal file. Personal letter, February 10, 1995, and interviews to Summer 2017.

Moore, Herb (son of a home child). Interview, 2007.

Nevard, (Pownell) Mick (a former Fairbridgian). *Fairbridge Gazette*, Summer 2000, 6.

Preece, Mollie (a former Fairbridgian). Interview, 2007, and Fairbridge Farm School personal file.

Skidmore, Marjorie (Arnison). Fairbridge Farm School personal file. Personal letter, February 20, 1995, and interviews, 1999–2016.

POEMS AND SONGS

"A Partial Eclipse." Patricia Skidmore, 2012.

"Down on Misery Farm." Both the boys' and girls' versions.

"The Eagle." Alfred, Lord Tennyson, 1851.

"Fairbridge March." Words and music by John Rowland, Victoria, B.C. This song was copyrighted in the name of the Fairbridge Farm School. A copy of this song was accepted by His Majesty the King.

"Fairbridge Tears." Patricia Skidmore, 2012.

"Fairbridge the Founder," in D.A. Rutherford, "Follow the Founder: An Account of the Fairbridge Society at Molong, NSW." Forster, Australia: D.A. Rutherford, 1983, 43.

"Farming." Leon Mendoza (a former Fairbridgian). *Fairbridge Gazette*, Autumn 1946.

"Full Circle." Patricia Skidmore, 2012.

"Home Sweet Home." Patricia Skidmore, 2012.

"Lost Love." Grace MacCollum, 2002.

"My Memory of Things Gone By." Tom Isherwood (a former Fairbridgian), 2003.

"Rule, Britannia!" James Thomson, set to music by Thomas Arne, 1740.

"There Is a Mouldy Home ..." a song that Marjorie recalls the children singing while working at the farm school.

"There's a Plymmy Running Back." Tony Branson, the games master, brought the song to the Prince of Wales Fairbridge Farm School. The original came from Australia (*There's a flivver running back down the old Pinjarra track ...*) and was changed to suit the Prince of Wales Fairbridge Farm School.

"Red Sails in the Sunset." Lyrics by Jimmy Kennedy and music by Hugh Williams, 1935.

"There'll Always Be an England." Words and music by Ross Parker and Hughie Charles, 1939.

"White Cliffs of Dover." Melody by Walter Kent and words by Nat Burton, 1941.

"Winifred's Children." Patricia Skidmore, 2012.

VIDEOS: FAIRBRIDGE FARM SCHOOL IN PUBLIC ARCHIVES OF B.C. PABC

V1988 0/10 & 10.2; F1987 20/1; V1980:76. *Prince of Wales Fairbridge Farm School 1938–1940*: Video and CBC Broadcast, May 22, 1942. Title: B.C. school broadcast. Fairbridge Farm School: [4 radio programs]. B.C. Archives. Call Number: T4216:0001–0002 of description AAAB6101.

WEBSITES

"Australia Opens National Child Abuse Inquiry." BBC News Asia. Accessed August 8, 2017. bbc.co.uk/news/world-asia-22011598.

Australian Parliament. "Lost Innocents: Righting the Record — Report on Child Migration." Accessed August 8, 2017. aph.gov.au/ Parliamentary_Business/Committees/Senate/Community_Affairs/ Completed_inquiries/1999–02/child_migrat/report/index.

"Blair, Frederick Charles." *Wikipedia*. Accessed August 8, 2017. en. wikipedia.org/wiki/Frederick_Blair.

British Columbia Archives. bcarchives.gov.bc.ca/index.htm.

"Canada Doesn't Have to Apologize for Britain's 'Home Children,' Minister Says." *Hamilton Spectator*. November 29, 2009. thespec.com/ news-story/2191369-canada-doesn-t-have-to-apologize-for-britain- s-home-children-minister-says.

Canadian Museum of Immigration at Pier 21. Accessed August 8, 2017. pier21.ca and pier21.ca/research/immigration-history/ immigration-act-1869.

"Canadians Not Interested in 'Home Children' Apology: Minister." *Star* (Ottawa). November 16, 2009. thestar.com/news/canada/2009/11/16/ canadians_not_interested_in_home_children_apology_minister.html.

Child's Migrant Trust. Accessed August 8, 2017. childmigrantstrust.com.

CORB Children's Overseas Reception Board. Accessed August 8, 2017. en.wikipedia.org/wiki/Children%27s_Overseas_Reception_Board.

Fairbridge Canada Association. Accessed August 8, 2017. fairbridgecanada. com.

Fintry. Accessed August 8, 2017. fintry.ca.

Global Case Law. Accessed August 8, 2017. canlii.org/en/ca/fca/doc/1980/ 1980canlii2563/1980canlii2563.html?resultIndex=1.

The Golden Bridge: Child Migration from Scotland to Canada. Accessed August 8, 2017. content.iriss.org.uk/goldenbridge/exhibition/why. html.

Governor General of Canada. Accessed August 8, 2017. gg.ca/honour. aspx?id=65711&t=3&ln=Arnison.

Home Children, 1869–1930. Library and Archives Canada. Accessed August 8, 2017. bac-lac.gc.ca/eng/discover/immigration/immigration-records/home-children-1869–1930/Pages/home-children.aspx.

"Home Children." *Wikipedia*. Accessed August 8, 2017. en.m.wikipedia. org/wiki/Home_Children.

Hudson, Sophie. "The Prince's Trust and Fairbridge to Merge." January 26, 2011. thirdsector.co.uk/princes-trust-fairbridge-merge/governance/ article/1051693.

Independent Inquiry into Child Sexual Abuse with Regard to British Child Migration Programmes. Accessed August 15, 2017. iicsa.org. uk.

Library and Archives Canada. Accessed March 17, 2018. bac-lac.gc.ca/ eng/Pages/home.aspx.

National Archives of Australia. Accessed August 8, 2017. naa.gov.au.

Old Stone Butter Church. Accessed August 8, 2017. waymarking.com/ waymarks/WM699H_Old_Stone_Butter_Church__Duncan_BC.

Prince's Trust. Accessed March 17, 2018. princes-trust.org.uk/.

Royal Commission into Institutional Responses to Child Sexual Abuse (Australia). Accessed August 8, 2017. childabuseroyalcommission. gov.au/about-us/terms-of-reference.

Rudd, Kevin. "Transcript of Rudd's 'Apology to Forgotten Australians and Former Child Migrants.'" Parliament House, Australia. November 16, 2009. theaustralian.com.au/archive/politics/apology-by-prime-minister-kevin-rudd-to-the-forgotten-australians-and-child-migrants/story-e6frgczf-1225798266181.

Slavery Abolition Act 1833. Accessed August 8, 2017. anti-slaverysociety. addr.com/huk-1833act.htm.

U.K. Parliament. "British Prime Minister Gordon Brown's Transcript of the 24 February 2010 Apology to All British Child Migrants." Accessed August 8, 2017. publications.parliament.uk/pa/ld200910/ldhansrd/text/100224-0002.htm#10022468000373.

"Waugh, Benjamin." *Wikipedia.* Accessed August 8, 2017. en.wikipedia.org/wiki/Benjamin_Waugh.

Photo Credits

8   University of Liverpool Archives, Special Collections Branch, Fairbridge Fonds, Arnison Family Records, D 296.E1.

10   *The Times* (London), November 29, 1934.

12   University of Liverpool Archives, Special Collections Branch, Fairbridge Fonds, D 296.F1, and Fairbridge Farm School, *Annual Report*, circa 1949.

14   Photo by Patricia Skidmore.

18   Remembrancia V (LMA ref: COL/RMD/PA/01/005), printed with permission from the London Metropolitan Archives).

25   Victoria and Albert Museum, London.

44   (top and bottom) University of Liverpool Archives, Special Collections Branch, Fairbridge Fonds, Arnison Family Records, D 296.E1.

59   Photo by Patricia Skidmore.

60   (top) Skidmore family collection.

60   (left and right) Skidmore family collection.

62   University of Liverpool Archives, Special Collections Branch, Fairbridge Fonds, Arnison Files, D 296/f/4/1/5.

69   Photo by Patricia Skidmore.

71   Skidmore family collection.

74   Skidmore family collection.

80   (top) Skidmore family collection.
     (bottom) Fairbridge Farm School, *Annual Report*, "Fairbridge Farm School's Thirty-Sixth Year, 1945," 3.

92   Fairbridge Farm School, "Fairbridge Farm School's Thirtieth Year, 1939," 13.

101   (top) Skidmore family collection.
      (bottom) Fairbridge Farm School, "Fairbridge Farm School's Twenty-Seventh Year, 1936," 5, 13.

120   Skidmore family collection.

125   (top) "From Tyneside to Vancouver Island," Fairbridge Farm School, *Annual Report*, "Fairbridge Farm School's Twenty-Eighth Year, 1937," 29.
      (bottom) "English Youngsters Learn Canadian Farming Methods at Fairbridge Farm School," *Cowichan Leader*, March 14, 1946, Duncan Studio.

128   "Fairbridge Glimpses," Prince of Wales Fairbridge Farm School Fiftieth Anniversary, 1935–1985, booklet of the Old Fairbridge Alumni Committee, 51.

136   Skidmore family collection.

141   Photo by Patricia Skidmore.

158   Garnett family collection.

160   Photo by Vera Hance, Skidmore family collection.

165   Photo by Vera Hance, Skidmore family collection.

168   Skidmore family collection.

195   Fairbridge Farm School, "Fairbridge Farm School's Twenty-Seventh Year, 1936," 6.

207   Courtesy of Jean Conlon.

213   Photo by Patricia Skidmore.

229   Skidmore family collection.

232   (top) Photo by David Arnison.
      (bottom) Skidmore family collection.

233   Skidmore family collection.

Index

BOOK CREDITS

Acquiring Editor: Beth Bruder
Developmental Editor: Dominic Farrell
Project Editor: Elena Radic
Copy Editor: Melissa Churchill
Proofreader: Tara Tovell

Cover Designer: Laura Boyle
Interior Designer: Jennifer Gallinger
E-Book Designer: Carmen Giraudy

Publicist: Michelle Melski

DUNDURN

Publisher: J. Kirk Howard
Vice-President: Carl A. Brand
Managing Editor: Kathryn Lane
Director of Design and Production: Jennifer Gallinger
Marketing Manager: Kate Condon-Moriarty
Sales Manager: Synora Van Drine
Publicity Manager: Michelle Melski

Editorial: Allison Hirst, Dominic Farrell, Jenny McWha, Rachel Spence, Elena Radic
Design and Production: Laura Boyle, Carmen Giraudy, Lorena Gonzalez Guillen
Marketing and Publicity: Kendra Martin, Kathryn Bassett

dundurn.com   dundurnpress
@dundurnpress   dundurnpress
dundurnpress   info@dundurn.com

FIND US ON NETGALLEY & GOODREADS TOO!

DUNDURN